A Business and Labour History of Britain

A Business and Labour History of Britain

Case Studies of Britain in the Nineteenth and Twentieth centuries

Edited by

Mike Richardson

and

Peter Nicholls

First published 2011 by
PALGRAVE MACMILLAN

Palgrave Macmillan in the UK is an imprint of Macmillan Publishers Limited,
registered in England, company number 785998, of Houndmills, Basingstoke,
Hampshire RG21 6XS.

Palgrave Macmillan in the US is a division of St Martin's Press LLC,
175 Fifth Avenue, New York, NY 10010.

Palgrave Macmillan is the global academic imprint of the above companies
and has companies and representatives throughout the world.

Palgrave® and Macmillan® are registered trademarks in the United States,
the United Kingdom, Europe and other countries

ISBN 978–0–230–28092–2

This book is printed on paper suitable for recycling and made from fully
managed and sustained forest sources. Logging, pulping and manufacturing
processes are expected to conform to the environmental regulations of the
country of origin.

A catalogue record for this book is available from the British Library.

A catalog record for this book is available from the Library of Congress.

10 9 8 7 6 5 4 3 2 1
20 19 18 17 16 15 14 13 12 11

Printed and bound in Great Britain by
CPI Antony Rowe, Chippenham and Eastbourne

Contents

Illustrations

Tables

Acknowledgements

The editors of this volume wish to thank the contributors for the development of this book, and all those colleagues who lent help and criticism. Three chapters originally appeared in *Historical Studies in Industrial Relations* (HSIR) for which copyright has been kindly granted: Chapter 4: Mike Richardson '"Murphyism in Oxfordshire' – the Bliss Mill Strike 1913–14"' (HSIR, Vol. 25/26, Spring/Autumn 2008, pp. 78–103); Chapter 5: Mike Richardson 'Rapprochement and Retribution: The Divergent Experiences of Workers in Two Large Paper and Print Companies in the 1926 General Strike' (HSIR, Vol. 22, Autumn 2006, pp. 27–53); and Chapter 8: Stephanie Tailby 'Taylorism in the Mines? Technology, Work Organization and Management in British Coal Mining before Nationalization' (HSIR, Vol. 10, Autumn 2000, pp. 71–99).

Chapter 9 draws on material previously published by the authors with the inclusion of some new data. Copyright permission has been kindly granted by Palgrave Macmillan for selected material reproduced from: 'The Legacy of Trade Union Power' in A. Danford, M. Richardson, P. Stewart, S. Tailby and M. Upchurch, *Partnership and the High Performance Workplace: Work and Employment Relations in the Aerospace Industry* (2005). We are grateful to Pluto Press, www.plutobooks.com, for the use of selected material from P. Stewart, M. Richardson, A. Danford, K. Murphy, T. Richardson and V. Wass, 'The Prehistory of Lean Production: Employee Relations in the British Automobile Industry since the Second World War' in *We Sell Our Time No More: Workers' Struggles Against Lean Production in the British Car Industry* (2009).

Contributors

Andy Danford is Professor of Employment Relations at the Centre for Employment Studies Research, University of the West of England, Bristol. He is co-author of *Partnership and the High Performance Workplace* (2005); *The Reality of Partnership at Work* (2008); and *We Sell Our Time No More: Workers' Struggles against Lean Production in the British Car Industry* (2009); and co-editor of *Flexibility at Work. Critical Developments in the International Automobile Industry* (2008).

Peter Nicholls is Principal Lecturer in Employment Studies at the University of the West of England, Bristol. He is an international coordinator for overseas programmes. He has taught on the MBA Programme at University of Shenzhen, China. He has co-edited *Employee Relations*, First and Second Editions (1999, 2003). His publications include 'Bolivia: Between a Rock and a Hard Place', *Capital and Class* (Autumn 2003).

Mike Richardson is Associate Fellow at the University of the West of England, Bristol. His recent co-authored publications include *Partnership and the High Performance Workplace: Work and Employment Relations in the Aerospace Industry* (2005); *The Reality of Partnership at Work* (2008); *We Sell Our Time No More: Workers' Struggles against Lean Production in the British Car Industry* (2009). He has also co-edited *Flexibility at Work. Critical Developments in the International Automobile Industry* (2008).

Paul Stewart is Professor of Sociology of Work and Employment at the University of Strathclyde, Glasgow. He is the co-author of *Partnership and the High performance Workplace* (2005); *We Sell Our Time No More: Workers' Struggles against Lean Production in the British Car Industry* (2009); and co-editor of *Flexibility at Work: Critical Developments in the International Automobile Industry* (2008).

Stephanie Tailby is Professor of Employment Studies and Director of the Centre for Employment Studies Research (CESR) at the University of the West of England, Bristol. Her research interests include public sector employment and employment relations reform; contingent employment in cross-national and inter-industry comparative perspective; women's self-employment in 'old' and 'new economy' service occupations; and employee voice and the theory and practice of workplace partnership.

She is the co-author of *Partnership and the High Performance Workplace* (2005) and *The Reality of Partnership at Work* (2008).

Peter Wardley is Principal Lecturer in Modern Economic and Business History at the University of the West of England, Bristol. His research interests include modern economic history, business history, local history and applications of information technology (computing) in history. He is co-author of 'Banking on Change: Information Systems and Technologies in UK High Street Banking 1919–1979' in J-G Degos (ed.) *L'entreprise, le chiffre et le droit: itinéraires parallèles, itinéraires croisés*, (2006).

1
Introduction: Themes and Historical Backdrop

Mike Richardson and Peter Nicholls

The business and labour history case studies presented in this edited collection provide valuable insights into the field of work organization, the social relations of production, and the detailed division of labour in some key British industries and workplaces between the 1830s and the 1990s. These studies reveal the constant ebb and flow of power and influence between capital and labour, and the initiatives both sides took to defend their interests. Over this extended span of history such cases identify a series of constants that have come to reflect the unique qualities of the relationship between British capital and labour, and the sectors and industries that have given Britain such a distinctive and, as some might argue, skewed economic structure. Through the assemblage of key historic data, and the exploration of significant dynamics of change, each case contributes to the continuing debates about factors related to control over the labour process.

The case studies

For the first case, in Chapter 2, Peter Nicholls examines the early organizational and employment policies in the British railway industry. The chapter explores how the early railways pioneered ideas and systems of management organization and control that foreshadowed theories of organization, socialization and culture. Strong forms of paternalism, sectionalism and hierarchy all combined to create an all-pervasive culture of control. These regimes of control often provided a template for geographically contingent industries, and demonstrated some of the logistical advantages of adopting the status a of joint stock form.

Peter Wardley, in Chapter 3, explores how new technology in the British financial services industry impacted on the gender division of labour during the twentieth century. The introduction of electromechanical aids, including office equipment before 1914 and 'mechanical banking' in the interwar years progressing to computer technology in the late 1950s and beyond, was associated with the employment of greater numbers of low-cost female labour and the ability to centralize managerial decision making that enabled the implementation of new control systems.

The fight for union recognition that led to a six month strike is the subject of Chapter 4. Mike Richardson presents a micro level study of the conflict that took place in 1913–14 in the one-industry market town of Chipping Norton. Richardson examines the causes, conduct and consequences of this dispute. Changes in management style are explored as ownership of Bliss Mill moved from a seemingly benevolent proprietor to a public limited company under stricter managerial control. He concludes that, despite defeat, union activists were politicized and became involved in the formation of a local Labour Party branch.

The experience of two paper and print companies, John Dickinson and E. S. & A. Robinson, in the 1926 General Strike is the focus of the next study in Chapter 5. It examines the operation of management authority and the experiences of their workforces, before, during and immediately after the Strike. Despite the similarities in industrial relations strategy in Dickinson and Robinson, their responses to the General Strike took markedly different forms. The chapter explores why management at Dickinson derecognized trade unions after the General Strike and utilized a house union with which to consult workers on workplace and industrial relations issues, while Robinson continued to recognize and bargain with independent unions.

The way in which J. W. Arrowsmith, a traditional family-owned printing firm, conducted industrial relations from the beginning of the twentieth century to the end of the 1930s is the main focus of Chapter 6. Ownership control, as opposed to managerial control, features here where authority concerning long-term strategy and day-to-day decision making stayed with the individual owner. The mechanization of composing, the economic recession in the early 1920s, and the 1926 General Strike, proved to have a significant impact on the conduct of industrial relations and ownership authority. The 'soft' paternalistic management style practiced before the First World War was replaced first by an authoritarian approach and then, in response to workers' resistance, by pragmatic solutions to industrial relations and aspects of control over the labour process.

In Chapter 7 Peter Nicholls explores the manner in which the British Broadcasting Company (BBC) evolved into a powerful public sector broadcaster possessing a range of distinctive features which were to shape its organization and work practices. The case study provides an analysis of the formation and development of the BBC as an agency of the State. It demonstrates the existence of an uneasy relationship within itself, and with the central State, as its role emerges in the 1920s and 1930s when the first Director General set out to secure a degree of independence from political control. It also reveals some of the key features of the style of management control which appeared to recreate many attributes of Edwardian thinking in its forms of paternalistic methods of control.

In light of the debates on scientific management and the influence of Taylorism on British industry, in Chapter 8 Stephanie Tailby surveys changes in production technology, work organization and management in British coalmining in the first half of the twentieth century. She evaluates management interpretations of the work and production management systems that had been fashioned in mechanizing mines, and highlights the role of machine manufacturers in proselytizing a more complete reconstruction on Taylorist lines. Her analysis is concluded by assessing reasons why the take up of Taylorist techniques was rarely applied.

The final chapter, co-written by Mike Richardson, Andy Danford and Paul Stewart, is concerned with changes in production practices in automobile and aerospace manufacture across Britain 1950–82, and the considerable impact these changes have had on labour relations and control over the labour process. Despite disparities both between and within these respective industries, particularly the higher skill levels required by the aerospace sector, common experiences of the transformation of labour conditions of work were discernable. In mapping some key historical struggles of automobile and aerospace workers against management forms of authority and control, this chapter charts the critical dynamics prevalent in both industries.

The labour process

Notwithstanding the diversity of these cases, extending over both time and place, the common thread which connects them is that they examine changes in aspects of the labour process; such as scientific management, mechanization, deskilling, microtechnology, gender division of labour, work organization and labour relations in differing industries. The concept of the labour process is derived from Marx's analysis.[1] Marxian theory shows that the organization of the labour process, in its specific historical form under the capitalist mode of production, is premised on the need to extract and realize surplus value. Marx emphasized that capitalism is based on commodity production for exchange values. Labour power is purchased and used to generate more value in commodities than it is paid. The measure of value is 'socially necessary labour-time...required to produce an article under the normal conditions of production, and with the average degree of skill and intensity prevalent at the time'.[2] Marx points out that after the capitalist has purchased the means of production and workers' labour power, the labour process comes under direct capitalist control.

Accumulation of capital as the employer's main objective is central to both neoclassical and Marxist theories of value. Marx stressed that the profit needs of capital, and the periodic crises that accompany the accumulation of capital, conflict with the social needs of workers. The exploitative situation that exists at the point of production is hidden through the cash nexus: 'necessary and surplus labor time are not distinguished within the labor process...the wage conceals such a distinction.'[3] Yet, as Burawoy argues, the obfuscation of this exploitative situation is not sufficient to secure surplus value. Workers often pursue disparate interests from those of their employers and, therefore, 'the labor process...must be understood in terms of the specific combinations of force and consent that elicit cooperation in the pursuit of profit'.[4]

For around one hundred years, until the 1970s, the labour process as a subject of study was overlooked or dealt with scantily. Then, in 1974, Harry Braverman's seminal work on labour process theory was published stimulating a debate that is still ongoing in the twenty first century.[5] Braverman developed Marx's theory by focusing on the degradation of work and tightening of managerial control under monopoly capitalism. He maintained that the ever-increasing pace in the introduction of automation and new technology, combined with new techniques in the organization of work, had resulted in an acceleration of deskilling. He argued that the simplification of craft work, through the separation of conception and execution of work tasks, had inevitably led to the diminution of craft control over the labour process, and increasing levels of alienation at work, as tedium replaced skill in the workplace. Subsequent contributions to the labour process debate have marked out areas of weakness in his analysis. For example, he does not take into full account variation and diversity, nor does he acknowledge the increase in semi-skilled workers who acquired 'significant forms of expertise' which they defended rigorously.[6] Furthermore, he omits the impact of class struggle and worker resistance. Yet, Braverman's thesis remains influential, is central to establishing the terms of the labour process debate, and, as such, provides the framework for understanding many of the issues raised in the case studies presented in this book.

The British economy and the power relations between business and labour, pre-1914

In concluding this introduction we provide a brief reading of the changing situation regarding labour relations, the maturation of capitalism and the economic position prevailing in Britain in the second half of the nineteenth century. Space prevents us from extending this review into the twentieth century; but the object is to touch on important advances in the development of monopoly capitalism, and concerns facing capital and labour, in order to comprehend key issues that continued to surface at the point of production during the twentieth century.

Britain's domination of the world market, following the repeal of the Corn Laws in 1846, was predicated on its technological lead, manufacturing monopoly, monetary orthodoxy,[7] free trade imperialism,[8] and high returns on foreign investment.[9] The economic recovery following the 1847 banking crisis, and the collapse of Chartism in 1848, resulted in the Liberal Party, the party of industrial capitalists, being sufficiently self-assured to grant reforms that it previously regarded as obnoxious in the realization that it needed the assistance of the working class to complete its victory over the landed aristocracy. Thus,

> [t]he Factory Acts, once the bugbear of all manufacturers, were not only willingly submitted to, but their expansion into acts regulating all trades, was tolerated. Trade Unions, lately considered inventions of the devil himself, were now petted and patronised as perfectly legitimate institutions....[10]

Primarily, this volte-face succeeded in bringing about the acquiescence of the 'protected' elements of the working class, the labour aristocracy, represented principally by the new model unions.[11] They were attracted to the Gladstonian form of liberalism that mixed its belief in free trade with social and political reform. To a limited extent, these craft workers did gain some benefits from free trade imperialism in the golden age of Victorian capitalism; 1850–73. Real wages grew, particularly for skilled workers. Profits boomed and, for those in regular employment, the standard of living increased especially in comparison with the 1840s. The scale of manufacturing ballooned. Britain was indeed the workshop of the world.

The demand for fixed capital (plant and equipment), increased as industrialization gathered speed and large industrial enterprises emerged. Key to the development of the latter was the consolidation, in 1862, of the Joint Stock Companies Acts of 1844, 1855 and 1856 which 'allowed the liability of partners to be limited to the extent of their stake in the company without having to seek parliamentary approval'.[12] These legal reforms mark another important point, as they make possible the separation of ownership and control in large enterprises by means of the formation of publicly traded companies. This 'functional differentiation' emerged 'as a means of raising the ever-increasing amount of capital' required to sustain and expand the profitability of public companies.[13] Financial institutions, however, were accused of not providing long-term funds for British industry. Attracted by the promise of high returns, they 'exhibited a strong predilection for holding overseas assets and financing international trade'.[14]

In the last quarter of the nineteenth century, Britain faced increased competition from the United States of America and Germany as these nations rapidly industrialized, establishing large modern enterprises. By the beginning of the twentieth century, while Britain had advanced economically, Germany and the United States, now its main rivals, forged ahead to become the world's leading industrial powers pushing Britain into third place.

Thus the period 1873–93 witnessed the relative decline of the British economy apropos the United States, Germany and, indeed, Japan. This era is often referred to as the Great Depression. Britain endured a fall in prices and profits, increased unemployment, and an end of its industrial monopoly. Yet the standard of living for those in work rose, and mass production and mass consumption quickened. Firms began to expand faster than markets could grow. Price wars broke out. Competition intensified. This marked the end of the Gladstonian era of free trade. Modern British industry had to adapt to survive. Concentration of production followed. Mergers and acquisitions produced large industrial conglomerates. Trade associations were utilized to manage cartels in order to control prices and output. These were attempts to escape the laws of capitalist competition.

The emergence of monopoly capitalism in Britain should not be exaggerated, however, as this development was mild when compared to the American and German experience. Moreover, scientific management, adopted by several large plants in the United States before the First World War, did not attract the same level of interest in Britain. According to Craig Littler 'this was because of the pattern of demand for many engineering products in Britain'.[15] Despite attempts to promote 'the value of scientific management', such as the address given by Frank Gilbreth to the Production Managers Association in London on 12 July 1913,[16] its appeal was limited; partly because there was little demand for standardized repetition work in Britain until the outbreak of the First World War.[17] Nonetheless, workshop reorganization and the introduction of new payment systems (piecework and the closely related premium bonus system), was a particular feature of the engineering industry after 1890 and generated opposition from workers and their unions.[18]

Thus, as well as the strike waves of 1889–93 and 1910–14 executed primarily by non-craft workers, workers' resistance took the form of restrictive practices; particularly in the engineering industry. Here, employers sought to gain greater control over the labour process through the introduction of new payment systems. In 1896, to counter what they deemed as powerful and aggressive trade unions and to maintain managerial prerogative, they formed its Employer' Federation of Engineering Associations. Unified, its employer were powerful and able to inflict defeat on the union, the Amalgamated Society of Engineers (ASE), in the national lockout of 1897–98. This victory paved the way for employers to weaken craft control through exerting tighter supervision of manufacturing operations and compelling the ASE into the formal acceptance of piecework.[19] Dismay from ASE rank-and-file members led to a shift of power from union officialdom to work committees and shop stewards. Where this occurred, greater independence at the local level emerged enabling shop stewards and works committees to resist some of the worst excesses of the strike settlement by securing collective bargaining rights over piece-rates.[20]

Elsewhere, during 1880s and 1890s, many employers' organizations bolstered managerial authority by providing what the Shipping Federation termed 'a permanent battle-axe' against the emerging 'socialistic unions'. By 1914, employers' organizations 'were relatively strong in coal, cotton, engineering, shipbuilding, printing and construction'.[21]

The aspects of the British economy described above are some of the recurring themes that feature throughout the twentieth century. The persistence of relative economic decline, the rise of the corporate economy,[22] the evolution of giant firms,[23] and conflict and consent between capital and labour is the background against which the company or industry specific cases in this book are set.

Notes

1. K. Marx, *Capital, Vol. 1* (Lawrence and Wishart: 1977), Chapter Seven, pp. 173–93.

2. *Ibid.*, p. 47.
3. M. Burawoy, *Manufacturing Consent: Changes in the Labor Process under Monopoly Capitalism* (University of Chicago Press: 1982), p. 28.
4. *Ibid.*, p. 30.
5. H. Braverman, *Labor and Monopoly Capital* (Monthly Review Press: 1974).
6. T. Elger, 'Braverman, Capital Accumulation and Deskilling', in S. Wood (ed.), *The Degradation of Work? Skill, Deskilling and the Labour Process* (Hutchinson: 1982), p. 37.
7. The Bank Charter Act of 1844 established a tighter connection between note issue and gold reserves. The adoption of the gold standard, the convertibility of the pound sterling to gold at a fixed exchange rate, instituted monetary orthodoxy in nineteenth century Britain.
8. A good example of free trade imperialism was the enforcement of free trade upon India, the jewel in the crown of the British Empire. India's local textile industry was demolished allowing the Lancashire cotton industry to penetrate the Indian market. See E. J. Hobsbawm, *Industry and Empire* (Penguin: 1985), p. 149.
9. See A. N. Offer, 'The British Empire, 1870–1914: A Waste of Money?', *Economic History Review* XLVI:2 (1993), pp. 215–38, for the debate on the costs and benefits of empire. The concern of this article is whether 'the British Empire was producing an economic return lower than investment in Britain itself…'. Offer concludes that, on balance, the benefits of empire, particularly 'from a private point of view', outweighed the costs.
10. F. Engels 'England in 1845 and in 1885' in K. Marx and F. Engels, *Articles on Britain* (Progress Publishers: 1975), p. 388.
11. For a recent contribution to the debate on the labour aristocracy see J. Foster, 'The Aristocracy of Labour and Working-Class Consciousness Revisited', *Labour History Review* 75:3 (December 2010), pp. 245–63.
12. K. Watson, 'Financing Industry in the Nineteenth Century', *ReFRESH* 22 (Spring1996), p. 3.
13. M. De Vroey, 'A Marxist View of Ownership and Control' in T. Nichols (ed.), *Capital and Labour* (Fontana: 1980), pp. 225–26.
14. M. Collins, *Banks and Industrial Finance in Britain 1800–1939* (Macmillan: 1991), p. 18.
15. C. R. Littler, *The Development of the Labour Process in Capitalist Societies* (Heinemann: 1982), p. 95.
16. *The Times*, 14 July 1913, p. 10.
17. Littler, *The Development of the Labour Process in Capitalist Societies*, p. 95.
18. *Ibid.*, pp. 84–94.
19. E. Wigham, *The Power to Manage: A History of the Engineering Employers' Federation* (Macmillan: 1973), pp. 29–62.
20. R. Price, *Labour in British Society* (Croom Helm: 1986), p. 146.
21. A. J. McIvor, *A History of Work in Britain, 1880–1950* (Palgrave: 2001), p. 89 and 92.
22. See L. Hannah, *The Rise of the Corporate Economy* (Methuen: 1976).
23. See S. J. Prais, *The Evolution of Giant Firms in Britain* (Cambridge University Press: 1976).

2
Labour, Management and Control: The Early Railway Industry in Britain

Peter Nicholls

Introduction

With Britain's early pattern of industrialization characterized as erratic and chaotic, it is interesting to consider how the period from the nineteenth century onwards became a period of capitalist development and transition where the very idea of an urban industrial economy moved from an aberration to be avoided or side-stepped to a more permanent reality transforming itself into something more sophisticated and recognizable from the position of the present day.

As part of that account this chapter will look at one of the earliest attempts to modernize both the structure and organization of work that contributed to the labour process within one particular industry; and its choice is significant because of its unique ability to set an example and influence a vast range of industrial and commercial organizations at that time. At the age of 91 Samuel Smiles wrote:

> The iron rail proved the magicians' road. The locomotive gave a new celerity to time. It virtually reduced England to a sixth of its size. It brought the country nearer the town, and the town to the country.... It energised punctuality, discipline and attention; and proved a moral teacher by the influence of example.[1]

These changes to the culture, organization and structure of work and enterprise, took many forms and are matters central to this discussion for understanding the formation and dynamic of this labour process. The period under consideration spans the era prior to any major reforming legislation being adopted. From the mid-1820s through to the mid-1860s legislation remained piecemeal and based upon the principle that the railway companies, once they had obtained their Acts, were sufficiently constrained by those conditions.[2]

This chapter also questions the argument by Howlett[3] and Savage[4] that internal labour markets were really only established on the railways after 1870. The evidence from the period under consideration suggests that, though hardly comprehensively planned, the very adoption of a variety of strategies such as hierarchy, paternalism and sectionalism alongside many facets of military organization combined to form elementary career paths and opportunities for long-term employment albeit in a period of high labour turnover.

Joint stock companies, engineers and salaried managers

The building and organization of the railways in Britain made an incalculable contribution to the pace and direction of the industrial revolution and, in most histories of the period, the railways are portrayed as amazing feats of civil engineering and, subsequently, technological and business success. It is easy to understand this emphasis when the enormity of the project is understood.

Compared to the canal system, railways were a relatively straight forward method for conveying freight for long distances and accessing railheads for coal and other minerals. The actual numbers of dray and cab horses increased much more than the numbers of coaching horses declined. The building of the railways resulted in an expansion of shorter journeys as long distance coaching declined, but was more than compensated for by the additional business generated by substantial increase in the number of rail destinations. Before the Stockton to Darlington line was opened in 1825, 23 railways acts had already been passed. By 1840, 2390 kilometres of track had been laid and, by 1880, 25,060 kilometres.[5]

With so many startling statistics and profound changes taking place in the economy as it became knitted into a national system by the railways, it is easy to miss the extraordinary significance of the railway as an industry in its own right and the profound affect it would have on labour relations both in the UK and overseas. Completely new regimes of labour control emerged as the industry invented a labour process unique to its own conditions.

An extensive literature on the lives and achievements of the early pioneers who built and managed these early railways certainly exists.[6] The novelty, scale and sheer complexity of the challenges facing this emergent industry were without parallel in Britain and it is perhaps these challenges that confronted the early business leaders that have provided a fascination and distraction for many seeking to understand work and control in early railway history.

The very idea of a salaried management answerable to a board was a novelty, and the detail of how the new senior hierarchies were devised is a comprehensive area of study in its own right. By comparison, the details of the workforce that would actually do the work to confront and overcome these challenges have remained partial and fragmented. Nonetheless, without some understanding of the type of management that was being created at this time, it is difficult to appreciate the very distinctive features of early railway organization. The question as to how the labour process of railway work was designed, implemented and sustained at this time has remained largely unexplored while factory regimes have tended to capture the attention of writers in this tradition.

Unsurprisingly, the first half of the industrial revolution had been characterized by small and medium sized enterprises growing constantly to fill an ever expanding market. The apparent dream of Adam Smith had been supplied with investment capital from local, equally small-scale 'country banks'. These informal arrangements had grown up around the need for modest sums of money where family, friends or partners, the traditional source of finance, had failed. Usually based within an industry, the more successful enterprises were in possession of some level of retained profits. The owners of these local enterprises were, therefore, experienced within their own trade or industry and in a strong position to judge the competence of others in their region to manage a line of credit. Understanding something of the nature of their own business success meant that these regional entrepreneurs were in a strong position to evaluate the position and plans of others in the same regional industry and supply the appropriate scale of loans to achieve these objectives. Confronted with scale and complexity of the new railway organizations, this localized form of banking could not possibly cope with the extraordinary demands for mobilizing capital on a scale to cope with the colossal costs associated with building and subsequently operating these completely novel organizations.

If the reality of the market at this time was of large numbers of small and medium sized enterprises supported by an informal and highly flexible regional banking system, then it was clear that this structure was reinforced by the belief that to be a successful and a respected entrepreneur meant owning your own enterprise. Ownership conferred status within this newly emerging business class. In practical terms it meant complete discretion and control over all aspects of the operations of the enterprise. In a sense, the provision of local small-scale finance reinforced this arrangement and its underlying beliefs.

Confronted by the enormity of the costs of constructing the railways, and subsequently equipping and operating them, such arrangements were totally inadequate.[7] In the future, investment capital would have to come in the form of joint stock companies which, though outlawed at this time, could be created by an Act of Parliament. The pressure for large-scale finance would provide the pressure to force the government to repeal the earlier Acts and establish joint stock companies as a normal vehicle for generating investment capital. There was real concern about creating a divorce of ownership from control on the railways expressed early on by Lieutenant Peter Lecount in his treatise on Railways in 1841 in *Encyclopaedia Britannica:*

> The first question which arises is by what system can a joint stock company be so managed as to obtain the same amount of alacrity, vigilance, and industry in its Service, as characterizes the conduct of individuals when acting for themselves, and to combine with these qualities an honest and economical administration.

Concern that the traditional board of management, benefitting from a variety of contributions from a number of individuals, might be undermined by the reliance on one particular 'salaried' officer continued to worry the early architects of these railway companies.[8]

In the same treatise, Lecount finally confronts the need to rest authority in a single individual even though they might not be the direct owners of the company:

> In the management of railways, such an officer is more especially required where the heads of departments are necessarily numerous, consequence of the several branches of business into which the working of the railway is divided; where each department employs considerable numbers of men, two alone, those of the police and porters, amounting to almost a regiment, and where all are to be brought to act with the precision and regularity of a steam engine. It would be impossible to produce unity of action amidst such conflicting elements, without a close, active, and unremitting personal superintendence, such as may be accompanied by an individual, but can never be affected by a [management] board.[9]

Contained in this statement is the essence of the approach to railway management in Britain in the 1840s.[10] Faced with the enormity of the task, the scale of employment, and complexity of these new organizations there really was no choice but to break with the past and embrace the joint stock company form, and use a single leading position to execute the policies of the company. In reality the failings of the earlier engineers (who had built the railways) to switch into operating them, left the railway boards with a managerial vacuum. To confront the next stage of operating these companies a new type of manager and management system would have to be found.[11]

The transfer of military experience into a commercial setting

Returning to the original question of company structure and finance, it is possible to see the pressure for the development of this revolutionary new form of transport to be a major catalyst for forging this new form of finance, which would in turn be adopted by the banking industry itself for precisely the same reasons: mobilizing larger volumes of capital, harnessing the resulting economies of scale, and rationalizing the organization and administration of the enterprise. As Hobsbawm[12] points out, Britain was awash with surplus capital which 'surged' into the railways for want of anything equally capital-absorbing, and turned a valuable innovation in transport into a major national programme of capital investment.

To connect this through to the core concern for understanding the labour process within this industry, and the rapid changes to it, is to make the connection to the emergence of these new procedures for raising finance and the consequent alterations to company structure. This resulted in the switch from direct owner management to the recruitment of salaried managers on a grand scale. The sheer enormity and complexity of these organizations required more than an engineer or skilled craftsman to manage the enterprise. The British navy was being run down in this period releasing many officers at a time of recruitment to these nascent companies. A background as an officer trained in strategy, logistics, accounting, training, discipline and controlling a large uneducated workforce would equip these men with a set of skills wholly appropriate for these new positions in the rapidly expanding railway organizations.

A position as a salaried manager answerable to the board of the company was not an easy option when so little was known about this new technology and means to organize it. Those responsible for making these appointments were equally ignorant of how to design a post, its area of responsibility, and the tasks to be pursued. As such, these early managers often made up their own role through using earlier experience and trial and error.

> The captain and the lieutenant from both army and the navy had the experience of accounts and book keeping and were also familiar with the control of large staffs. Captain Huish entered the railway industry after service with the East India Company's army, but it was the navy which provided the majority of these important railway recruits.[13]

Earlier manufacturing had relied upon internal subcontracting and a range of informal methods to get the earliest workshops and factories to work; relying on craftsmen to handle the decisions for most of the production process. In time, changes and developments on the shop floor accumulated to form chains of logic that became apparent to those with a mind to see them.[14] Here was a situation in a brand new industry where a complete lack of experience existed across the entire enterprise. Considerable hostility against the industry from canal and stage coach companies, landowners, and many others existed at this time. Within the organization, directors and members of the board were often completely unrealistic about how much could be achieved within particular periods of time. If managerial decisions were not based upon sound information there was little chance of finding reliable data. Cost accounting was rudimentary and accounts were kept sporadically and usually inaccurately. Into this situation managers had to be found who would be loyal to the company yet display considerable initiative where those who appointed them had little relevant advice as to how to proceed. It was a matter of finding someone who had experience in some parallel area of management that could be transferred in to the railways, and who was capable of handling the immediate pressures confronting those responsible for operating newly built lines.

Not only was there a lack of reliable information for a new general manager, but also there were high expectations to generate cash as fast as possible. The costs of purchasing the land for the route and building the line were colossal: in the case of Britain, the most expensive in the world. From the earliest stages of forming a company costs were high, as Klingender points out in referring to cost associated with passing the individual bills to establish each company:

> After an enormous amount of time, energy and money had been wasted, and after each major railway Bill had been thrown out of

Parliament at least once, the most apparently embittered opposition invariably vanished quite suddenly. The lawyers, experts, journalists and caricaturists pocketed their fees. The landlords consoled themselves for the spoliation of rural England with the inflated compensation they had succeeded in extorting from the railway companies. And the British railways were saddled from the start with non-productive overhead costs, far higher than those of any other system in the world.[15]

At £40,000 per mile, British railways were four times more expensive than American and continental lines. Willing to pay excessive amounts to purchase the land to build the railway, further large sums were lost in gaining the support of politicians to ensure the successful passage of a particular company bill. As Mathias records: 157 Members of Parliament (MPs) were subscribers in new companies in 1845 and 99 railway directors were sitting in both Houses of Parliament by 1852.[16]

So, from the point of raising capital through to the sale of shares, finance had been drained by these arrangements before even confronting the significant building costs. The result was that there was often little left to plough into operational departments of the enterprise. Once the original engineers who were responsible for building the railway (and had themselves added unnecessarily to the costs by building highly decorative or ornate structures to reflect their own reputations) were replaced by these salaried officers, the pressure was on to achieve a rapid return to set against the huge debts which had often ballooned out of control.[17]

The pressure upon companies associated with the high capital cost of railways invited a dangerous policy of parsimony. An attitude of cheeseparing harmed many lines, especially in their first few years of working when repair and maintenance costs were particularly high. The companies were often torn between reducing operating costs, and thus meeting the demands of those investors who desired temporary high dividends, and using profits to offset future expenses.

Ideas and systems for designing company structures and administrative systems could be drawn from the nearest relevant industries including the canal, road-coaches, carriers and mining companies, but most railway companies advanced very slowly in their grasp of effective organization and administration. In this vacuum of knowledge and experience, the early ex-naval and later ex-army managers were able to pursue their careers almost unfettered. Transferring entire systems from their military backgrounds into these companies provided an immediate structure and operating logic.[18]

Controlling labour, hierarchy and grades

With a predominantly agricultural workforce at this time, recruiting labour was relatively easy especially where railway wages were well ahead of those in agriculture. The steady supply of rural workers to the railways was to provide a sustained advantage from the 1820s right through to the early twentieth century. Like many developing countries in the early stages of industrialization, this vast migration from the land to the newly emerging cities would contribute to sustaining modest wages and the constant threat that there was always someone else to replace the employee.

Of the many forms and varieties of control transferred into this civilian setting, it is perhaps the navy that made the most significant contribution.[19] Of all the systems that made their way in into the railways it is conceivably the system of rank and hierarchy that had the most profound impact upon the labour process of railway workers. The rural squirearchy was being transformed at this time and the old boundaries of rural life were being broken down by the growth of the burgeoning middle class merchants and entrepreneurs. At the same time a small skilled working class was emerging in the early workshops and factories. Ideas of rank, status and authority were well enshrined in a society still escaping from the rigid structures of its feudal past. For those rural workers confronting an organization, where up to a hundred grades existed from the humblest position of horse boy right up to the senior station master or head engine driver, there was unlikely to be much surprise. One hierarchical system of work would merely be replaced by another however different in form.

Even with an almost insatiable desire for labour, the railway companies were resolute about maintaining high standards for the process of recruitment. Selecting the most suitable labour force where no system of education existed removed the possibility of relying on exam grades or being able to conduct rudimentary tests (this was to change by the 1840s). In the absence of such measures, personal statements or references would be one of the few sources of evidence for selecting between candidates. Figure heads in the local community who were literate; clergymen, lawyers or doctors, would be expected to provide an honest assessment of their nominee. Should their account appear inaccurate they might be called in for a meeting with senior staff within the company to explain and justify their testimony.

Personal interviews were quite normal requiring applicants to remember and rehearse sections for the company's rule book. Rudimentary medical examinations were conducted and limits were set for the maximum and minimum heights for staff. In one company, anyone with red hair was excluded due to the known connection between red hair and the proclivity for wild tempers and mood changes![20]

Once the candidate had obtained a position he (for there were few women recruited at this time; in the 1850s, out of 61,005 employees on the London and North Western Railway Company, 180 women and girls were employed in ticketing and food provision) would be allocated to a particular director of the company who sat on the board of management.[21] With every employee identified with a director of the company, from the very commencement of their career, railway employees were located within a highly personalized relationship and one which would determine annual bonuses, annual reviews of their behaviour, and future career opportunities. This relationship would last for the duration of the employees' working career.

Identified with a senior manager, the newly recruited employee would then be allocated to one of a hundred grades within the company. Like the military system from which they were drawn, each grade was distinguished from those either side of it in the hierarchy by minute gradations in pay and status. Described by Kenny[22] as complex as a caste system, this type of sectionalism would send powerful messages of the identity, expectations and behaviour associated with each railway 'servant'. For, under the existing Masters and Servants legislation at this time, this is exactly what they expected to be: servants of the railway company.

The addition of a uniform modelled very closely on military design could change as the individual progressed up the career ladder. Additional pieces of embellishment would reflect fine distinctions in seniority. The addition of a full length coat and the type of hat worn would all serve to mark out the rank of the individual employee. The new recruit was locked into a form of employment and a labour process that dictated a particular desired outcome for every minute of the day, 7 days a week and 365 days of the year.

Paternalism, sectionalism and discipline

In the railway towns, like Crewe or Swindon, entire communities were built by the railway companies to house their staff. Schools for their children were provided alongside housing, libraries, parks, churches and other amenities.

Sectionalism and the rank of the individual were reflected in the design and size of the houses provided. Those in the most junior positions would be in possession of the most humble terrace buildings, based upon the most practical designs of the day, while the station master would live in a detached villa with the most ornate decorative features.[23] Attendance at church on Sunday was a requirement where the 'railway' clergyman was likely to deliver the sermon in a direction supportive of company objectives.

This form of paternalism was not new with plenty of examples reaching back into the eighteenth century; often originating in religious beliefs. But railway paternalism was distinguished by its comprehensiveness and complexity. Organizing paternalism on this scale was not cheap and clearly such a level of investment reflected a long-term vision of the benefits of this type of investment. Becoming an employee on the railways at this time could be entering a career for life; you might get married in a railway church, baptize your children, and have your funeral in the same building.

Each year the progress of the individual was checked against the earliest personnel records. Much of the attention of these records dwelt on behaviour rather than work performance. Without the technologies of work measurement and performance tables, understanding, constructing and defining standards of good work performance was going to be difficult. This was especially so when senior management were kept busy with some very basic issues of control trying to maintain continuity and reliability of employment, and sustain an extensive surplus based upon the maximum effort to be extracted from labour.[24]

Notwithstanding what was said about sectionalism and paternalism, the earliest workers showed little respect for the newly experienced 'working day'.

Attendance at work was a real issue, as was sobriety. Confronting the regimentation of railway work, those from a rural background often looked to drink and absenteeism to cope with deadweight of authority and the end of any form of personal discretion.

Once the period of initial recruitment of a workforce had been completed, and the full weight of sectionalism, paternalism and control had been brought to bear on the workforce, it became apparent to management that the business of sustaining loyalty would be best achieved by encouraging staff to consider the prospect of a long and successful career through opportunities for training leading to the possibility of a progression up the hierarchy to more senior positions with enhanced remuneration and status. As one early commentator put it:

> The practice adopted by the London and North-Western Company, and it is, in the main, the one which is observed by all English Railway Companies, is to appoint lads about fourteen years of age as boy porters, telegraph boys, and for other similar employments; these lads grow up in service, and by the time they reach manhood they have become experienced in railway duties in their various branches, and are eligible for filling such posts as become vacant.[25]

For engine drivers the journey from 'lads' in the engine sheds to cleaners, firemen and eventually drivers of the highest rank on the express passenger trains would take years. Literally growing up in this railway world from living in railway houses, going to railway schools, reading in railway libraries to the daily experience of railway work could have left little space for imagining an alternative way of working. As in the military setting, order, duty and respect were all reinforced at every opportunity to leave little space for an alternative perspective on the world.

To reinforce compliance with all these controls, weighty rule books were drawn up to ensure every aspect of behaviour was itemized and prescribed, often running to several hundred pages with the finest of minute details of working life itemized and proscribed. Eventually these rule books would become part of the selection process where potential candidates would be required to learn the content and rehearse them in front of an interview panel. Issued to all staff, sections of these books would be pinned up on notice boards to constantly remind staff of what was expected of them.

McKenna comments extensively on the use of rules and rule books as a source of resentment amongst the workforce and, seeing the breadth of coverage, it is hardly surprising. This list appeared in the Railway Service Gazette in April of 1873 quoted in McKenna:
The Railwaymen's Ten Commandments

1. Thou shalt have no occupation but this.
2. Thou shalt not seek the benefits of a trade union.
3. Thou shalt make all thy applications in vain.

4. Remember the Sabbath day – work for nothing.
5. Honour thy official and carry tales.
6. Thou shalt use thy skill.
7. Thou shalt commit 300 rules to memory.
8. Thou shalt not have any times for meals.
9. Thou shalt not make any complaint, except for the waste-paper basket.
10. Thou shalt not covet any superior position – thou shalt obey thine official, be his manservant, his gardener, his ass, or anything short of being his neighbour. [26]

Not only were these rules reflecting the harsh conditions of work at that time, but it is a list that contains many features of the labour process so far discussed and still assumes, in 1873, 50 years after the earliest railway companies began, a complete sanctity of the managerial prerogative.

On the other side of this process of constant reinforcement was an elaborate system of fines and punishments. These could range from fines at the value of several weeks salary from poor time-keeping by a porter, to using too much coal as an engine driver. In the early 1840s, getting caught for drunkenness at work on the Great Western Railway would lead to average fine of £1.65p; for absence, 60p; and for theft 50p. At that time, the wages of a porter were £1 per week. At worst, railway workers could be arraigned before a Justice of the Peace (JP) and sent to jail for breaking the more serious regulations. Unjust treatment of engine drivers was revealed in Reynolds's Newspaper:

> [I]f the reports be true…there can be no doubt that this most useful, intelligent, and responsible class of workmen [railway engine drivers] are exposed to a series of grievances the most galling, oppressive, and intolerable that can well be imagined…have their locality on the Great Northern Line of railway.[27]

The source of one of the engine drivers' grievances was working 'the line cheap'. To ingratiate himself with his superiors the supervisor in question attempted to achieve 'cheapness' 'by *overworking* and *underpaying* the engine drivers' (emphasis as original). Engine drivers in this case were paid 'by the *hour* and not the *mile*', as it was and is the custom on every other railway'. As a consequence hourly paid men received much less remuneration than men paid by the mile. To make up their wages they had to work longer hours (working double and sometimes triple trips). Sleep deprivation often resulted with all the dangers that entailed to the general travelling public.[28]

Fines would continue right up to the twentieth century as a constant threat to workers. With the prospect of being thrown into debt from relatively minor infringements, and a harsh approach to dismissal, most employees would acquiesce rather than confront a dictatorial management. It was taken for granted that management had the right to determine all aspects of employment including recruitment, dismissal, promotion, wage determination, and discipline. Indeed, as mentioned earlier, each company designed its own set of regulations to reflect its own pattern of control over labour.

Any dissatisfaction was expected to be represented directly to management. With the force of law behind them there was little chance of a fair hearing. A report by the House of Commons Select Committee in 1839 on communication by railway informed that:

> It is essential to the safety of the Public and to the maintenance of regular intercourse by Railroads that the Companies should have a more perfect control over their servants.... Where the lives of many persons depend on the good conduct and ready obedience of subordinate officers, and where the smallest irregularity may be attended with fatal consequences, a system of exact discipline should be encouraged, and powers should be given to the directors for the purpose of upholding their authority.[29]

So not only was the railway worker a 'servant' under existing legislation, but he or she was also hemmed in by rules, regulations and fines. If that was not enough to severely constrain their working life, a whole onerous layer sat just above the immediate everyday regime of control. This layer was composed of the endless exhortations to comply with the existing controls for the sake of safety and efficient operation of the railway system. Into this labour process entered a new powerful addition to the vocabulary and techniques of management control, the idea of 'service'; particularly service to the public. Could there be any worthy argument against such an ideal? Associated with the incessant call for safety and regularity, this blandishment would echo right up to the present day.

Sustaining an extensive surplus

Odd then, that with all this weight of control bearing down upon employees, the company, or the controlling board for that company, while insisting upon safety and service, took no care to ensure workers were capable at the most fundamental level of being able to sustain this level of performance. Kenney reports on the motion promoted by Francis Channing as late as 1891 in the House of Commons on 23 January:

> That, in the opinion of this House, the excessive hours of labour imposed on railwaymen by the existing arrangements of the railway companies of the United Kingdom constitute a grave social injustice, and are a constant source of danger to the men themselves and the travelling public, and that it is expedient that the Board of Trade should obtain powers by legislation to issue orders, where necessary, directing railway companies to limit the hours of work of special classes of their servants, and to make such a reasonable increase in any class of their servants as will obviate the necessity for overtime work. [30]

The short-time movement of railway engine drivers and fireman, the aims of which were supported by Lord Shaftsbury, had been campaigning against long hours for decades. '[I]nstances were quoted in which it was proved that eighteen, twenty, and twenty-four, and even thirty hours day and night had been the term of one man's labour on his engine.'[31]

The Tory government opposed Channing's motion, but a select committee was appointed to investigate the matter. What they found was substantial evidence of long hours and revealed the case of James Choules, a goods guard who was killed on the London and South Western Railway after being on duty for 22 hours 18 minutes consecutively, and on the 11 previous days had averaged 19 hours 11 minutes. This was typical of the industry at this time and 50 years earlier had no doubt been even worse. As one director is reported as explaining to the government enquiry into long hours:

> '[L]ong hours were to a great extent more a nominal than a real strain on the men. Overtime was mere attendance, and was no actual strain on the faculties'. He produced elaborate calculations as to the seconds of time actually taken up in such operations as pulling levers in signal boxes, sending and receiving messages, and the like.[32]

The number of accidents and deaths on the railway were high even with under-reporting. In 1870, 244 employees were killed out of a workforce of 220,000. Not only were the figures for mortality high but also for morbidity. Both issues were connected to harsh working conditions and very long hours. Overall the experience of work at this time kept the men 'low' as cited by the Labour Research Department:

> The method chosen has been to 'keep the railway man low', to under-pay him, overwork him, refuse him his right to organise and where that fails, to bind him down by long-term sectional agreements. [33]

With such a sharp contrast with former agricultural forms of work, and the towering body of controls over them, it is small wonder that labour turnover in these early railway companies was so high.

The slow emergence of trade unions

Faced with all these controls, and long hours of work, it is odd to con-front such a slow growth of trade unionism in this industry. Many of the features for the growth of trade unions, superficially at least, appeared to exist in these companies. The existence of a relatively large workforce, and a degree of common experience in the hardship of work-ing conditions, should have provided the basis for some rudimentary form of trade union association, especially as this was a time of radical working-class politics:

> Chartism, the first independent political movement of the industrial workers, attained its widest influence and fought its most determined battles in 1837–42, and flared up again in 1847–48. And yet, during the whole period of strife and waste and bitter distress the produc-tion of coal increased fivefold and pig-iron tenfold. The import of raw cotton increased fifteen fold. But the most striking example of industrial expansion was the creation of the British railway system, precisely during the age of the Chartists.[34]

Yet, for the first 40 years of the railways there were only ten strikes and most commentators of the time believed labour relations were relatively positive. The strikes that did take place occurred in two waves, the first from 1845–50 and the second in the late 1860s. Both periods follow national periods of labour unrest and, for the most part, the railway strikes are said to be in pursuit of wages. Kingsford[35] classifies the strikes and identifies the first seven based upon claims for increased wages, two were against a reduction in wages, and the last was against discip-linary fines. In most cases the strikes were confined to a single grade and hence it was easy for the company to continue to operate.

Perhaps the sanguine understanding of labour relations fails to take into account just how difficult it was to mobilize a workforce so entrenched within a labour process so far outlined. In contrast to the number of strikes there is reason to believe that the incidence of petitions and memorials were far more frequent and were a more accurate measure of emerging resistance amongst the workforce.[36] Moreover, grievances persisted on what was perceived as the unjust imposition of fines (which in the case cited here resulted in a strike) 'for accidents over which they [railway engine drivers and firemen] neither had nor could have any control'.[37]

In this early period it is important to remember the gross inequality that existed in labour relations. Under near-military control, these early workforces were enmeshed in a relationship with management that shared similarities with Newby's[38] account of agricultural workers and their 'deference' to those with whom they closely worked. As Findlay indicates, care and concern for labour were a part of management vocabulary of paternalism:

> The Company are very far from being unmindful of the material welfare of the men they employ, and indeed it is their constant study to maintain the most cordial and friendly relations with them, and to make them feel that employers have a sincere interest in them and in their well-being at all times, apart from the mere buying and selling of their labour; in fact, they are taught to regard their employers as their best friends and advisers, as should be the case in every department of labour where proper relations exist between master and man.[39]

Hardly surprising then when, as a 'railway servant', every message, idea and written word around the employee reinforced the idea of compliance and subservience to an omnipotent management who were of course on 'friendly terms' with their workforce. For the earliest workforce, this cross cutting set of values must have been, at best, confusing and, at worst, demoralizing in the sense that it was almost impossible to articulate any genuine counter argument. Faced with the reality of a working life almost comprehensively designed and owned by the company, an educated employee would find the process of questioning wages, benefits, working hours, let alone the whole range of welfare provision, an almost insurmountable prospect. As Christopher Bassett Vincent explained:

> The development of a clear understanding of work relations is associated with the potential for Trade Union consciousness. It is of no

surprise, therefore, to find that the first railway union was not established until 1865, 35 years after the first companies were formed. Once formed, the strike record of the railway unions was very low in the nineteenth century.[40]

As if to add to this line of argument, by the 1850s many companies had the added inducement of offering superannuation funds and the prospect of a reasonable pension if a good record of service had been achieved.

The particular context for trade union activity was set by the unique bill under which each company had been licensed as a joint stock company. In most cases the tone of industrial relations would be set by the individual placed in charge of the operational divisions of the company; usually called the superintendent or general manager. Lecount argues that:

> [E]xecutive administration is best and most efficiently exercised by one and, one only, and accordingly, every board, whether of government commissioners or of a joint stock companies, or of charitable institutions, has some one to whom is entrusted the executive superintendence.[41]

Lecount's treatise on the railway management is just that. It is pitched at a technical and administrative level – where positions, roles and responsibilities are discussed, lists of duties and best practice abound – the assumption is clear; that labour would naturally comply with all the managerially defined tasks and the existence of a countervailing source of power was out of the question. The implication was that labour did not warrant any attention when so many other technical, engineering and administrative matters had to be discussed. It implies that the question of recruitment and control of labour could be taken as non-problematical. With the existing Master and Servant legislation alongside the local railway acts, and the almost universal belief in a form of Social Darwinism that elevated the decisions of business leaders as indisputable, why would such a document expend any time concerning itself with labour?

Many of the details governing the control of labour were contained within the individual acts of incorporation, such as the clauses giving them power to impose fines and details of punishments. The Regulation of Railways Act of 1840, after it was amended in 1842, embraced just about every contingency that could be construed as evidence for breaking rules which would lead automatically to being placed in front of a JP with a maximum penalty of two months hard labour or a £10 fine.

Trying to explain the slow emergence of trade unionism on the railways, therefore, raises a multitude of issues. Management rarely wrote down their thoughts about trade unions at this time; management drawn from the military clearly used their experience to design the systems of control within particular railway companies. The coincidence of these military practices filling the management vacuum could not be construed as a direct response to the politics of labour at this time, but the choice of these early managers and their military methods could not have been lost on the boards who appointed them.

Creating an entire social system of work, a labour process so complex and all-embracing, unwittingly insulated the railways from much of the political agitation surrounding them. Added to this advantage was the express policy of recruiting rural workers who were less likely to have experienced the rallying cry of Chartism.

As McKenna [42] points out, the Enclosure Acts and the Poor Law of 1834 were significant pressures for creating a pool of rural workers. The example of Swindon's rapid growth exemplifies the dynamics at the time. Building Swindon as a hub for the Great Western Railway at the centre of rural hinterland provided work for a growing concentration of unemployed rural workers. In 1841 it had a population of 2495 and by 1901 it grown to over 45,000.[43]

Faced with dire poverty or working for the railways left little choice for those forced out of their rural way of life. Beyond the necessity of working, McKenna makes the point that the class system and its symbols in rural communities provided an easy transition into the military hierarchies of the railway organizations:

> Trade Unions and working-class political agitation groups had little chance of success against the entrenched power of the landed gentry, often backed by the Church and the town merchants.[44]

If rural wages were notoriously low at this time, then even the lowest paid job on the railways could double that amount. Nonetheless, as described above, sectionalism on the railways guaranteed a huge disparity in pay. Those few skilled positions such as engine drivers might earn nearly a £100 per year in 1847 but the vast majority would earn more like £30 per year, unlike senior management who might earn in the region of £600 per year.

It is also a matter of the type of trade unionism that operated at this time. According to Hobsbawm, [45] only with the establishment of the railways did the permanence of the industrial revolution, and the world it was ushering in, become a reality to most working people. The early trade unions, in effect, tried to find ways around what felt like an impermanent world where unemployed members were encouraged to tramp to the next town in search of work, or debate the virtues of land reform, but not necessarily devise policies to confront the leviathan, the railway company, or other sectors of manufacturing industry. The contours and certainties of this new urban industrial capitalist economy were unclear for those wrestling with its earliest days. For the mass of working people adjusting and just surviving in this new world was a huge challenge. The rigid certainties that appeared to surround the experience of employment in these early railway companies may well have appeared better than most other alternative forms of employment.

It was as a result of the government action under pressure from the growing body of middle class entrepreneurs that the investigations into working conditions in Britain started in earnest. The reliance on very long hours was endemic in the railway industry as well as the well known examples in textiles and manufacturing. The Ten Hours Act of 1847 became a reality as much for the reasons of business efficiency as a concern for working conditions.

The evidence of long hours, low wages and dangerous working conditions were slowly emerging, and individuals like Bassett Vincent, having been removed from Worcester where he had tentatively established the first trade union, were now able to develop a fuller picture of working conditions on the railways from conducting extensive surveys drawing evidence directly from individual railway companies. Supported by M. T. Bass, the brewing magnate, Bassett Vincent set out with a Special Commissioner from the London Daily Telegraph, James Greenwood, to compile a report known as 'Mr Bass's Crusade'.[46] With the support of Greenwood, the press finally started to take an interest in the appalling conditions of railway workers. Bassett Vincent had finally built a body of evidence to support those in the House of Commons prepared to reform the ever more powerful railway companies.

Conclusion

The fundamental arrangements for work and employment introduced by these early companies between the mid-1820s and the mid-1860s were profound both in the scale and impact upon the economy. The technical difficulties to overcome absorbed several thousand engineers while business leaders, lawyers and financiers busied themselves both lining their own pockets and all those who needed convincing of the merits of the individual schemes.

As the period of construction came to a close, it became rapidly apparent that construction engineers did not possess the relevant experience for operating the lines. Into this vacuum arrived the military figures, made redundant at the end of the Napoleonic wars, and who appeared to be in possession of a set of skills and experience closely matched to the demands of the day.[47] These early railway companies had had to invent a new model of employment and control in the period under scrutiny, and the combination of paternalism, sectionalism and a body of extensive rules and regulations made resistance difficult to articulate. By the 1860s the weight of experience and information of working conditions started to provide an incontrovertible body of evidence that threatened the safety and efficiency of the industry.

This chapter suggests that the argument made by Howlett[48] and Savage[49] that internal labour markets were really only established on the railways after 1870 is more nuanced. Career structures were evident as early as 1840s even if they were undeveloped. Arguably this was designed precisely to address the problem of labour turnover and create an internal labour market.

The key argument of this chapter, however, has been to demonstrate the range and complexity of the labour process that frustrated the opportunities for resistance to such all-encompassing sets of controls, but this is not synonymous with the daily experience of harsh working conditions. This experience resulted in petitions and less visible forms of dissent, such as drunkenness, lack of attendance at work and various forms of insubordination which had in turn produced a climate of military discipline.[50] From this perspective, it is hard to agree with Kingsford when he suggests that 'In conclusion relations between labour and companies were notable for their peacefulness.'[51] Eventually, the companies had to confront the necessity to supply a safe and efficient service aided by more accurate financial and operating data that would lead the labour process to move inexorably from one dependent upon an extensive surplus to a more structured pattern of work based upon an intensive surplus.

Notes

1. Samuel Smiles quoted in F. D. Klingender, *Art and Industrial Revolution* (Paladin: 1968), p. 122.
2. G. Alderman, *The Railway Interest* (Leicester University Press: 1973), p. 15. Alderman points out that 'the railway companies had obtained their Acts

subject to certain conditions which had been well considered with a view to the protection both of public and private interests. The bargain had been made. Parliament had already sealed its conditions, and shareholders had invested their money under them, and it would not now be right to impose liabilities upon them'.

3. P. Howlett, 'The Internal Dynamics of the Great Eastern Railway Company 1870–1913', *Economic History Review*, LVII:2 (2004), pp. 396–422.

4. M. Savage, 'Discipline, Surveillance and the "Career": Employment on the Great Western Railway, 1833–1914' in A. Mckinlay and K. Starkey (eds), *Foucault, Management and Organisation Theory* (Sage: 1998), pp. 65–92.

5. H. J. Dyos and D. H. Aldcroft, *British Transport. An Economic Survey from the Seventeenth Century to the Twentieth* (Pelican Books: 1974).

6. R. S. Lambert, *The Railway King* (George Hudson) (Allen and Unwin: 1934); L. T. C. Rolt, *Isambard Brunel* (Longmans: 1957); A. Helps, *Life and Labours of Mr. Brassey* (London: 1872).

7. P. Mathias, *The First Industrial Nation. An Economic History of Britain 1700–1914* (Methuen: 1983).

8. P. Lecount, *Railways* (Encyclopaedia Britannica: 7th edition, 1841), p. 55.

9. *Ibid.,* p. 55.

10. The reason that the volume of railway police was so large was to ensure compliance with the regulations of the day.

11. M. De Vroey, 'The Separation of Ownership from Control in Large Corporations' *Review of Radical Political Economics* 7:2 (1975), pp. 1–10.

12. E. J. Hobsbawm, *Industry and Empire* (Penguin: 1969).

13. T. R. Gourvish, *Mark Huish and the London & North Western Railway: A Study of Management* (Leicester University Press: 1972), p. 26.

14. A. Gorz (ed.), *The Division of Labour. The Labour Process and Class Struggle in Modern Capitalism* (Harvester Press: 1978). Gorz traces the steps along which handicraft production finally gave way to early factory systems, clearly indicating that it was not the technology that forced the change but the need to subdue the refractory tempers of work people that provided the logic for forcing individual craft workers into a single place of work under one roof. In the case of the railways this concentration of the work force relied upon installing a complete military system to replace the walls of the factory.

15. Klingender, *Art and Industrial Revolution*, p. 123.

16. Mathias, *The First Industrial Nation*, p. 259.

17. Gourvish, *Mark Huish and the London & North Western Railway*, p. 29.

18. It is interesting to note that, in the case of early American railroad companies, the initial reliance on military order and indeed ex-military personnel for senior management positions in the 1840s is similar to the case of Britain: T. C. Cochran, *Railroad Leaders 1845–1890: The Business Mind in Action* (Harvard University Press: 1953)

19. C. Harvie, *Industrialisation 1830–1914*, Units 29–30 (Open University: 1970).

20. *Ibid.,* p. 65

21. G. Findlay, *The Working and Management of an English Railway* (Whittaker & Co: 1889).

22. R. Kenney, *Men and Rails* (T. Fisher Unwin: 1913).

23. W. H. Chaloner, *The Social and Economic Development of Crewe 1790–1923* (Manchester University Press: 1950). Chaloner provides an excellent detailed account of the development and structure of Crewe as a railway town and refers to four main categories of housing reflecting the very different echelons of company hierarchy.

24. C. Palloix, 'The Labour Process: From Fordism to Neo-Fordism', in *The Labour Process & Class Struggle* (CSE Pamphlet No. 1:1976). Palloix provides a helpful exposition on the nature of the labour process and its historical development and clarifies the transition from 'extensive' surplus to 'intensive' surplus. Essentially this chapter deals with the labour process of railways workers during the period of 'extensive' surplus where long hours and the lack of calculation and measurement are set within a climate when the keeping of records was an arbitrary activity. Even where rudimentary accounting procedures were introduced they were rarely standardized and hence high localized.

25. Findlay, *The Working and Management of an English Railway*, p. 26.

26. F. McKenna, *The Railway Workers 1840–1890.* (Faber and Faber: 1980), p. 39.

27. *Reynolds's Newspaper*, 15 January 1860.

28. *Ibid.*

29. Kenney, *Men and Rails*, p. 30.

30. *Ibid.*, p. 33.

31. *Reynolds's Newspaper*, 25 November 1860.

32. Kenney, *Men and Rails*, p. 34.

33. The Labour Research Dept. Studies in Labour and Capital Unit, *Labour and Capital on the Railways* (The Labour Publishing Company: 1923), p. 39.

34. Klingender, *Art and the Industrial Revolution*, p. 122.

35. P. W. Kingsford, *Victorian Railwaymen* (Frank Cass & Co: 1970).

36. G. D. H. Cole and R. P. Arnot, *Trade Unions on the Railways* (George Allen & Unwin: 1917).

37. *The Morning Chronicle*, 22 August 1850.

38. Newby provides an account of the employment relationship in nineteenth century agriculture, arguing that the close proximity of employer and employee made it difficult for a widely dispersed workforce in this industry to generate a level of organization to challenge working practices at that time. H. Newby, *The Deferential Worker* (Penguin: 1977).

39. G. Findlay, *The Working and Management of an English Railway*, pp. 28–9.

40. C. Bassett Vincent, *The Authentic History of Railway Trade Unionism* (National Association of General Railway Clerks and the Amalgamated Society of Railway Servants: 1902). Bassett Vincent provides a personal account of his move from the Railway Clearing House, where he worked to organize the huge range of services provided by the large number of companies at that time. He established the first official trade union for railway workers in Worcester in 1865.

41. Lecount, *Railways*, p. 55.

42. McKenna, *The Railway Workers 1840–1890*, p. 25.

43. Chaloner, *The Social and Economic Development of Crewe*, p. 39.

44. McKenna, *The Railway Workers 1840–1890*, p. 120.

45. Hobsbawm, *Industry and Empire*, p. 123. He describes: 'if the labouring poor hesitated to accept the system as permanent, even less were they likely – unless forced, often by extra-economic coercion – to adapt themselves to it, even in their struggles. They might seek to by-pass it, as the early socialists did by free communities of cooperative production. They might seek, in the short run, to evade it, as early trade unions did by sending their unemployed members 'on tramp' to some other city, until they discovered that 'bad times' in the new economy were periodic and universal'.

46. Having experienced directly the harsh working conditions and discipline of the clerks working in the Railway Clearing House in London, Bassett Vincent became increasingly concerned for the working conditions generally on the railways. Removed from his post in London he arrived in Worcester with the idea of setting up a trade union on the railways. It was at this time that two of the largest railway companies of the period, the Midland and London and the North Western, once aware of the growing number of employees joining the trade union, set out to intimidate workers by firing 'some fifty of the best men that ever stood on the foot plate, brake van, or signal box; men who had been honest and faithful servants of their respective companies from 5 to over 25 years!'. Bassett, *An Authentic History of Trade Unionism*, p. 27.

47. Bonavia, *The Organisation of the Railways* (Ian Allen: 1971); Gourvish, *Mark Huish and the London & North Western Railway*; Harvie, *Industrialisation 1830–1914*.

48. Howlett, 'The Internal Dynamics of the Great Eastern Railway Company 1870–1913', pp. 396–422.

49. Savage, 'Discipline Surveillance and the "Career": Employment on the Great Western Railway, *1833–1914*,' pp. 65–92.

50. McKenna, *The Railway Workers*, p. 67.

51. P. W. Kingsford, 'Labour Relations on the Railways, 1835–1875', *The Journal of Transport History* 1:2 (November 1953).

3
Women, Mechanization and Cost Savings in Twentieth Century British Banks and Other Financial Institutions

Peter Wardley

In the course of the twentieth century the British financial system was transformed. Although economic historians often prioritize the manufacturing companies that have delivered dynamic industrial performance, this drive for modernization of services provision was an essential element that underpinned the emergence of the British corporate economy and the consolidation of modern economic growth. While different components of the financial system, including the insurance companies, contributed to this development, the vanguard of the movement was provided by the 'High Street' banks, the familiar institutions that by the mid-century provided retail financial services on a mass scale. Each of the 'Big Five' high street banks (Barclays Bank; Lloyds Bank; Midland Bank; National Provincial Bank; and the Westminster Bank) realized its own strategic policy that had been designed to achieve its transformation.[1]

During the interwar years these companies, that 50 years before the First World War had been regionally based and moderately sized, were consolidated as large major employers of capital and labour to such an extent that informed contemporaries would naturally have considered them among the most significant firms in the world. The nature and extent of this transformation can be illustrated by a comparison of the British banking system at the beginning and the end of the twentieth century.[2] However, this transformation was not confined to questions of corporate size, be that indicators of scale or scope, though the magnitude of corporate growth indicated by such metrics is obvious. The achievement of this multifaceted expansion was dependent on two essential ingredients: the employment of women, and the deployment of capital equipment – physical investment in the form of business machinery. It was the integration of these two factors, female labour and capital equipment, that, in the course of the twentieth century, underpinned the expansion of the British financial sector and sustained the growth of its large corporate institutions, the banks, saving institutions, and insurance companies.

However, it is important to recognize in this context that in British banks the employment of women was a twentieth century phenomena (Table 3.1). From the beginning of the late Victorian period (from the 1870s onwards) women clerical workers provided an important and increasingly evident component of the British labour market.[3] Neither the nature of office work, nor the working conditions experienced by female clerical workers, offended contemporary middle class social sensibilities and the gainful employment of young educated women became more favourably regarded. Furthermore, for those who found themselves exposed to the realities of economic, social and personal distress, often caused by the misfortune, malfeasance, physical decline or death of a male provider, employment in such respectable circumstances was a welcome alternative to the unattractive options then available to women.[4] However, although many women found 'white blouse' jobs in the offices of small privately owned companies,[5] the most significant employer of female clerical staff was the British State. In the 40 years before the Great War, first the British Civil Service. and then the General Post Office (GPO) and the National Savings Bank (NSB) provided employment for tens of thousands of female clerical workers.[6] By contrast, and apart from data processing staff in the largest insurance companies, notably the Prudential, relatively few female workers in Britain found employment in financial services before 1914.

The data processing requirements of the exceptions noted here, the Civil Service, the GPO and the NSB,[7] even in the late nineteenth century, are significant here. In more recent years the use of computers by the high street banks has been an obvious feature of financial services provision. It is also one that has been recurrently re-emphasized by each cohort of senior managers that have overseen the implementation of the most recent generation of machines. However, it is important to recognize that this is a far from revolutionary development that has come in discrete stages over a long period of time. Furthermore, while it is all too easy at the beginning of the twenty first century to view the early stages of office mechanization with a condescending eye, there are strong and direct lineages that link the pioneering equipment installed before 1930 to the technology now in use in contemporary banks.[8] As the introduction of this technology by the 'Big Five' high street banks was a vital determinant of the large sale peace time entry of women into the labour force employed in the British financial sector, a brief history of its establishment is outlined below.

This transformation of Britain's banking industry has been the result of three connected long-term strategic decisions. First, this transformation had its origins in the late nineteenth century with the development of branch banking networks, at first regional and, eventually, national if not international in scope. Second, the branch network required the installation of uniform accounting and book keeping procedures, a development that has continued through to the latest, continuing, implementations of information technology-based managerial accounting systems. Third, and closely associated with this transformation of the financial sector, there has been the expansion of employment opportunities for women. While the closer focus here is directed at the initial stages of this evolutionary process, more general and longer term perspectives are highlighted to emphasize that these developments should be assessed in a proper historic perspective, one that reveals the interrelatedness of these phenomena. In fact, it appears that interconnectedness of these three factors has been especially manifest in banking.

By contrast, the literature of different historiographies identifies different aspects of these developments, but fails to integrate these developments in their full complexity. Here company histories emphasize developments specific to the one company, though sometimes indicating the experience of the financial sector. Financial historians, while investigating profitability, lending behaviour and costs, have tended to ignore questions that relate to internal organization and structure of the financial firm. Sociologists and labour historians have researched bureaucratization, labour composition and attitudes to work, but have been apt to award less attention to the determinants of corporate strategy that these reflect.

In the second half of the twentieth century this transformation also encompassed other elements of the British financial system, notably the building societies.[9] In Britain, building societies were created to facilitate house purchase by providing loans secured by mortgages financed by deposits paid into interest-bearing savings accounts or 'share' accounts held by members of the society (the latter, which are not equity shares, offering higher rates of interest on more constrained withdrawal terms). Originally spawned by activists in the Friendly Societies Movement as mutual organizations, some building societies (for example Abbey National) were demutualized and reorganized as shareholder companies in the late 1980s. Constraints on their trading activities were diminished by the permissive 1986 Building Societies Act and these companies then rapidly became similar to the banks in both structure and behaviour. In some cases, the difference between the two was extinguished completely when an amalgamation, such as that which combined the Halifax Building Society and the Bank of Scotland as HBOS, brought together institutions that had very different histories. However, fusion was not a necessary condition as the simultaneous deregulation of the banking sector permitted the banks to enter the mortgage market, an opportunity they seized along with other changes that permitted them to conduct more long-term business. Consequently, over the last two decades an obvious feature of Britain's financial sector has been corporate convergence.

Throughout the period considered here, banks, as indicated by their share of national financial assets, have always been the most important financial institution in the modern British economy; indeed, until 1990 their aggregate holdings amounted to more than half of the nation's financial assets. The residual assets were held by building societies, insurance companies, investment and unit trusts and pension funds. It was only in the last decade of the twentieth century, with the rapid growth of companies which provided pensions, that British banks ceased to be by far the largest collective owners of Britain's financial assets. The importance of the pension funds has even greater significance here given the nature of their function and the problems faced by interwar banks. Obviously, in the twentieth century, the financial sector was not only an essential element of the British economy but it was one that experienced substantial change: women, both as customers and employees, had a part to play in this process. Here, the significance and nature of female employment in this sector is reviewed.

In short, the thesis presented here is that the British financial companies have adopted a succession of long-term strategies that, taken together, have transformed the banking sector and, in so doing, have transformed themselves by adopting modern management techniques, including mechanization and its subsequent manifestation computerization, while at the same time introducing female labour so that they ceased to be solely employers of males. However, although it can be argued that there was 'feminization' of specific jobs in British banks, notably those associated with keyboard equipment and data input, the author doubts that it is sensible to conclude from the employment of increased numbers of females that British financial institutions can be depicted as being 'feminized' during this period.

The origins of office mechanization and antecedents of computers in the British financial sector

By 1914, banks, like many large commercial organizations in Britain and elsewhere, had introduced a number of different types of office equipment designed to 'modernize' clerical and administrative functions. These included: typewriters, telephones, voice recording machines, steel filing cabinets, safes and security systems, photographic records, duplicating presses and copying machines, card sorters and adding machines. Whereas some equipment, the typewriter for example, was capable of multiple uses, some machines, such as those that counted, sorted and packaged coins were specialist in function. A further development associated with some devices saw the adoption of electric motors so that human power was replaced or rendered less strenuous in its application to direct the process undertaken. Those implements designed to process numerical data were to undergo a continual process of improvement and technical development that, eventually, would lead to the electronic computer. For half a century after 1890 these machines were often fundamental to the implementation of managerial systems that depended on the analysis of copious quantities of data.[10] The information processing requirements of firms in the financial sector in Britain and the US in the late Victorian period are well documented,[11] as is the symbiotic relationship that developed over the next four decades between the commercial users of information, especially insurance companies, and the firms that manufactured data processing machinery.[12]

The introduction of these technologies to business occurred concurrently in each of the wealthier economies and encompassed companies that engaged in a wide range of activities so that these developments were shared by firms in both the manufacturing and services sectors. However, it was the USA that saw the most remarked upon changes, be these technical, economic or social, including the deployment of office machinery and the concomitant employment of women clerical workers and the consequences of these developments. It is not surprising that historians there have tended to write of an American experience,[13] rather than one that was international in its scope. Nevertheless, the global significance of these phenomena was recognized in Europe, as is evidenced by the multitude of articles published in the contemporary commercial press, trade journals and popular newspapers.

In August 1929 the author of an anonymously written article in *The Banker* did not regard it as news for a reader that 'inventors have devised calculators for interest, tax, exchange, and other arithmetical computations, for the posting of ledgers, passbooks, security books, and all the interlocking records which go to make up the system'. Indeed, he noted that the arrival of the first Burroughs adding machine in a British banking office had taken place 30 years before. However, what he did regard as news was this:

> Already several banks have launched schemes of mechanization covering more or less of the routine work of their branches; some have introduced machines for ledgers and pass-books statements; while others are committed to plans involving [these machines] besides many parts of the internal accountancy – with a view eventually to the supersession everywhere of the pen by the machine.

In the 1920s, in an effort to economize their administrative costs, many large corporations introduced more complex and specialist office technology. Banks were among the pioneers to adopt these new business machines that became a common feature of the British, French, German and American banking industries. However, banks in the USA were outliers: American banks were relatively small, restricted by legislation to activity within one state, and, not infrequently, to a single banking office. Whereas mechanization in the USA offered data processing economies within a single office, in economies where national branch banking was permitted these were supplemented by economies that came with the introduction of office machinery to service banking systems that operated at the national and regional level as well as within the local branch.

By the end of the 1920s British high street banks had introduced 'mechanized banking' by a variety of standardized accounting procedures and record keeping functions that provided the more rapid throughput of information fundamental for the achievement of economies of scale. This depended upon equipment produced by a number of manufacturing firms including Burroughs, Hollerith, Mercedes, National Cash Register, Powers-Samas and Remington; but at the heart of mechanized banking the most significant instrument was the Ledger Posting Machine and, within a relatively short time, most frequently its female operator.

Attitudes to women clerks by male staff in the British financial sector

Traditionally, banking as an occupation and profession had been the preserve of males; female bank clerks were almost unheard of before 1914. The Midland Bank, a pioneer in this respect, recruited its first female staff member, Miss Anne Tulloch, in 1907; thereafter a small number of typists and stenographers were employed at its major bank offices in London.[14] The Great War was to change attitudes in the banking industry, as in so many aspects of British life.

During the war there had been an almost universal acceptance that the recruitment of women workers was a necessary expedient that enabled senior management to fill the gaps caused by military service. Bank staff in Britain, as almost universally throughout the British Empire, proved remarkably enthusiastic when war broke out in 1914 and enlisted eagerly. While, no doubt, patriotism was an important determinant of their eagerness to enlist, another factor for many young bank clerks habitually faced with daily humdrum and routine office work was the excitement of active military participation in what was generally assumed to be a war of limited duration. As it was, many of those keen to enlist at the beginning of the war did have a short military career, though one that was cut short by their untimely demise rather than by the widely anticipated cessation of hostilities before the Great War's first Christmas. The sacrifice of these staff, of whom some were mourned as lost potential leaders, would weigh heavily upon those who made decisions within the banks for the next generation.[15]

Those staff who did act according to their patriotic inclinations were encouraged to meet the call to serve King and Country both by their colleagues, those male bank staff who worked on in their absence, and by their employers. Throughout the war the banks financially supported those of their employees who had joined up so that the service pay of bank staff was augmented with a supplement that brought their income up to the level that would have experienced had they remained in the bank's employ.

As a consequence of the perceived obligations created by the war, senior managers accepted that, as employers, the banks had a responsibility to their male staff who had served in the armed forces. This was evident in both the salaries and conditions of work implemented by the banks throughout the interwar years and beyond. The banks also accepted as a social norm the concept of the family wage, a belief that justified enhanced payments for older male employees because they were likely to be married men whose income also supported a wife and children. The latter principle also determined an attitude to promotion as the banks specified payment systems that corresponded to the expectations of male staff that they would have promotion opportunities above, beyond, and different from female staff.

Nevertheless, and despite these perceptions, senior bankers readily acknowledged the contribution made during the war by female staff,[16] fully recognized the capabilities of female bank clerks, and greatly regretted the limited loyalty they were able to demonstrate in their treatment of female workers, many of whom had their employment terminated when demobilized male bank staff returned to civilian employment. The bankers seem to have been consoled, at least in part, with the thought that, at least on their part, the work had only been offered to women as a temporary measure pending the return of men on military service.

By 1922, with peace time conditions restored, in many sectors of the economy there was a reappraisal of working conditions in the labour market. In this context, the banking industry was no exception. The position and status of women employees offered an opportunity to senior managers because they provided a source of cheap labour and, for the same reason, they posed a threat to existing male employees who had not been promoted and held junior positions. In the banking industry the development and refinement of technology, in the form of machine banking and associated mechanical devices for the conduct of clerical and office work, was considered in association with female labour that offered opportunities for cost-cutting innovation.

It is important to note that all of these views were not unconscious consequences of unthinking acceptance of traditional values; on the contrary, contemporaries frequently recognized that these positions were social constructs that could be disputed and deliberated upon. This was manifest as early as January 1923 when the Debating Society of the Institute of Banking heard a discussion of the proposition 'that the permanent retention of women clerks in the banks, on the lines of the Civil Service, is desirable, both from the point of view of male staffs, and that of the economical conduct of banking business'. In the Opener's speech that started the debate, E. R. Long presented a reasoned case that fully reflected this caution.[17] Moreover, it is significant that this debate occurred before most banking staff had a clear appreciation of the scope and extent of the technological transformation that would occur in the financial industry over the next 15 years.

Long prefaced his remarks with two questions: first, was it desirable that women were permanently employed as bank staff? To this he replied that many of the 'temporary lady helpers' had 'become more or less permanently enrolled on our staffs'. Second, if women were to be made permanent staff, under what conditions were they to be employed?

To the latter, he insisted that the time had arrived when an honest response was required, and he proposed that three alternative policies existed: First, that any sex barrier should be rejected such that the whole range of banking activity was thrown open to all; women as well as men. To adopt this policy, he suggested, was to follow the example of the learned professions. However, he opined that although this was theoretically plausible, and could not be discounted in perpetuity, it was a sweeping innovation for the 'notoriously conservative world of finance' that could not be regarded as practical policy. Second, that the banks should act to remove female staff immediately, either with or without compensation, or that recruitment of women cease and wastage be allowed to diminish their number. He opined that this policy was strongly supported among 'certain sections of the junior male staff' and that possibly it was more evident in the north of England than in the south.[18] Acceptance of this strategy, at least to a limited extent, can be demonstrated by the example of Lloyds Bank where female employment declined from 3300 in 1918 to 1380 in 1927.[19] Third, that women should be accepted as permanent employees, 'but that their services should be conditional on certain clearly defined limitations being observed'.[20]

Long presented the third option as the 'middle road' and the policy he advocated in accordance with the qualifying clause specified by the proposed resolution: based on the conditions of female employment by the English [*sic*] Civil Service. In modern parlance his proposal recommended for the finance industry a gender determined segmentation of internal labour markets. The characteristics that he drew to the attention of his audience were that:

> women clerks entered the (Civil Service) under well-understood conditions, they are given recognised commencing salaries and annual increments; and a definite maximum (of salary and position) beyond which they cannot go, save in exceptional cases of women employed appointed to supervisory work over other women, in positions that cannot be filled by men.[21]

Unsurprisingly, this work was routine and demanded little in the way of responsibility, such that 'a great mass of clerical labour which would otherwise have to be done by men [was] done by women'.[22] However, he also drew attention to additional conditions that applied in the Civil Service that were to prove a little more problematic for the banks. For example, in the Civil Service women were assigned work that was gender specific and distinct from that allocated to men and they were allowed working conditions, including holidays and overtime, that differed from those enjoyed by men. A similar policy was adopted by Lloyds Bank in the early 1920s when it abandoned general recruitment of female bank clerks, but continued to employ female typists and filing clerks.[23] As a consequence, women disappeared from the bank's counter and were either relocated to clerical tasks or left the bank's employ.

Long's prescriptions were prescient in that they not only predicted many of the conditions to be adopted almost immediately by England's high street banks, but forecast conditions that were to remain in force for the next 50 years; as he spoke:

> I only desire to suggest that the recruitment of women for bank service should be on a recognised scale, with regular increments up to a suitable point and an adequate pension on retirement; but that it should not hold out any possibility of the appointment of women – however capable and deserving – to the higher positions of executive responsibility.[24]

Long regarded this a candid position because, although it did not perhaps reflect the ambitions of some women who had already joined the banks, it did not break any promises of advancement that had been made to them and those potential recruits who were more ambitious or specially talented would recognize that they should look elsewhere. For the banks, it was not a problem if the girls with large ideas or big ambitions looked elsewhere for employment because there would 'remain plenty of girls of the right type' who would be 'glad to secure employment under conditions' which, if they 'did not promise affluence, at least [did] provide a reasonable livelihood in the event of their avoiding the common fate of matrimony'.[25]

He also suggested that the employment of women on these terms was in the best interest of young junior staff because, with routine tasks delegated to women with no prospects of promotion, it would improve the chances of advancement for each junior male staff member:

> It is the belief that these better paid appointments are awaiting him, sooner or later, which makes it worthwhile for the bank clerk to

remain for so many years in a service which, but for these rewards ahead, is apt, in its earlier stages, to offer little encouragement to his enthusiasm, and small return for his fidelity.[26]

Long also identified benefits that would accrue to the bank: first, a high proportion of women would be paid at the lower points of the female scale because newly employed junior women would constantly replace those experienced female workers who left to get married; and, second, women would be remunerated on a scale that had a more shallow gradient than that of male staff, who required higher salaries 'to meet the normal family requirements of men'.[27] These two features were salient characteristics of the incremental pay scales for women that were adopted in the mid-1920s and maintained, with subsequent modifications, until the early 1970s. At Lloyds Bank, for example, it was not until 1957 that a woman doing work comparable to that of a man received four-fifths, rather than two-thirds, of his pay.[28]

Furthermore, gender discrimination was systematic in other respects. Whereas a man could be requested to defer from marrying until he had reached a point on the salary scale that provided his family with a middle class life style and guaranteed an appropriate social status, only single women were welcome as bank employees. A strictly applied marriage bar stipulated that a woman's wedding marked the end of her career at the bank. At Lloyds, for example, this was not revoked until 1949, when the labour market was extremely tight. At the Ulster Bank, an affiliated subsidiary of the Westminster Bank that had engaged its first women employees in 1915,[29] the marriage bar persisted until at least 1963; though, by then, immediate re-employment on a temporary contract was not uncommon.[30]

However, as women were obliged to wear an official uniform a more immediately evident form of gender discrimination was also apparent at the Ulster Bank. Originally this was a light blue overall that 'resembled a washed-out blue bag'. This was very much a garment of its time, as women employed in many different occupations during the Great War, be they civilians or members of the armed forces, worked in such apparel. Since then, although largely true to delphinium blue, the uniform has been evolved through 1960s 'air hostess' to 1990s corporate chic.[31] Although it is far from uncommon for women employed by many large companies to be obliged to wear a corporate uniform, the general requirement that men dress in grey or blue suits of their choice is much less restrictive and also less reminiscent of school adolescence and teenage immaturity.

Given the developments at the end of the decade, it is striking that mechanization plays no part in Long's analysis of the prospects of women bank clerks in 1923. Once machine banking was adopted extensively by the English high street banks in the late 1920s, the logic of his position appeared all the stronger. There was a widespread belief that women were more dexterous and more accurate keyboard operators. Women were also viewed as more patient workers, who were more careful, who worked more conscientiously throughout the working day and who were more accepting of the limited promotion prospects imposed by the conditions of their employment over their career.

Once mechanization was widely diffused across a bank branch network, there was a necessity that young male bank clerks learnt to operate the various machines employed by the bank. After their promotion it was important that senior staff should know how to operate all the elements of the bank's organization, in order that they could not only supervise all the staff in their section but that they could also respond appropriately to local emergencies. However, senior staff were determined that exposure to these technical requirements was not to deter or discourage aspirant younger male staff and it was also perceived that those with talent should then be moved on quickly to other more demanding tasks that required responsibility and talent.[32]

Consequently, the junior ranks of the bank staff came to comprise newly recruited women and men, more experienced women who had no possibilities of promotion, and older men whose less than promising performance had caused their employer to deny their expectations of promotion. In the latter case, given the almost unheard alternative of employment by a competitor bank, at least some senior bank managers appear to have the view that only an adequate pension on retirement guaranteed anything that could resemble adequate performance.

For the building societies, at least before 1940, their limited size and geographical spread restricted the opportunities for female employment. Additionally, these characteristics also sharply curtailed their opportunities for mechanization. However, at the outbreak of the Second World War, the building societies, now much larger than they had been in 1914, substituted female labour for male staff who joined the forces, thus following a path similar to that pioneered by the banks in the First World War. In the new economic conditions of the post war period, with the expansion of home ownership and full employment, the building societies grew and extended their branch networks.[33] Thirty years after the 'Big Five' banks, and again replicating to some extent the patterns exhibited by the banks in the interwar years, building societies in the

1950s and 1960s employed larger numbers of female staff and under-took programmes to mechanize their internal accounting functions. A very similar story can also be told for Britain's smaller banks, especially those that conducted most of their business in the 'provinces', Scotland[34] and Ulster.[35]

In the 1950s labour shortages, exacerbated by the relatively high rates of labour turnover particularly among young women,[36] provided further stimuli to the search for automated accounting procedures in the financial sector. By the early 1960s both the banks and the building societies were large employers of female labour and pioneering users of the newly developed mainframe computer.[37]

When the pay and working conditions of female workers became a contentious political issue in the 1960s, it was the State that once more provided the framework, if not the role model, for the equalization of employment opportunities. Where banks had adopted the employment mores of the British Civil Service in the 1920s, mores that had been followed by the building societies in the 1950s when women were employed for the first time in larger numbers, the advancement of equal opportunity policies by the British State, legislated as the Equal Pay Act of 1970, required major policy changes in these institutions. The Equal Pay Act narrowed, even if it did not eradicate, the salary gap between men and women. Thereafter, unequal opportunities would reflect mainly discrimination caused by favouritism in promotion and merit payments rather than institutionalized gender biased salary schemes.

Female employment in twentieth century Britain and its financial institutions

How important was female labour for the British economy in the twentieth century? And how did the female labour force become important in the British financial services industry? Table 3.1 provides an essential preliminary perspective on the importance of female labour, firstly in the British economy and, secondly, in the broadly defined financial and business services sector. Overall, this reveals a steady increase of female employment commensurate with the growth of the British population.

From 1901 the female participation ratio, the proportion of women recorded as active in the labour market by each successive Census of Population, was remarkably stable at *circa* 25 per cent until the Second World War whereupon it rose to 27 per cent in 1951 and reached 31 per cent in 1971. The male participation rate was also stable at *circa* 65 per cent until the interwar Great Depression, when it fell to *circa*

Table 3.1 Employment in the British insurance, banking, finance, and business services industries, 1901–71

	1901	1911	1921	1931	1951	1971
Population	36,999,946	40,831,396	42,685,157	44,706,903	48,854,303	53,978,545
Total employment	16,311,539	18,351,366	19,006,598	18,907,945	22,134,689	23,732,610
Participation rate	0.441	0.449	0.445	0.423	0.453	0.440
Male population	17,902,368	19,754,447	20,382,348	21,418,159	23,449,991	26,197,610
Male proportional of population	0.484	0.484	0.478	0.479	0.480	0.485
Number of males employed	11,548,164	12,927,422	13,369,600	13,117,617	15,309,022	15,031,550
Male participation rate	0.645	0.654	0.656	0.612	0.653	0.574
Female population	19,097,578	21,076,949	22,302,809	23,288,744	25,404,312	27,780,935
Female proportion of population	0.516	0.516	0.522	0.521	0.520	0.515
Number of females employed	4,763,375	5,423,944	5,636,998	5,790,328	6,825,667	8,701,060
Female participation rate	0.249	0.257	0.253	0.249	0.269	0.313
Total employed in insurance, banking, finance and business services	165,774	242,456	332,810	389,323	435,121	952,520
Males employed in IBFB	162,558	233,061	246,976	300,889	285,367	475,100
Females employed in IBFB	3,216	9,395	85,834	88,434	149,754	477,420
Female workers as proportion of IBF&BS total	0.019	0.039	0.258	0.227	0.344	0.501
Female IBF&BS as proportion of female total	0.001	0.002	0.015	0.015	0.022	0.055
Male workers as proportion of IBF&BS total	0.981	0.961	0.742	0.773	0.656	0.499
Male IBF&BS as proportion of male total	0.014	0.018	0.018	0.023	0.019	0.032
IBF&BS as proportion of employment total	0.010	0.013	0.018	0.021	0.020	0.040

Source: Adapted from C.H. Lee, *British Regional Employment Statistics 1841–1971* (Cambridge University Press: 1979)

61 per cent, recovered to its early twentieth century rate in 1951 before falling to 57 per cent in 1971. In aggregate, taking both sexes together from 1901 until 1971, the proportion of the population actively engaged in employment was virtually constant, bar the very small fall of about 2 per cent associated with the high level of unemployment of 1931, at circa 44 per cent. Between 1901 and 1951, at each of the population censuses, women comprised *circa* 30 per cent of the labour force; thereafter in 1971 the share of employment taken by women's rose to 37 per cent.

However, despite the stability suggested by these statistics, a major feature of the twentieth century British economy was structural change. By 1971 a large and significant shift in employment had seen services emerge as the largest of the three major components of the British economy and this shift was consolidated and augmented over the next 30 years such that by 2001 for every four jobs, three could be classified as service activities. Within the services sectors, a conspicuous change was that domestic service was much reduced in importance and commercial services became increasingly important.

Disaggregate data highlights the nature and extent of this shift for the British financial sector; here the Insurance, Banking, Finance and Business Services (IBF&BS) is the relevant major industrial order identified by Clive Lee from the British Censuses of Population. In the nineteenth century total employment in the sector was relatively small: 6281 in 1841; 5694 in 1851; 17,248 in 1861; 29,243 in 1871; 48,444 in 1881; and, 73,772 in 1891. Furthermore, female employment was insignificant in this sector in the nineteenth century; the British Census of Population only recorded 47 females employed in the IBF&BS sector in 1841; none in 1851; 1 in both 1861 and 1871; 419 in 1881; and, 793 in 1891.[38] Despite the appreciable growth of male employment evident in this sector in the second half of the nineteenth century, the IBF&BS sector employed remarkably few women before 1901.

This expansion of employment continued into the new century and in the two censuses before the First World War the workforce employed in the IBF&BS sector was recorded as 165,000 in 1901 and 242,000 in 1911. Substantial growth in the sector resulted in employment increasing to 333,000 in 1921, though slower growth is indicated by the 389,000 employees recorded in 1931. The impact of the First World War remains ambiguous. After the Second World War, however, growth was re-established so that 435,000 were recorded as active in the IBF&BS sector in 1951 and 953,000 in 1971.

As Table 3.1 demonstrates, although the number of males employed in the IBF&BS sector grew from 162,558 in 1901 to 233,061 in 1911, the same decade saw the number of females increase from 3216 to 9395. In 1901, at a time when the IBF&BS sector employed 1 per cent of the British workforce, female employment in the sector was only a tenth of 1 per cent of the British total and only 2 per cent of the employment in IBF&BS. Between the wars, the IBF&BS sector had grown to employ 4 per cent of total British employment recorded by the Census of Population. Female employment for this sector increased significantly relative to its pre-Great War level, from 85,834 in 1921 and 88,434 in 1931; a quarter of all employment in the sector was now taken by females.[39]

However, as we will see, though the increase in both employment and the number of females employed relative to the late Edwardian period was real, the stability suggested by these data, and others provided by the Census of Population, is in some ways misleading, if not contradictory. The latter aspect is demonstrated by Table 3.2. Taken at face value, this would suggest that in English banks and discount houses there was: first, a conspicuous increase in total employment (a 16 per cent increase); second, a significant increase in male employment (a rise of 25 per cent); third, a significant fall in female employment (down 10 per cent); and, consequently, a major shift in the ratio of male:female banking staff between 1921 and 1931 (a 40 per cent shift in favour of males). Were this the only evidence available, it would not be suggestive of a major change in the gender balance of the workforce employed by these institutions during the interwar years. *Prima facie* it might even be taken to indicate a partial restoration of the *status quo ante* World War One when the financial institutions employed a predominantly male bank office workforce. However, this was not the case.

Although there are no complete statistics of bank staff and their compositions, contemporary concern, particularly on the part of junior male banking staff, prompted an investigation in 1935 undertaken by the Bank Officers' Guild; an employees' organization established to

Table 3.2 Employment in banks and discount houses in interwar England

	1921	1931	Change	% Change
Males	58,043	72,673	14,630	25
Females	20,842	18,783	–2,059	–10
Total	78,885	91,456	12,571	16
Ratio of males per 100 females	278	387		

Source: *Census of Population in England and Wales, 1931* (HMSO).

Table 3.3   Bank Officers' Guild employment survey of junior bank staff

	1928/9	1934/5	Change	% Change
(1) Junior staff (2+3 adult + Junior)				
Males	29,064	23,797	−5,267	−18
Females	12,302	14,347	2,045	17
Total junior staff	41,366	38,144	−3,222	−8
Ratio of males per 100 females	236	166		
(2) Adult junior staff				
Male	27,454	23,064	−4,390	−16
Female	12,060	14,031	1,971	16
Total adult junior staff	39,514	37,095	−2,419	−6
Ratio of males per 100 females	228	164		
(3) Juvenile junior staff				
Boys	1,610	733	−877	−54
Girls	242	316	74	31
Total juvenile junior staff	1,852	1,049	−803	−43
Ratio of males per 100 females	665	232		

Sources: *Bank Officers' Guild Report*, 1935. "A Banker", 'Bank Mechanization as Affecting Personnel and Public', *The Banker*, (October 1938) Vol. xliii, no. 153, p.59. *Note*: Compiled for the Bank Officers' Guild from the annual reports of the Banking Unemployment Board; the BUB surveyed only persons with salaries of £250 and under.

represent junior male staff. This survey utilized the annual reports of the Banking Unemployment Board, a government body established to review the labour market and assess the unemployment entitlements of persons in the industry who earned £250 and under. Its findings are summarized in Table 3.3. The implications of the Bank Officers' Guild report differ greatly from those suggested by the Census of Population taken only five years earlier. In particular, it revealed a decline in the number of male junior staff, an increase in the number of female junior staff, and, consequently, a fall in the ratio of male:female junior staff. All these data suggest that a major shift in the gender balance of bank staff occurred during this period.

In detailing juvenile employment these data also provide some indication of recruitment patterns, but, for this purpose, they have to be read with care and the longer term dynamics are not without ambiguity. This is due, in major part, to the segmented internal labour market, where there was discrimination by gender that operated within each of the banks. Not only did senior managers expect the exit rate of female workers to be higher than that of male staff, because females were obliged to leave employment on marriage, but females also tended to be employed at a slightly older age than boys who were more often recruited directly as school leavers to a career ladder that potentially provided a route to senior management for those males who obtained preferment and promotion.

Table 3.3 also speaks to the recruitment of juvenile staff in this period. Even during the bleakest years of the interwar Great Depression, a period when bank expansion virtually slowed to a halt, the actions of senior bank managers confirmed the new gender balance. While recruitment of boys fell by more than a half, the number of newly appointed girls increased by a third. 'A Banker' summarized these changes with the comment that 'the reduction in male staff naturally took place through a check to recruiting, and the net decrease of 3222 in the total staff within the lower salary grades was no doubt attributable as much to depression as to mechanization'.[40]

'A Banker' also opined that 'displacement consists also in the substitution of female for male labour, since machines are operated more efficiently and economically by women clerks', adding that '[a]lthough boys may be trained to operate machines with equal efficiency it cannot be economic from the point of view of succession to tie them to the machine for a substantial period of their early banking careers'.[41] Here his view was typical of many senior bank officials. Female staff would 'man' the equipment that made possible the economies promised by machine banking throughout the years of their employment. By contrast, once familiar with the operation of banking routines and the associated mechanical apparatus, male staff, who showed aptitude in appraisal that suggested they were candidates for senior positions, were selected for promotion according to extended career ladders that reached much greater heights. One beneficial consequence of this pattern of work organization, not infrequently commented on by senior managers in the banks, was that promising 'boys' would not be deterred from entering the bank by excessive exposure to boring and routine machine work. Almost absent was any mention of the consequences of continuous contact with this tedious drudgery for the female staff who did not even have the consolation that one day their talents might be recognized; they faced no prospect of a hard earned promotion to 'better things'.

What changed in interwar British banks?

Three elements stand out as the most significant in this transformation: first, the development of a coordinated network of outlets that permitted unified branch banking across the institution as a whole; second, the introduction across this system of a new system of managerial organization that was closely supervised from the head offices of the bank; and, third, the introduction of female labour. The implementation of these three factors was closely related. However, development was a sequential and iterative process that saw in the second and third elements; the implementation of new control systems and the introduction of female labour. This was a tripartite strategy and only the successful execution of each of the three elements allowed its successful implementation. The consolidation and expansion of the branch network was associated with both new internal record keeping systems and new technology; originally machine banking which would later become computerized banking, and a gendered labour force.

Before 1850 British banks were small-scale businesses, usually partnerships held by a small number of partners rather than joint stock corporations, organized according to relatively simple principles and employment was resolutely a male preserve. Within these small organizations banking operations were relatively simple, easy to supervise, and conducted for the most part without recourse to anything but the most simple and traditional technology that required little beyond pens, ink, ledger books and, perhaps, a set of scales. It was the development of extensive networks of branch banking offices in the second half of the nineteenth century that necessitated the development of a centrally directed supervisory regime. Adherence to the policies stipulated at headquarters by senior managers was scrutinized and enforced by bank inspectors who travelled from bank to bank to ensure that the rigorous, codified regulations were applied consistently and accurately across all the offices of the bank. At Queen Victoria's death in 1901 the financial sector was much changed in some respects but in others it still exhibited many of the features that had been characteristic 50 years earlier. Perhaps the most obvious of these traditional aspects was that it was determinedly a male world. As in some other respects, this was to change, and to change remarkably quickly. At the time the contribution of the First World War appeared significant but more fundamental underlying factors internal to the banks were, in reality, much more significant.

By the third quarter of the twentieth century the British high street banks, the major retail banks that had achieved a ubiquitous presence in the country's urban centres of any significance, were large consolidated financial institutions operated by senior managers through highly centralized organizations. Proficient management of these organizations became increasingly reliant upon advanced and complex information technology. By 1919 substantial changes had already ensured that in the leading large financial corporations, senior bank officers already commanded management systems that demonstrated features that have persisted through to the present.

To some extent it is justifiable to view the high street banks as pioneers, significant corporations that led the field in the development of the 'Corporate Economy'. One feature of the twentieth century was the introduction of significant changes in managerial structures of large companies, which emerged before the First World War and continued to grow in size and economic significance throughout the rest of the century. Inevitably, an important aspect of this was the organization of work and labour processes within these corporate giants. Although these developments are often highlighted for firms that operated in industrial sectors of the developed Western economics,[42] many large corporations in the services sectors contemporaneously experienced similar changes. However, these developments are often overlooked and neglected by those who have recorded the emergence of the large industrial corporation, the classic 'Chandlerian' firm.[43]

Analysis of mechanization by the British high street (retail) banks raises essential questions about the nature of gendered technical change in the services sectors: the nature of work, organization of the labour process, the substitution of male labour by female labour and, eventually, questions of equality and opportunity both in the workplace and within the large corporation. In the interwar years these questions were even starker than they appeared in the 1960s and 1970s, when mainframe computing was introduced by the British retail banks and building societies. In both eras, the introduction of new technology had important consequences for the gendered division of labour and, in each case, this was a direct result of a conscious decision making process that initiated and oversaw the implementation of managerial strategies that is worthy of historical attention in its own right.

The senior managers of the large banks were confident, and with good reason, that the combination of female labour and mechanized banking would cut costs. The most recent historical researchers, while examining the structure and extent of competition, measuring profitability and investigating the introduction of management accounting, have found scant evidence of either productivity growth or cost reductions.[44] These studies have, however, had little to say about the methods or the strategies adopted by the banks to *either* achieve cost reductions *or* to prevent costs rising as fast as senior managers might otherwise have anticipated. Nevertheless, the combination of woman and machine was a vital part of the strategy uniformly adopted by the British high street banks.

The managerial changes implemented by the 'Big Five' high street banks in England during the interwar period were designed to raise efficiency and reduce costs. Rouse, the senior manager charged with implementing policy at the Midland Bank, was convinced that substantial economies had been achieved by mechanization, the associated recruitment of female staff, and managerial reorganization in general. His original assessment was that two male clerks could be released for the cost of one female machine operator. Six years after the initial implementation of mechanical ledger posting, Rouse was able to refine his earlier estimate to suggest more definitively that the employment of one female operator for every ledger posting machine installed allowed the release of 2.1 male clerks to be redeployed to alternative work. Significant saving in labour costs were achieved as female salaries (*circa* £150 p.a.) were half those of their male counterparts (*circa* £300 p.a.). As the price of the ledger posting machines was *circa* £420, and the equipment had a life expectancy of about ten years, even after allowing for the cost of the capital equipment, substantial cost savings were made. Rouse's initial evaluation of staffing redeployment suggested that the break-even point, after investment in all aspects of the system (that is including training, accommodation, sundry expenses and so on), would occur about two years after the installation of accounting machines. In crude terms, though, the saving achieved by the installation of each machine approximated to the salary of a male staff employee.[45]

Overall, it would appear that by 1939, through the introduction of machine accounting, the 'Big Five' had collectively made annual net savings on costs in excess of £1 million.[46] This was a reduction equivalent to about 7 per cent of total labour charges and *circa* 3 per cent of total costs. Although all the savings achieved through related managerial and employment changes are not included in this estimate, it does represent an initial, though approximate and admittedly conservative, financial estimate of the economies of scale achieved by the 'Big Five' through the operation of national branch banking systems supervised centrally from a head office.[47]

Conclusion

The twentieth century saw the transformation of the British financial system that began with the implementation of a strategic policy at each of Britain's largest financial companies that provided retail banking; 'High Street' banks. This transformation was achieved by the implementation of long-term strategies applied by individual companies so that it now embraces the financial sector in its entirety, albeit that minor local variations peculiar to specific institutions have been apparent and can continue to persist.

The comprehensive nature of this transformation is indicated clearly by a comparison of the British financial sector in the early years of the twentieth century and the beginning of the twenty first century. Here the leading role of the high street banks is emphasized not only to indicate the nature of this process within these institutions but also to highlight the subsequent impact on the other elements of the financial sector. The banking sector also stands representative of the major components of the process of Modern Economic Growth. Such is the absolute and relative expansion of the service sector, measured both by value of output and employment of labour, that these activities have now surpassed the primary and industrial sectors, both separately and taken together, to form the largest component of the British economy.[48]

One major change was the restructuring of employment patterns within the major British financial institutions; during a period when employment at banks grew significantly, the female labour force grew from negligible numbers to one that equalled the male labour force in numbers, though not in status or influence. Although often regarded as passive, conservative, and of less significance relative to the supposed dynamic, progressive and paramount industrial sector,[49] the service sector has to be recognized as a source of productivity growth and technical change.[50] The transformation of the British financial sector was achieved by firms that adopted and executed innovative long run corporative strategies. However, it is important to recognize that gender, as well as managerial innovation and technology advance, has been an important causal factor.

The story presented here takes the long run view and asserts that the attempts by British financial institutions in the twentieth century have been complex, strategically managed and gendered. These factors are inter-related and each plays an important role in the drama. In the English banking sector at the end of the 1930s, and after two decades of significant managerial and organizational change, female banking staff could be found everywhere, bar only the smallest of branches. Where female labour was found in the banks after 1922, it was usually accompanied by banking machinery. In the building societies, at least until the Second World War, female employment was inconspicuous. After 1950, the building societies and the smaller British banks followed an expansionary path that resembled in many aspects that which the 'Big Five' English banks had adopted after the First World War. Inevitably, this was not a case of history repeating itself as macroeconomic conditions were very different in the two eras and the building societies were responding to changes in their segment of the financial market, where customer expectations were changing substantially.

At the end of the 1980s, as the 'IT Revolution' became a popular topic for discussion and popular awareness of the potential of computers became increasingly apparent, Robert Solow remarked famously that the computer age could be seen everywhere except in the productivity statistics.[51] One consequence of his comment was an increased awareness among economists that the fruits of technical change were much harder to identify than had been previously believed. There was also an enhanced attentiveness to significance of long run technical change. When economists looked for a gauge against which calibrate the impact of computers, they were obliged to consider the impact of other technologies that had, at least apparently, had a transformative effect on economies and their constituent industries.

A conspicuous element here was the discussion of the role of the services sector that become so important in terms of their relative contribution to the modern economy; and within the services, the producers of financial services figured strongly, both as user of computers and as computer users whose productivity was notoriously difficult to measure. However, historical developments in the banking sector were relatively neglected and the long run history of technological innovation and gendered employment was overlooked. Quite correctly, on this some economists were eager to take the long run view and adopt a historically informed perspective:

> We looked at the new products and new technologies at the end of the 20th century, and we are impressed. We should be. But are they increasing at an increased rate? Is the number of new products increasing more rapidly on a logarithmic scale? I think it safe to assert that the empirical work in economic history that would confirm the increasing rate hypothesis has not been carried out.[52]

However, the nature of labour employed to complement that new technology is also an important concern, and that this issue has been neglected. The expansion of female labour employed by the building societies, another major component of the financial services sector, was achieved from a low base over a similar length of time by an analogous process to that undertaken by the high street banks, but one that was delayed for a generation, occurring 20 years later. Although world wars, by removing men to the armed forces, played a part here, major changes came about in peace time and were the result of managerial decisions, made at the most senior level within these organizations, that determined strategy. The two comparable strategies that occurred in both sets of institutions were associated with the adoption of machinery that allowed the oversight and management of large financial organizations and were associated with the greatly increased employment of women.

An expansion of both scale and scope, *a la* Alfred Chandler, by both institutional types necessitated the substitution for male labour of the combined and complementary inputs of female labour and machinery in the form of, first, mechanized banking equipment in the decade after 1928, and then mainframe computers after 1958. Whereas the high street banks implemented both phases, it was in the second phase that the building societies implemented a similar expansive strategy, augmenting their branch networks and extending their product range. As both institutions implemented these strategic initiatives in periods of business expansion, this strategy of substitution did not require that men were made redundant but it did curtail the expansion of male employment.

Without the increased employment of a less expensive female labour force, the introduction of new technology, both in the interwar years and during the post war 'Golden Age', the economics of change associated with the introduction of new technology would have been very different. Without the savings made on the additional male salaries that would otherwise have been required, the introduction of new technology would have been much more expensive and, therefore, much less attractive to those who sponsored its introduction. At the heart of this very rational managerial strategy lay a very explicit and largely unapologetic policy of gender discrimination.

At the end of the twentieth century, British financial institutions had less opportunity to exploit workers by discriminatory labour practices. Women now had equal employment rights and, part-time workers and students apart, there is no domestic segment of the labour force that could be substituted as a 'third gender'. However, recent technological advances have made it possible to employ in the services sectors workers who are located geographically outside the United Kingdom and employed in separate labour markets; and the providers of financial services, including both the banks and institutions that were historically recognized as building societies, have taken advantage of these opportunities. New technology, in the form of call centres and improved telephony, has provided yet another opportunity for capital to be introduced in association with labour substitution. While new technologies may be developed, and with globalization now well established, it has become difficult to envisage alternative sources of labour that the British financial services industry might find that could be substituted for those that are now drawn upon for recruitment of new employees. At least in one respect, could this be yet another example of the end of history?

Notes

1. My thanks to Nicola Verdon and my colleagues, Bernardo Bátiz-Lazo, June Hannam, Moira Martin and Philip Ollerenshaw for comments on the initial draft of this chapter which was presented at the International Economic History Association XIV Conference, Helsinki in 2006, and to the archivists at the HBOS for their advice and assistance.
   P. Wardley, 'The Commercial Banking Industry and Its Part in the Emergence and Consolidation of the Corporate Economy in Britain before 1940', *Journal of Industrial History* 3:2 (2000), pp. 71–97.
2. F. Capie, 'Structure and Performance in British Banking, 1870–1939' in P. L. Cottrell and D. E. Moggridge (eds), *Money and Power: Essays in Honour of L.S. Pressnell* (Macmillan: 1988); British Banking Association, *Abstract of Banking Statistics* (British Banking Association: 2001).
3. Lady John Manners, *Employment of Women in the Public Services* (William Blackwood and Sons: 1882).
4. M. Zimmeck, 'Jobs for the Girls: the Expansion of Clerical Work for Women, 1850–1950' in A. V. John (ed.), *Unequal Opportunities* (Macmillan: 1997), pp. 153–77.
5. R. G. Wilson, 'Women's Work in Offices and the Preservation of Men's Breadwinning Jobs in Early Twentieth Century Glasgow', *Women's History Review* 10:3 (2001), pp. 463–82
6. Zimmeck, 'Jobs for the Girls'.
7. M. Campbell-Kelly, 'Data Processing and Technological Change: The Post Office Savings Bank, 1861–1930', *Technology & Culture*, 39 (1998), pp. 1–32.
8. Wardley, 'The Commercial Banking Industry'; A. Booth, 'Technical Change in Branch Banking at the Midland Bank, 1945–75', *Accounting, Business and Financial History* 14:3 (2004), pp. 277–300.
9. Building societies were established to provide finance for home purchase and were not construction companies.
10. J. Yates, 'Co-Evolution of Information-Processing Technology and Use: Interaction between the Life Insurance and Tabulating Industries', *Business History Review* 67:1 (1993), pp. 1–51.
11. M. Campbell-Kelly, 'Large-Scale Data Processing in the Prudential, 1850–1930', *Accounting, Business and Financial History* 2:2 (1992), pp. 117–39.

12. Yates, 'Co-Evolution of Information-Processing Technology and Use'.
13. A. Baron (ed.), *Work Engendered: Towards a New History of American Labor* (Cornell University Press: 1991); C. Goldin, *Understanding the Gender Gap: An Economic History of American Women* (Oxford University Press: 1990); A. Kwolek-Folland, *Engendering Business: Men and Women in the Corporation Office: 1870–1930* (John Hopkins University Press: 1994).
14. A. R. Holmes, and E. Green, *Midland, 150 year of Banking Business* (Batsford: 1986), p. 128.
15. During the First World War 685 Lloyds Bank staff were killed or died on active service (R. J. Winton, *Lloyds Bank 1918–1969* (Oxford University Press: 1982), p. 37) while the Midland Bank staff losses were 717 (Holmes and Green, *Midland, 150 year of Banking Business*, p. 128); many more staff were wounded or injured. In the Second World War, 326 of the *circa* 5,000 Lloyds Bank staff in the armed forces were killed or died while on military service while another 18 civilian employees, men and women, died in air raids (Winton, *Lloyds Bank 1918–1969*, p. 117); for the Midland Bank 420 of the *circa* 9,000 staff in the forces were killed on active service and 25 civilian staff were killed by enemy action (Holmes and Green, *Midland, 150 year of Banking Business*, p. 204).
16. Arthur Marwick suggests that the number of female employees in the financial services increased from 9500 in 1914 to 63,700 in 1917; of these, female bank staff increased from 1500 in 1914 to 37,600 in 1918. A. Marwick, *Women at War 1914–1918* (Fontana & the Imperial War Museum: 1977), pp. 74, 166.
17. E. R. Long, 'The Future Position of Women Clerks in Banks', *Journal of the Institute of Bankers*, xliv (1923), pp. 114–23. E. R. Long was, I assume, a middle ranking bank clerk, well-respected for his articulate views, but not a director or policy determining bank employer.
18. *Ibid.*, pp. 114–15.
19. Winton, *Lloyds Bank 1918–1969*, p. 11.
20. Long, 'The Future Position of Women Clerks in Banks', p. 115.
21. *Ibid.*, p. 116.
22. *Ibid.*
23. Winton, *Lloyds Bank 1918–1969*.
24. Long, 'The Future Position of Women Clerks in Banks', p. 115.
25. *Ibid.*, pp. 116–17.
26. *Ibid.*, p. 119
27. *Ibid.*
28. Winton, *Lloyds Bank 1918–1969*, p. 166.
29. In 1915 the Ulster Bank employed five 'lady clerks', its first female employees. Almost 200 women were taken on before recruitment was suspended in 1919. No new women were employed by the bank before the outbreak of the Second World War: L. Gallagher, *The Ulster Bank Story* (Ulster Bank Limited: 1998). p. 169.
30. Gallagher, *The Ulster Bank Story*.
31. *Ibid.*
32. Wardley, 'The Commercial Banking Industry'; Wardley, 'Perceptions of Innovation, Receptions of Change: responses to the introduction of machine banking and mechanization in interwar British Retail Banks'.

Paper presented at Information Systems and Technology: in Organizations and Society (ISTOS). Session IV: IST in the Banking Sector. Barcelona, 2003

33. O. R. Hobson, *A Hundred Years of the Halifax* (Batsford: 1953); R. Redden, *A History of the Britannia Building Society 1856–1985* (Franey & Co: 1986); B. Ritchie, *We're With the Woolwich: The Story of the Woolwich Building Society 1847–1997* (Woolwich plc & James & James: 1998).

34. R. Saville, *Bank of Scotland: A History 1695–1995* (Edinburgh University Press: 1996); Wardley, 'Perceptions of Innovation, Receptions of Change'.

35. Gallagher, *The Ulster Bank Story.*

36. Winton, *Lloyds Bank 1918–1969,* pp. 151–2.

37. B. Bátiz-Lazo, and P. Wardley, 'Banking on Change: Information Systems and Technologies in UK High Street Banking, 1919–1969', *Financial History Review* 14:2 (2007), pp. 177–205

38. C. H. Lee, *British Regional Employment Statistics 1841–1971* (Cambridge University Press: 1979).

39. *Ibid.*

40. 'A Banker', 'Bank Mechanization as Affecting Personnel and Public', *The Banker*, xliii:153 (October 1938), p. 59

41. *Ibid.*

42. A. D. Chandler Jr., *Strategy & Structure: Chapters in the History of the American Enterprise* (MIT Press: 1962); L. Hannah, *The Rise of the Corporate Economy* (2nd ed., Methuen: 1976).

43. Wardley, 'The Commercial Banking Industry'.

44. F. H. Capie, and M. Billings, 'Profitability in English Banking in the Twentieth Century', *European Review of Economic History* 5:3 (2001), pp. 367–401;
F. H. Capie, and M. Billings, 'Accounting Issues and the Measurement of Profits – English Banks – 1920–1968' *Financial History Review* 11:2 (2001), pp. 225–51. M. Billings, and F. H. Capie, 'The Development of Management Accounting in UK Clearing Banks, 1920–70', *Accounting, Business and Financial History* 14:3 (2004), pp. 317–38.

45. Wardley, 'The Commercial Banking Industry'.

46. This is an estimate of annual salary savings, minus machine costs, including depreciation, at the 'Big Five' banks in 1939. Based on information contained in contemporary sources, including articles cited here and numerous internal reports concerning mechanization, it is a smaller saving than that suggested either by *ex ante* predictions or by savings reported by the staff closely associated with mechanisation.

47. Wardley, 'The Commercial Banking Industry'.

48. C. H. Lee, *British Regional Employment Statistics 1841–1971* (Cambridge University Press: 1979); C. H. Lee, *The British Economy since 1700: A Macro-Economic Perspective* (Cambridge University Press: 1986); C. H. Lee, 'The Services Industries' in R. Floud and D. McCloskey (eds), *The Economic History of Britain Since 1700, Vol. 2: 1860–1939* (2nd ed., Cambridge University Press: 1994); M Thomas, 'The Service Sector' in R. Floud and P. Johnson (eds), *The Cambridge Economic History of Modern Britain, Vol. 2: 1860–1939* (Cambridge University Press: 2003), pp. 99–132.

49. S. Broadberry, *The Productivity Race: British Manufacturing in International Perspective, 1850–1990* (Cambridge University Press: 1997).

50. S. Broadberry and S. Ghosal, 'From the Counting House to the Modern Office: Explaining Anglo-American Productivity Differences in Services, 1870–1990', *Journal of Economic History*, 62 (2002), pp. 967–98.

51. R. Solow, 'We'd Better Watch Out', *New York Times Book Review*, 38 (1987).

52. J. E. Triplett, 'The Solow Productivity Paradox: What Do Computers Do to Productivity' Paper presented at the 1998 Chicago meetings of the American Economic Association, in a session titled 'Is Technological Change Speeding Up or Slowing Down?'

4
Bliss Tweed Mill Strike 1913–14: Causes, Conduct and Consequences

Mike Richardson

The 1910–14 strike wave in Britain is generally associated with the infamous and intense industrial battles in the coal, cotton, transport, metal, engineering, shipbuilding, and building industries.[1] It is not surprising, therefore, that localized disputes involving a single employer, especially in rural areas not renowned for militancy, tend to be overlooked or underestimated except in the annuals of local history.[2] A six month strike, involving just 237 woollen textile workers (125 women and 112 men) which took place at Bliss Tweed Mill in Chipping Norton, Oxfordshire, is one such dispute. Yet, as the Oxford academics G. N. Clark and G. D. H. Cole argued at the time, there was much riding on this strike not only for those directly involved, but also for workers in Oxford, the nearest city to Chipping Norton:

> The strike now in progress at Chipping Norton is of exceptional significance. Wages in Oxfordshire are notoriously low. The Oxford tram strike of last year showed conclusively that there is no hope of improving the deplorably bad conditions of workers in Oxford unless there is a general upward movement in the surrounding country districts. Till the country worker is better off, he will always be tempted into towns to take the place of any town worker who endeavours to raise his wages.[3]

This strike was not just of local significance. As this chapter will argue, it captured the mood of workers in this period of widespread labour militancy. It is an example of the difficulties, complexities and contradictions that emerged as workers' wrath burst in a confrontational dispute with what turned out to be a very obdurate employer. In fact, some contemporaries referred to this dispute as 'Murphyism in Oxfordshire',[4] a reference to the Dublin transport strike of 1913–14 led by James Larkin, secretary of the Irish Transport and General Workers Union, and his understudy James Connolly, against the anti-union employer William Thomas Murphy.[5]

George Dangerfield characterized this period of industrial unrest in the UK as 'the workers' rebellion'. He sought an explanation to the conundrum:

> The workers of England, united neither in their politics nor in their grievances, with no single desire for solidarity, yet contrived to project a movement which took a revolutionary course and might have reached a revolutionary conclusion; and how is this to be explained?[6]

George Askwith, Board of Trade Chief Industrial Commissioner during this period, identified two principal causes of labour unrest; economic and unions organizing campaigns. Similarly, Hugh Clegg later concluded that the main causes of strike activity were, first, the 'boom in union organization' and, second, the resistance of key employers in the coal and rail industries to concede wage demands because of the perceived adverse impact on profit margins.[7] While many observers of this period, including Clegg, felt that the fall in real wages during 1900–10 contributed to the intensity of industrial unrest,[8] firm evidence is lacking on whether this was actually its cause.[9] Dangerfield's analysis considered the failure of wages to rise proportionally with prices from a different perspective: it was not the fall in real wages *per se*, but rather fairness and the ability of workers to provide for their families free from charity or state provision that mattered. Downward pressure on wages was an attack on the pride and dignity of the working class and this fuelled a sense of injustice. Moreover, he argued that, despite the Labour Party's initial political progress, by 1910 its impact in Parliament was seen as largely ineffective, and he offered this as one reason why workers turned to trade unions to secure justice and fairness via improvements in wages and conditions. In the process 'the Trade Unions became the not too willing repository for instincts, for feelings, for a kind of vital unreason'.[10] Therefore, some workers followed those leaders with syndicalist aims or sympathies advocating direct action;[11] and syndicalists were indeed influential, especially in the disputes in Dublin, London, Liverpool and South Wales,[12] but syndicalism 'was never a mass movement'.[13]

Dangerfield argued that syndicalist tactics conducted during the strikes of 1910–14 were based on instinct rather than reason, which was the attraction for some rank-and-file workers. Moreover, he maintained that little attempt was made by syndicalists to raise workers' class consciousness, a view that corresponds with Joseph White's later assessment.[14] This analysis bears some resemblance to Vladimir Lenin's characterization of strikes in Russia in the late nineteenth century. Lenin insisted that these strikes were spontaneous and devoid of revolutionary consciousness: such consciousness, he argued, could only be brought to the masses from without, that is by a revolutionary party and such a party, trained in the dialectical materialist method, was absent in the UK. [15] Seen in this light, while the 1910–14 strike wave created a revolutionary situation, without the development of revolutionary consciousness the strike movement was destined to remain at the level of spontaneity. While this analysis is open to debate – Standish Meacham, for example, argues that as well as economic grievances workers were developing a sense of class consciousness[16] – it was trade union consciousness that prevailed and on which success in the fight for improvements in wages and conditions depended.[17] What is of interest in this study is how workers' experience of the Bliss Mill strike fits with this picture and whether instinct and a sense of injustice, under the leadership of the Workers' Union, could carry workers to victory.

So, what were the root causes of the strike at Bliss Mill? How was the strike organized and conducted? What were the effects of the strike on those directly concerned and its impact on the local community? Appraisal of this dispute will focus on the tenacity of men and women to fight together in circumstances of adversity. The Bliss Mill conflict was fought in difficult conditions as a significant minority of the workforce refused to join the strike. There was no long and unbroken tradition of industrial solidarity and militancy, one factor that helps to explain why just over a third of the workforce continued to work, seriously weakening the strike's effectiveness. While this strike has received some attention from local historians,[18] and is remembered in the town itself, it has not been subject to an in-depth analysis.

This chapter will seek to determine the underlying causes of the strike, its course and outcome. First, the development of Bliss Mill will be outlined; the changing economic condition of the company; and the level of wages received by its employees relative to elsewhere in the woollen industry. Second, changes in management style will be delineated, as ownership of Bliss Mill moved from a seemingly benevolent proprietor to a public limited company under stricter managerial control. Third, consideration will be given to the standpoint of the company both to the demands for union recognition and its response to strike action;

the influence of the Workers' Union; the divisions in the local community; the role of the police and courts; and the resistance of the strikers, their families and supporters. Finally, some observations will be made on how Bliss Mill strikers dealt with having to concede defeat after six months of struggle.

The historical development of Bliss Mill

Chipping Norton, an ancient market town 19 miles north west of Oxford and 13 miles south west of Banbury, built its prosperity on the wool trade during the middle ages. In the mid-eighteenth century, Thomas Bliss was given a small cloth business (known as the upper mill and powered by a 'horse engine') located in the town. It was his son, William (1764–1825), who, on taking over the business in 1790, orchestrated its transition from a cottage industry to a factory system. In 1810 he bought and converted an old flour mill into a water mill (known as the lower mill) for fulling and spinning.[19] And it was his son, William Bliss (1810–83), who developed and expanded the business from employing just 11 hands, excluding family, and eight water-powered machines in 1839, to 700 employees working in a fully integrated steam-powered mechanized factory in 1870.[20]

Exports of English woollen products increased substantially between 1835 and 1870 and Bliss Mills shared in this boom, focusing on selling to the USA and Germany in particular, as well as the domestic market. The rapid adoption of power looms in the woollen industry, despite some technical difficulties, provided an additional lift to the trade in this golden period for Britain's manufacturing industry.[21] However, in 1872, disaster struck the company. A fire totally destroyed Bliss's lower mill, killing three employees in the process. Bliss had to borrow heavily from the Birmingham Banking Company in order to rebuild the mill.[22] This took place just as the woollen industry was about to enter a decade of recession.[23] Demand for Bliss Mill products fell, especially from the USA and Germany.[24]

It was not until William Bliss's death in 1883 that the severity of the company's trading position and financial situation began to emerge. His son, also named William, took over a business that was bankrupt and, therefore, investment and expenditure decisions had to be approved by his creditor, the Birmingham Bank Company and, later, the Metropolitan Bank, a joint stock bank, which had taken over the Birmingham Bank in 1889. It sent in its own representatives to monitor the business. Changes that were introduced during his time (1884–95) included product diversification and economic measures such as the employment of more boy and girl labour.[25] A steep decline in the value of trade in 1890 signalled the onset of a severe depression in the woollen trade that was to last five years.[26] In 1893, Bliss was forced to sell the upper mill and cut numbers employed significantly to 300. In addition to these measures, the firm was formed into a limited company in December 1895, with William and his two sons kept on as co-directors. This arrangement lasted only a year. In 1896, the Bliss family left the business and the town and the Metropolitan Bank took full control appointing Arthur. H. Dunstan, the mill's general manager, as managing director. Born in Nottingham, and trained in Birmingham as a chartered accountant, the 29-year old Dunstan had established a reputation for his single-mindedness and forceful manner in running the mill.[27]

It was 1901 before the woollen trade began to show clear signs of a revival and, apart from a relatively poor year in 1908, trade was brisk between 1901 and 1912. By the end of 1913, however, clear signs of a downturn in trade were apparent. In fact the timing of the strike at Bliss Mill, in December 1913, coincided with the start of a significant slump in trade, reflected in the decline in output of woollen goods in the UK. This decline continued up to the outbreak of the First World War, in August 1914, following which the demand for military attire soared and the woollen trade recovered.[28] During the prosperous years, the company invested in electricity for lighting (1904) and powering machinery (1910). The old beam engine was replaced by a gas engine.[29] However, investment in employees was not given the same priority. Wages were 'undoubtedly low'.[30] In 1913, employees perceived that they were 30 per cent lower than elsewhere in the woollen industry,[31] although Dunstan contested his employees' claim that pay was inadequate.[32]

There was no uniformity of wage rates in the woollen trade and, indeed, no uniformity of rates at Bliss Mill, making it difficult to ascertain with any accuracy the merits of the respective claims. But wage rates paid to men employed in various jobs at Bliss Mill in 1914 are available. Notably, and this excludes boy labour, office workers and those paid by the piece, 19 out of 64 men (30 per cent) were paid 21 shillings (£1.05) or less per week.[33] Thus for a significant minority of men wages were indeed very poor. A complaint made in 1909 by the General Union of Textile Workers (GUTW) in a letter to the *Yorkshire Factory Times*, recorded what it perceived as shockingly low earnings received by workers in the woollen and worsted industry: 'Out of 31,000 men … 5,200 earn less than a pound a week'.[34] Four years later the indication was that on this measure at least 30 per cent of men employed at Bliss Mill were indeed very badly paid considering inflation had increased by approximately 4 per cent between 1909 and 1913 (3 per cent out of 4 per cent of this increase occurred in 1912).[35]

Changes in management style and managerial control

The changing fortunes of Bliss Mill in the nineteenth and early twentieth century took place in the context of different management regimes and the ways in which managerial authority over labour was exercised. Contemporaries accredited the success of Bliss Mill in the golden years 1839–70 not only to William Bliss's entrepreneurial skills, but also his paternalistic style of management; views shared by the later writings of local historians. They conveyed his apparent concern with the social issues of the community in which he lived, peaceful labour relations, and his business acumen in similar tones to those exponents of paternalism in the nineteenth century.[36] Patrick Joyce has argued that social relations in the nineteenth century textile industry rested on employers' commitment to secure workers' subordination at the workplace through the practice of shared rights and obligations and that commitment carried with it 'the expression and validation of a sense of superiority, of being master in one's own factory'.[37] In some ways Bliss fits this description. After the fire in 1872, he rebuilt the lower mill in Palladian style, an economical form of classicism, which he most likely felt would assist his 'social self-aggrandisement' as was the practice of many industrial entrepreneurs.[38] Preceding this, his company was awarded a gold medal at the Amsterdam International Exhibition of Domestic Economy in 1869 for providing:

> a sufficiently striking illustration of the inseparable nature of the interests of the workgiver and the workman … None of the workmen had joined trade unions … no hands had been allowed to go to the workhouse – families had worked for three generations – the duration of life had been above the average … School, reading-rooms, lectures, concerts, cricket, football, had been liberally promoted.[39]

Bliss was instrumental in bringing the railway to Chipping Norton, which opened in 1855, facilitating easier and cheaper delivery of coal to fuel his newly converted steam-powered mill.[40] He built cottages for some of his employees; he was an active member of the Baptist church where his brother was the pastor; and he was mayor of Chipping Norton on four occasions. His philanthropy and paternalist approach in regulating relations with his workforce should not be exaggerated; workers toiled long hours for low pay and their quiescence can be explained by their dependence on Bliss as an employer rather than their deference to and willing engagement with his paternalist overtures.[41] And the period in which these ostensibly good Christian practices occurred was short-lived, largely confined to the 1850s, 1860s and 1870s, the boom years for British manufacturing.

The well-publicized attack on Chipping Norton police station in 1873 illustrates that the degree of worker acquiescence to subordination and deference in the town, and at Bliss Mill, was far from absolute. Sixteen women were charged under the 1871 Criminal Law Amendment Act for obstructing and coercing two men, hired by a local farmer in Ascott–Under–Wychwood to replace those he had fired for joining the Agricultural Workers' Union, with a view to inducing them to leave their employment. They were found guilty and sentenced to imprisonment with hard labour. They were being held at Chipping Norton police courts and when this news spread:

> the roughs of the neighbourhood in which there is a manufactory (Bliss Tweed Mills) assembled in considerable force. After much shouting an onslaught was made on the police station and the windows and doors were broken and some of the tiles ripped off the roof[42]

Such was the ferocity of the attack the police had to send for reinforcements to remove the women from Chipping Norton to take them to Oxford in the small hours of the morning. Bliss challenged this account of the proceedings in a letter to *The Times*, claiming that his employees were just curious observers and did not participate in any riotous behaviour.[43]

There is evidence that Bliss Mill employees held some affection for their employer, although whether the statement signed on behalf of 254 employees in 1896, after the announcement that Bliss and his family were going to emigrate from England to Australia, is an accurate expression of their feelings is open to question:

> We, the employees of Wm Bliss & Son, feel that we cannot allow you to leave Chipping Norton without expressing in a humble manner the great respect and admiration we have for you, and a deep sense of indebtedness for many kindnesses extended to us during all the years it has been our pleasure to be in your employ.[44]

Bliss's response to this statement, made at his leaving presentation in November 1896, was a portent of events to come and a condemnation of the new management style introduced after his bankruptcy, the formation of Bliss Mill into a limited company, and the transition from ownership control to managerial control:

> He [Bliss] had always felt and acted upon the principle that there was a difference between the machine and the person who worked it. In future, however, all present must scarcely expect to find the same consideration, which from the exceptional nature of the case had previously been accorded to them. Their services at the same time should be just as conscientious straightforward and honest, as it had been for him, even if there could not be mingled with the service a little sugar in the cup represented by affection and regard.[45]

Indeed, after Bliss's departure the new managing director, Dunstan, soon became a figure of hate.[46] Despite his position as director rather than the owner of the business, he, like Bliss, thought himself superior to those he managed, but, unlike Bliss, he displayed no signs of concern for his workforce; a product of his role of representing shareholders' interests, assisted by his training as an accountant. Conditions at the mill have been described as 'disgraceful' and the way in which Dunstan managed the business as 'tyrannical'.[47] To affirm and assert his authority and feeling of self-importance Dunstan moved into Bliss's former residence in New Street, close to the upper mill, and named it Dunstan House. He resided here with his wife, three children and three servants; nursemaid, housemaid and cook.[48] Thus, by 1913 the majority of workers harboured feelings of dislike for Dunstan and his management regime, and having shouldered poor working conditions and low pay Bliss Mill workers were ripe for union organization.[49]

Demands for union recognition and the subsequent conflict

In November 1913, building on their success in nearby Witney, representatives of the Workers' Union initiated a recruitment campaign in Chipping Norton. By mid-December at least 230 Bliss Mill workers had joined the union,[50] despite Dunstan's threat that employees risked losing their jobs if they did so. He offered to establish a company union in order that workers could air and settle their grievances. However, 'workers seemed to regard this as an effort to crush their union' and refused to buckle under intimidation.[51] Dunstan stepped up the pressure. A deteriorating trading environment was utilized as an excuse to make three prominent union men redundant. This action was perceived by Bliss Mill workers as 'a further move against their organization', and they demanded that these men be reinstated.[52] The company refused and on Thursday morning, 18 December 1913, around two-thirds of the workforce (237) came out on strike.[53] The strength of feeling must have been high, given that Christmas was only a week away. Bliss Mill's union representative, John Hieatt, stated that the reason behind the strike was 'the sinister design that their liberty should be curtailed'.[54] Dunstan insisted that 'conditions of employment here [Bliss Mill] are such that a Workers Union is quite unnecessary – I mean, outside agitators'.[55]

In the face of Dunstan's countervailing action to break union organization at Bliss Mill the union's leadership, represented by John Beard, the newly elected president of the Workers Union, and, at the time, a member of the Independent Labour Party (ILP), faltered. Despite the members' call for work-sharing as an alternative to redundancy, as was the custom in the industry, Beard struck an agreement with Dunstan that conceded forgoing the demand for the men's reinstatement in exchange for union recognition. On this basis a return-to-work plan was established. This agreement, recommended by Beard, was endorsed by the Chipping Norton Branch of the Workers Union in its 'anxiety to reach a settlement'.[56] It was signed on 2 January 1914. There is little doubt that this was a climb down. It might indicate the union leadership's lack of confidence in its members to sustain the strike, given the signs of a downturn in the company's trade. Another, and more likely, possibility is that Beard was eager to get his members to return to work once union recognition was achieved.[57] None of the strikers had been members of the union long enough to be in benefit. As a proxy for strike pay the Workers' Union made a grant of £50 per week, which was then distributed by the local strike committee.[58] This cost factor would have been taken into consideration by union officials.[59] The sacrifice of a few militants, who no doubt could receive victimization payments from the union, would have been more cost-effective.

The detail of back-to-work arrangements is unclear, but whatever was agreed it was interpreted differently by the two parties concerned. On the 5 January 1914, strikers turned up at the mill to apply for re-employment only to be told that not all of them would re-engaged at once and 'it could be weeks or even months before they would be taken back'.[60] The union's understanding was that the settlement was based on re-employing strikers within a certain time limit. Dunstan said that would be a month for the majority of strikers, but not all.[61] The strike committee claimed that:

> It is only Mr Dunstan who had broken the agreement. The strikers understood the settlement to mean that **all the workers** [my emphasis] would return to work as soon as things could be got into proper running order (Mr Dunstan's own words).[62]

The settlement made on 2 January, in Dunstan's opinion, 'was repudiated by the strikers on the following Monday…It is now the intention to fill up from suitable applicants all the places they have vacant'.[63] In effect this was a lockout. It is from this moment that Bliss Mill strikers realized that they were no longer prepared to buy peace at any price. They stepped up their determination to remedy, in the face of adversity, what they perceived as a great injustice and took their opportunity to vent their long repressed feelings of discontent. The injustice they suffered was recognized by, among others, Charles Gore, the Bishop of Oxford, who had sent a letter of support accompanied by a small financial contribution.[64] His letter was read out at a meeting of the strikers on 30 December 1913:

> I am convinced that nothing is of more importance than that of workers of all grades and all trades should be encouraged to combine freely in trade unions with the view to collective bargaining. I am sure that the proposal of Messrs Bliss to form an inside association of their workers and to exclude membership of an outside organisation or trade union, is a proposal that should be strongly resisted.[65]

The sense of injustice, attributed directly to Dunstan, and shared by all the strikers, was reason enough for them to vigorously pursue effective action in the form of picketing, parades and assemblies.

The strike committee established itself at the Fox Hotel, just a short distance from the Town Hall and, utilizing the Workers' Union resources, set in motion a plan to complement and buttress their daily picketing of the mill. It publicized the dispute through meetings (usually finishing with a rendition of the Red Flag) and marches both locally and around the country to gain support from the labour movement and politicians and put pressure on the company. On 12 January 1914, small delegations of strikers were sent to Birmingham and London to publicize their case.[66] They appealed for financial donations to supplement union strike pay and establish and sustain a soup kitchen at the Fox

Hotel. Donations were also used to keep up a constant supply of tea and food for the pickets,[67] particularly welcome given the heavy snowfalls at the end of January.[68] Dunstan too busied himself in looking to hire new labour[69] and organizing police protection. Initially, he called in around 40 extra police from Oxford and had them stationed at the town. At a meeting of the town council on 8 January 1914 a council member questioned who was going to pay for their presence. The town clerk replied that 'they had better wait until they were asked to pay. It was the company [Wm. Bliss & Son] who applied for extra police'.[70] Divisions in the community had opened up.

Bliss Mill was the largest employer in the town. In 1911, the total population of Chipping Norton Parish was 3972, forming just 918 households. This is significant because although the 237 strikers represented just 6 per cent of all the local people many more households would have contained strikers and indeed non-strikers.[71] It was young workers who formed the majority of the strikers. An examination of Bliss Mill's wages book,[72] 1914–18, gives some indication of the proportions of the workforce that came out on strike based on age. This book does not include those 137 strikers who were never taken back by the company and there is a discrepancy over the number of non-strikers. Bearing this in mind it seems that at least 77 per cent of those men and women employed at the mill aged between 18 and 34 years actually came out on strike (57 out of 74) on 18 December 1913. This compares with at least 36 per cent of those over 35 years of age who struck (30 out of 83) and 54 per cent of those aged between 12 and 17 years of age (12 out of 22).[73] Strikers comprised a cross section of all grades and skills. Only 100 strikers were taken back, 67 of these after the strike was officially over.

The strike's impact on the local community was huge. 'Some families were split, parents working and children striking.'[74] Given the fact that significant numbers of young men and women were strikers does suggest a shift in values. Most of this generation would not have experienced Bliss's paternalist style of management, the features and benefits of which, in any case, were overblown. The new-found assertiveness was given voice, organization and purpose through the Workers' Union. This came as a huge shock to the local petty bourgeoisie. A letter from the town's trade people to the *Oxfordshire Weekly News*, in January 1914, revealed indignation and some anxiety in its complaint about being terrorized by strikers:

> A strike has never yet been successful which is only of a partial nature, and which does not command the sympathy of a large section of the

public…all told, including their dependents, they cannot represent more than ⅛ of the population of the town. Why should ⅞ be terrorised by such a hopeless minority?[75]

This was written in response to the 'processions parading the streets singing battle songs of various descriptions…largely comprised of the female element…raising their voices to the highest possible pitch' and of particular concern a spate of window smashing.[76] This complaint did not deter the strikers. Action escalated and non-strikers were pilloried. Effigies of them were paraded through the town. Signs of frustration at the lack of success, however, turned to revenge against their bosses, not at their place of work, which was well protected by the police, but at their homes. During one of the nightly processions the strikers and their supporters targeted the houses of Dunstan and J. S. Hall, the mill's general manager, in New Street, smashing their windows; 24 panes in all.[77] This triggered a stronger reaction. Another letter to the press in January 1914 demanded action:

> It is about time the authorities stepped in seriously and put down these organised bands of cowardly males and foul mouthed females going about insulting and threatening all those who only want to go quietly about their business.[78]

The policing of public order was very much apparent in Chipping Norton yet the Town Council complained in a letter to the Secretary of State that '[n]umerous assaults on the police have taken place, but it has been difficult to secure evidence of the identity of the assailants'.[79] A number of strike-related incidents did go to court, attracting large gatherings of supporters.[80] One early prosecution against Thomas Horwood, the father of a female striker, reveals how family members were inevitably drawn into the dispute whether for or against. He was accused of assaulting a policeman. He admitted hurling the policeman to the ground, but in his defence he alleged that this was in retaliation, as this policeman had taken him by the shoulders and thrown him into the gutter.[81]

Strikes produce leaders and sometimes martyrs. This was no exception. Horwood received a heavy fine of £5, more than four week's wages for most male workers in the area. He chose to default and was sentenced to 21 days' hard labour. At the strikers' open air meeting, on Friday night 16 January, Horwood was 'loudly applauded' for taking this stand.[82] In the meantime Thomas Winnett, a weaver, 49 years of age, emerged as a militant leader, able to mobilize disaffected workers. He led from the front. He was known to his work mates as Chippy Larkin after James Larkin, leader of the 1913 Dublin transport strike. Legal proceedings were taken against him, together with four other strikers, William Hieatt, younger brother of John the union representative, Charles Dixon, Herbert Griffin and Charles Simms, for intimidation against a mill foreman, Frank Shephard. The accusation was that on 16 January 1914 they:

> did compel a certain person to wit one Frank Shephard to abstain from doing an act which he had every legal right to do [to work for Wm Bliss & Son Ltd.]. Unlawfully, wrongfully and without legal authority [the accused] persistently followed the said F. Shephard about from place to place.[83]

Similar charges were brought against the same strikers for intimidation against Edward Garton, an engine driver at the mill.[84] Moreover, a month later Winnett was brought before the Justice of the Peace at the Petty Sessional Division of the Borough of Chipping Norton, together with five other named persons, on a more serious charge. They were accused that on the night of 18 February 1914:

> together with divers other evil disposed persons to the number of fifty and more unlawfully, riotously and routously assemble to disturb the Public Peace and then did make a great riot and disturbance to the terror and alarm of his Majesty's subjects.[85]

Winnett, Hitchman, Bowen, Reeves, Gee and Spencer, all of Chipping Norton, were committed for trial at Oxfordshire Assize Court.

The first willing martyr from the strikers' ranks, however, was a woman, Annie Cooper, who had worked at the mill for 26 years. On 14 February 1914, she was summoned for assault on a strike-breaker, Arthur Malpass, the mill lamp lighter. She was accused of attempting to pull him off a ladder from which he had to jump to avoid injury. She was found guilty and sentenced to 14 days in prison for refusing to pay the fine. Cole addressed a meeting of the strikers two days later, praising the courage of the strikers commenting that:

> the spirit shown by the strikers was a revelation to him, and it augured well for the future of the whole neighbourhood. The future was in their hands ... by the use of the powers which were theirs they could win a brighter and fuller life.[86]

On her release, on 28 February 1914, Cooper was met by 1000 jubilant supporters. Julia Varley, the full-time organizer for the Workers' Union presented her with a silver teapot inscribed to commemorate the occasion and then Cooper was paraded through the streets, with her father and husband, in a wagon pulled by the strikers and accompanied by a brass band. That evening a packed meeting greeted her in the Town Hall.[87]

Around the same time Frederick Shephard, a 26 year old striker, was accused (unjustly as it turned out) of assaulting two women strike-breakers. He was found guilty and ordered to pay a £5 fine or, on default, 28 days' hard labour. He protested his innocence and refused to pay. He served three weeks in jail before receiving a free pardon from the Home Secretary. Angered by this decision, a letter was sent to the Home Office from the Chipping Norton Clerk of Justices asking for confirmation that they were justified in convicting Shephard.[88] In contrast, J. S. Hall, the general manager at Bliss Mill, was treated leniently by the law. He was summoned before the court for an alleged assault on one of the strikers, Lizzie Bradbury, on 24 March 1914. It was reported that without provocation he 'seized her by the arms, threw her violently into the road, and strode on without any explanation'. He was found guilty of a technical assault and the case was dismissed.[89]

Given the daily picketing, confrontations with police, demonstrations and public meetings, ordinary town life was severely disrupted. A petition, dated 20 February 1914, signed by 140 residents (many of them non-strikers, including Frank Shephard the mill foreman Winnett had allegedly harassed) was sent to Chipping Norton Borough Magistrates urging them to do something about 'organised and unruly mobs … being allowed to parade the town and district', insulting and attacking people and causing considerable damage to property.[90] Tension was high. This was a town divided. Significant numbers of strikers were fighting for their dignity against the power of an employer, backed by the police, the courts and strike-breakers. Friction was further intensified as the company employed a few new strike-breakers who were joined by a trickle of strikers who broke ranks and returned to work. Police protection of strike-breakers seriously hindered the ability of strikers to picket them out. The one opportunity they had to disrupt production at the mill, which did not involve confronting the police, was to target the Huddersfield Power Loom Tuners' Association (HPLTA) and coerce it to instruct its members to withdraw their labour.

At a public meeting on Friday 23 January 1914, Varley addressed the strikers and their supporters (including students from Ruskin College,

Oxford), alleging that four power loom tuners[91] belonging to HPLTA were strike-breaking. Given that most of the tuners' labourers were on strike, she concluded that their work was being covered by these tuners. Moreover, she charged that 'one of the tuners' daughters was also blacklegging'.[92] In fact, evidence indicates that there were six tuners strike-breaking, but it may be that only four of them belonged to the union.[93] Significantly, it seems that not only did Dunstan accept their membership of HPLTA, but he paid the going rate expected by that association which was at that time around two pound per week, [94] nearly twice as much as most Bliss Mill workers. He had little choice, as the likelihood of finding power loom tuners in Oxfordshire was probably non-existent. Nevertheless, he must have felt reasonably secure that he would retain the loyalty of these workers given their relatively high wages and the fact that, according to GUTW, the HPLTA was more like a friendly society than a trade union, favouring cooperation with employers over supporting non-craft unions in struggle.[95]

A delegation of strikers took its case to the Huddersfield Trades and Labour Council which ruled that three of the four Yorkshire tuners should strike. The one foreman should not as it was an accepted custom that foremen were exempt in these situations.[96] The GUTW intervened. Although it had little time for the HPLTA, it argued that the Workers' Union had not substantiated the charge against HPLTA tuners and, therefore, the Trades Council was not justified in making the ruling it did. The GUTW went on to make the case for one textile union for the industry. Clearly, there was little support coming from this quarter. The GUTW felt that the Workers' Union had encroached on its territory and believed that the union at Bliss Mill was 'trying to run before it had learned to walk'.[97] In effect, the GUTW, a significant although not the most powerful union representing textile workers, sent the message that they would support neither Bliss Mill workers nor the Trades Council ruling, and therefore HPLTA escaped censure.[98]

Behind the scenes, Eustace Fiennes, Liberal MP for the division, and Frank Gray, who after the war was elected as a Liberal MP, attempted to mediate with the company. The best they could do was to get Dunstan to formally offer to re-engage 100 of the strikers, which would have left around 80 out. This offer was put to the strikers in the middle of March and it was rejected in a secret ballot; 179 for and just one against.[99] This was unsurprising given this overture was little advancement on the position they found themselves in on 5 January. By the end of March, 23 strikers had returned to work and many others had left the area to seek employment elsewhere. An undated report recorded: 'left the town, men 19 women 15. Leaving the town this week men 5 women 9.'[100] This explains the fall in the number of strikers to 180. In April, the possibility was explored of the strikers opening a mill of their own to produce the famous Chipping Norton Tweed. Some interest was shown, but the poor trading situation in the industry put a stop to this idea.[101] By the end of May, although only 12 more strikers had returned to the mill, it was clear that the struggle was over.

Reflections and conclusion

Despite the tenacity and commitment of the strikers and the challenge they made to achieve recognition of the centrality of labour, a feature of labour disputes in urban industrial areas since the late 1880s, they were forced to concede defeat. Thus 'the first trial of trade unionism in rural Oxfordshire since the days of Joseph Arch' came to a close.[102] Yet workers had demonstrated their willingness to combine and the ability to maintain discipline and solidarity. They had quickly adopted trade union methods of organizing strike activity: picketing, demonstrations and public meetings. In this they had faced powerful forces. Dunstan's obdurate resistance, assisted by the police and the courts, was made possible by access to the resources of the company's owners, the Metropolitan Bank. Notably, in 1917, Dunstan purchased the business from the bank and sold it three years later to Fox Brothers, a Quaker company located in Wellington, Somerset.

The end of the strike was a painful affair. The strikers could see no way forward. Faced with such a hardened anti-union employer, and having given their all, destitution drove the remaining strikers to defer to Dunstan in the hope that some of them could obtain work. The strike committee wrote to Dunstan at the end of May conceding defeat and requesting work if and when it became available:

To A. H. Dunstan
Dear Sir,
At a meeting of the men and women in dispute at Messrs Bliss & Son, held this afternoon, it was decided to bring the dispute to a close. The deputation is sent by the men and women in dispute to ascertain if you would receive the original forms with a view of having those back when the firm needs. We hope and believe you will take a sympathetic view of the course.

Yours sincerely
J. Hieatt, A. Woodward, F. Titcombe[103]

In concluding his reply to this request Dunstan, in a letter dated 29 May 1914, said that the company were still open to placing job applications on the waiting list:

> You must, however, be prepared for a great many disappointments, as owing to your action in taking part in the ill-advised strike, and your persistent refusal to return to work, many of your places have had to be filled, and, in addition, the business cannot accommodate anything like the number of hands it did before the strike.[104]

There was an outstanding court case against Winnett and others, arising out of the strike, for unlawful assembly that was yet to be heard, but the prosecution called for lenience given that the that the strike was over. They were bound over for a period of 12 months.[105]

This struggle for respect, recognition and reward could not be sustained. Union membership and the strike offered a remarkable remedy to isolation in their fight against harsh conditions and a ruthless employer. It produced leaders, martyrs and workers with organizational ability. Collective identity was forged through union membership and strike-related activity: picketing, demonstrations, discourse, meetings, soup kitchens and raising funds. Women showed courage and tenacity and did much in lifting morale. But in a small market town, particularly, dependency for employment on one or two relatively large companies made disputes doubly difficult to win. Despite the great strides made by trade unions in the conflict between capital and labour in the late nineteenth and early twentieth centuries, the former held, and still does, disproportionately more power. Trade union struggles were won and lost and it would be wrong to draw either overly optimistic or pessimistic conclusions from such struggles. Nonetheless, the strike at Bliss Mill is one example, among many others, of the creative element, initiative and fighting spirit of workers even when the odds were against them.

Lessons from such disputes, even from those of nearly a century ago, are still relevant. Social relations of production were being realigned before the First World War, but, by and large, trade union struggles were tied to spontaneity. Whether class consciousness can automatically develop out of such struggles is a debate that cannot be addressed here. But, by the same token that E. P. Thompson discerned, that defeat in the 1890–91 Manningham Mills strike in Bradford positively contributed to and accelerated the development of the independent Labour movement,[106] many of those activists involved in the Bliss Mill strike were drawn into working-class politics, after the First World War, in order to address their problems. A Chipping Norton Branch of the Labour Party was formed with Winnett as chair and Woodward as secretary. William Hieatt[107] and Titcombe were also members together with other former strikers. In 1920 the Chipping Norton Branch boasted 120 Labour Party members.[108] The fight for dignity among the working class in Chipping Norton took a different path, one of gradualism through parliamentary politics.

Notes

1. J. E. Cronin, *Industrial Conflict in Modern Britain* (Croom Helm: 1979); J. E. Cronin, 'Strikes 1870–1914' in C. Wrigley (ed.), *A History of Industrial Relations 1875–1914* (Harvester, Brighton: 1982), pp. 74–98; R. Holton, *British Syndicalism 1900–14: Myths and Realities* (Pluto: 1976); G. Dangerfield, *The Strange Death of Liberal England* (Serif: 1997); Lord George Askwith, *Industrial Problems and Disputes* (John Murray: 1920).
2. Richard Hyman makes a passing reference to the strike at Bliss Mill in his doctoral thesis 'The Workers' Union 1898–1929' (Ph. D. University of Oxford: 1968, p. 90). There is a wonderful collection of photographs available that gives a visual depiction of the strike, both helpful in the construction of, and providing supportive evidence to, the events directly related with this dispute. See Oxfordshire Photographic Archive, Frank Packer collection, Bliss Mill Strike, Oxfordshire Studies, Central Library, Westgate, Oxford. The Workers' Union (WU) reported on the strike in its journal, WU *Record*, February 1914. There are also a couple of brief references in the March and May editions of the journal. The *Oxfordshire Weekly News*, however, provided the most detailed accounts.
3. G. N. Clark and G. D. H. Cole, 'The Strike at Chipping Norton' (unpublished document: 1914), Oxfordshire Studies.
4. *Oxfordshire Weekly News*, 24 December 1913.
5. For an analysis of the causes of the Dublin transport strike see E. O'Connor, 'What Caused the 1913 Lockout? Industrial Relations in Ireland, 1907–13', *Historical Studies in Industrial relations (HSIR)* 19 (Spring 2005).
6. Dangerfield, *Death of Liberal England*, p. 179.
7. H. A. Clegg, *A History of British Trade Unions since 1889, Vol. 2: 1811–1933* (Clarendon Press, Oxford: 1987), pp. 24–74.
8. *Ibid.*, p. 73.
9. R. Bean and D. A. Peel, 'Business Activity, Labour Organisation and Industrial Disputes in the UK, 1892–1938', *Business History*, 18 (1976), pp. 205–11.
10. Dangerfield, *Death of Liberal England*, p. 193.
11. R. Aris, *Trade Unions and the Management of Industrial Conflict* (Macmillan, Basingstoke: 1998), p. 94.
12. Clegg, *A History of British Trade Unions, Vol. 2*, pp. 72–74; Holton, *British Syndicalism 1900–1914*.
13. J. White, 'Syndicalism in a Mature Industrial Setting: the Case of Britain' in Marcel van der Linden and Wayne Thorpe (eds), *Revolutionary Syndicalism: An International Perspective* (Scolar, Aldershot: 1990), p. 117.

14. White argued that syndicalist leaders 'at no time sought to counterpose their agenda to the consciousness of the workers themselves', 'Syndicalism in a Mature Industrial Setting', p. 105.

15. The beginning of spontaneous upsurge was analysed by Lenin in 1903: V. I. Lenin, *What Is To Be Done?* (Progress Publishers, Moscow: 1947).

16. S. Meacham, '"The Sense of an Impending Clash": English Working-Class Unrest before the First World War', *The American Historical Review* 77:5 (1972), pp. 1343–64. Lenin also showed some optimism that class consciousness was emerging in Britain. See his brief comments on 'Class War in Dublin' in *Lenin on Trade Unions* (Progress Publishers: 1970), pp. 254–58: 'The masses of workers are slowly but surely taking a new path [...] And once on this path the British proletariat, with their energy and organisation, will bring socialism about more quickly and securely than anywhere else.'

17. Roy Church concludes that in the period of labour unrest, 1890–1914, 'those who envisaged as the outcome a transformation of society and the advancement of class, as distinct from industrial, trade union aims, were a small minority'. R. Church, 'Edwardian Labour Unrest and Coalfield Militancy, 1890–1914, *The Historical Journal* 30:4 (1987), p. 855.

18. J. R. Hodgkins, *Over The Hills To Glory: Radicalism in Banburyshire 1832–1945* (Clifton Press, Southend: 1978), Ch. 11, pp. 126–37; E. Meades, *The History of Chipping Norton* (2nd ed., Bodkin, Chipping Norton: 1984); R. Evans, 'The Bliss Mills and the Bliss Family in Chipping Norton, 1758–1920' in *Oxfordshire Local History,* 20 (1975). Also see the video 'Needs Must When The Devil Drives' Concord Video and Film Council: Ipswich.

19. Meades, *The History of Chipping Norton*, p. 89.

20. H. Hurrell, *The Bliss Mill Chipping Norton: Industrial Lancashire in the Cotswolds* (Chipping Norton Local History Society: 1996), pp. 3–5.

21. Technical difficulties were associated with the characteristics of woollen cloth. It was necessary to spin the yarn feebler and looser than cotton, making weaving more susceptible to break on the power loom. See D. T. Jenkins and K. G. Pointing, *The British Wool Textile Industry 1770–1914* (Heinemann: 1982) Ch. 5, pp. 92–125, for a fuller explanation and a comprehensive examination of the importance of raw materials, technology and power in the English woollen industry 1835–70.

22. S. Laidlow, *A Brief History of the Manufacture of Cloth in Chipping Norton* (unpublished and unpaginated account from an employee of Bliss Mills: late 1940s approx.), Chipping Norton Museum.

23. W. Hoffman, *British Industry 1700–1950* (Blackwell: 1965).

24. Meades, *The History of Chipping Norton*, p. 91.

25. During its heyday the company boasted that it did not knowingly employ any child under the age of thirteen. In the 1880s, however, this avowal was relaxed in order to employ boys on half-time at eleven years for two shillings and sixpence (12.5 new pence) per week (Laidlow, *A Brief History of the Manufacture of Cloth in Chipping Norton*).

26. Hoffman, *British Industry 1700–1950*; Jenkins and Pointing, *The British Wool Textile Industry*, p. 235.

27. Laidlow, *A Brief History of the Manufacture of Cloth in Chipping Norton*; Meades, *The History of Chipping Norton*; 1901 Census of England and Wales online, www.1901censusonline.com

28. Hoffman, *British Industry 1700–1950*; Jenkins and Pointing, *The British Wool Textile Industry*, pp. 238–41.
29. Laidlow, *A Brief History of the Manufacture of Cloth in Chipping Norton*
30. *Ibid.*
31. Hodgkins, *Over The Hills To Glory*, p. 126; Laidlow, *A Brief History of the Manufacture of Cloth in Chipping Norton.*
32. In a letter dated 22 December 1913, published in *Oxfordshire Weekly News*, 24 December 1913, Arthur Dunstan claimed that between 1896 and 1913 wages had increased by 60 per cent.
33. Bliss Mill Wages Book, 1914–18, Chipping Norton Museum.
34. *Yorkshire Factory Times*, 22 April 1909, cited in T. Jowitt, 'The Retardation of Trade Unionism in the Yorkshire Worsted Textile Industry' in J. A. Jowitt and A. J. McIvor (eds), *Employers and Labour in the English Textile Industries 1850–1939* (Routledge: 1988), p. 98.
35. The position was much worse for women. However, most women employed at Bliss were on piece work so wage data are unavailable for comparison.
36. J. Foster, *Class Struggle and the Industrial Revolution: Early industrial capitalism in three English towns* (Methuen: 1974), pp. 188–89.
37. P. Joyce, *Work, Society & Politics; The culture of the factory in later Victorian England* (Methuen: 1982), p. 140. For a discussion on the meaning, strengths and limitations of the concept of paternalism see P. Ackers, 'On Paternalism: Seven Observations on the Uses and Abuses of the Concept in Industrial Relations, Past and Present', *HSIR* 5 (Spring 1998), pp. 173–94.
38. Hurrell, *The Bliss Mill Chipping Norton*, p. 34.
39. Report of the Amsterdam Exhibition of Domestic Economy, cited in Meades, *The History of Chipping Norton*, p. 90.
40. S. C. Jenkins, B. Brown and N. Parkhouse, *The Banbury & Cheltenham Direct Railway* (Lightmoor Press: 2004), pp. 261–64.
41. H. Newby, *The Deferential Worker* (Penguin: 1979), p. 414.
42. *The Times*, 26 May 1873, cited in Hodgkins, *Over The Hills To Glory: Radicalism*, pp. 66–67. For an account of the Ascott Martyrs see K. Sayer, 'Field-Faring Women: the Resistance of Women Who Worked in the Fields of Nineteenth-Century England', *Women's History Review* 2:2 (1993), pp. 189–95. Also see the video 'Needs Must When The Devil Drives'.
43. *The Times*, 27 May 1873.
44. Statement signed by Sarah Jacques and Walter Thomas Hawkins on behalf of 250 Bliss Mill employees, 31 October 1896, cited in Laidlow, *A Brief History of the Manufacture of Cloth in Chipping Norton.*
45. A report of William Bliss's final speech at his leaving presentation, November 1896, cited in Laidlow, *A Brief History of the Manufacture of Cloth in Chipping Norton.*
46. Meades, *The History of Chipping Norton*, p. 119.
47. Correspondence from local Chipping Norton historian, and former head of history at Chipping Norton Comprehensive School, Ralph Mann, 9 February 1985, to Aaron Tyler Bliss, Lake Oswego, Oregon, USA, Chipping Norton Museum.
48. 1901 Census of England and Wales.
49. This fits with mobilization theory: grievances and holding employer or management responsible for bringing about such grievances are preconditions

for employees to become collectivized. See J. Kelly, *Rethinking Industrial Relations* (Routledge: 1998), p. 45.

50. Hodgkins, *Over The Hills To Glory*, p. 127. A photograph of members the new branch of the Workers' Union at Chipping Norton, linking arms in a show of solidarity, and holding banners saying 'MANY MINDS ONE HEART WE FIGHT for RIGHT' and 'We Fight For LIBERTY, Down With OPPRESSION' reveals the strength feeling of Bliss Mill workers, Oxfordshire Photographic Archive, Frank Packer collection.

51. *Oxfordshire Weekly News*, 24 December 1913.

52. *Ibid*; Meades, *The History of Chipping Norton*, p. 119–20

53. *Oxfordshire Weekly News*, 24 December 1913; Meades, *The History of Chipping Norton*, p. 128.

54. John Hieatt, union representative, cited in *Oxfordshire Weekly News*, 24 December 1913. Hieatt's name is wrongly spelt (Hiatt) in *Oxfordshire Weekly News* and in Hodgkins, *Over The Hills To Glory*. Hieatt, an engineman at Bliss Mill, was a local Wesleyan Methodist preacher and a member of the management committee of the local Cooperative Society. After the strike the Workers' Union employed him as an assistant organizer in the Bedfordshire area, WU *Record*, November 1914, p. 9, Modern Records Centre (MRC), MSS. 126/WU/4/2/1.

55. Correspondence from Arthur Dunstan to the *Oxfordshire Weekly News*, dated 22 December 1913, published in *Oxfordshire Weekly News*, 24 December 1913.

56. Clark and Cole, 'The Strike at Chipping Norton'; Hodgkins, *Over The Hills To Glory*, p. 128.

57. Following the outbreak of war, Beard advocated that the union should adopt a conciliatory approach to employers. See R. Hyman, *The Workers' Union* (Clarendon: 1971) p. 82.

58. From this grant, and voluntary contributions from supporters, strike pay was set at 8/- a week for married men and 7/- a week for married women, with an additional six pence for each dependent. Single men received 5/6d and single women 5/-, Laidlow, *A Brief History of the Manufacture of Cloth in Chipping Norton*.

59. WU officials felt 'it is important to note and to watch that the income of the union increases [in line with increases in membership]'. WU *Annual Report*, 1914, MRC, MSS. 126/WU/4/1/10.

60. Report on the mass meeting of strikers and sympathizers held in Chipping Norton Town Hall on 10 January 1914, *Oxfordshire Weekly News*, 14 January 1914.

61. An open letter from the Wm Bliss & Son Ltd. to the strikers, dated 21 January 1914, and published in *Oxfordshire Weekly News*, 28 January 1914.

62. The strike committee's response to the company's open letter, *Oxfordshire Weekly News*, 28 January 1914.

63. A. H. Dunstan, quoted in *Oxfordshire Weekly News*, 14 January 1914.

64. Other notable contributors included Gilbert Murray, Regius Professor of Greek at Oxford, the Fabian Societies at Oxford and Cambridge, the Ruskin College Dramatic Society, and Eustace Fiennes, Liberal MP, Laidlow, *A Brief History of the Manufacture of Cloth in Chipping Norton*.

65. Charles Gore's letter cited in *Oxfordshire Weekly News*, 31 December 1913. Charles Gore was the first bishop to take the Labour Whip in the House of Lords.

66. *Oxfordshire Weekly News*, 14 January 1914.
67. In February 1914, a firm of tea dealers, Salmon's of Reading, donated to the strike committee 500 quarter pound bags of tea and five pounds to purchase food for the strikers, WU *Record*, March 1914, p. 4, MRC, MSS. 126/WU/4/1/10.
68. British Winter Snowfall Events 1875–2004 reports that there was heavy snowfall in Oxfordshire on 22 January 1914, www.napier.eclipse.co.uk/weather/bonacina, accessed 14 September 2007. For visual evidence see Oxfordshire Photographic Archive, Frank Packer collection.
69. Only three new employees were taken on in January 1914 and seven in February, Bliss Mill Wages Book, 1914–1918, Chipping Norton Museum.
70. *Oxfordshire Weekly News*, 14 January 1914.
71. 'A Vision Of Britain Through Time: Chipping Norton', www.visionofbritain.org.uk, accessed 9 September 2007.
72. The Bliss Mill Wages Book, Chipping Norton Museum.
73. This estimation was calculated from the number of non-strikers, those strikers who returned to work during the dispute, and those who were re-employed after it finished; therefore, this underestimates the proportion of workers who came out on strike. Records show that eight returned in January, three in February, eight in March, two in April and twelve in May, Bliss Mill Wages Book.
74. Laidlow, *A Brief History of the Manufacture of Cloth in Chipping Norton*.
75. *Oxfordshire Weekly News*, 14 January 1914.
76. *Ibid.*
77. *Ibid.*, 21 January 1914.
78. *Ibid.*, 28 January 1914.
79. Correspondence from the Town Clerk's Office, Borough of Chipping Norton to The Secretary of State, Home Office, Whitehall, London, Ref. BORI/4/A1/7, bundle of papers re Bliss Mill strike, Oxfordshire Record Office (ORO), Cowley, Oxford.
80. See Oxfordshire Photographic Archive, Frank Packer collection.
81. *Oxfordshire Weekly News*, 21 January 1914.
82. *Ibid.*
83. Petty Sessional Division of the Borough of Chipping Norton papers, 16 January 1914, Ref. BORI/4/A1/7, ORO.
84. *Oxfordshire Weekly News*, 11 February 1914.
85. Petty Sessional Division of the Borough of Chipping Norton papers, 23 February 1914, Ref. BORI/4/A1/7, ORO.
86. *Oxfordshire Weekly News*, 25 February 1914.
87. *Ibid.*, 4 March 1914. See Oxfordshire Photographic Archive, Frank Packer collection for a photograph inside the hall of this meeting.
88. Ref. BORI/4/A1/7, ORC; J. R. Hodgkins, *Over The Hills To Glory*, p. 131. Fred Shephard returned to the mill after the strike was over in June 1914 and went on to complete 50 years' service.
89. *Oxfordshire Weekly News*, 8 April 1914.
90. Ref. BORI/4/A1/7, ORO.
91. Power loom mechanics.
92. *Oxfordshire Weekly News*, 28 January 1914.
93. Herbert Brook, John Kaye, and Fred Lee all originated from Yorkshire (1901 Census of England and Wales), William Brinkworth originated from

Gloucestershire, William Hodgkins and William Moulder originated from Chipping Norton, Salaried Staff Wages Book, Bliss Mill, 1914–18, Chipping Norton Museum.

94. Richard Biernacki,. *The Fabrication of Labor: Germany and Britain, 1640–1914* (University of California Press: 1995), p. 464. Bliss Mill tuners' weekly wages in 1914 were Herbert Brook, John Kaye and Fred Lee who all earned £2 per week or more, William Brinkworth £1/-17/-6d, William Hodgkins £1/-14/-4d, William Moulder £1/-15/-4d, Salaried Staff Wages Book, Bliss Mill, 1914–18, Chipping Norton Museum.

95. *Yorkshire Factory Times*, 5 March 1914.

96. *Oxfordshire Weekly News*, 4 March 1914.

97. *Yorkshire Factory Times*, 5 March 1914.

98. Membership of GUTW was 4535 in 1910, Jowitt, 'The Retardation of Trade Unionism in the Yorkshire Worsted Textile Industry', p. 89.

99. *Oxfordshire Weekly News*, 18 March 1914; The Ruskin College Dramatic Society: Appeal on behalf of the Chipping Norton Strikers, 7 March 1914, Oxfordshire Studies; Laidlow, *A Brief History of the Manufacture of Cloth in Chipping Norton*.

100. Report by A. Woodward, cited in Hodgkins, *Over The Hills To Glory*, p. 133.

101. Hodgkins, *Over The Hills To Glory*, pp. 132–33.

102. Clark and Cole, 'The Strike at Chipping Norton'.

103. *Oxfordshire Weekly News*, 3 June 1914.

104. *Ibid.*

105. *Ibid.*, 10 June 1914.

106. E. P. Thompson, 'Homage to Tom Maguire' in Briggs, A. and Saville, J. (eds), *Essays in Labour History* (Macmillan: 1960), pp. 276–316.

107. His brother John was recruited by the WU as a full-time organizer.

108. Chipping Norton Labour Party, 1920–1969, ORO, Ref. 0141/2.

5
Rapprochement and Retribution: The Divergent Experiences of Workers in Two Large Paper and Print Companies in the 1926 General Strike

Mike Richardson

There is a vast literature on the General Strike which has covered most aspects of the conflict and assessed its aftermath.[1] The best known discussions of its impact have estimated its effects on trade unionism in general terms.[2] Yet, as one recent commentator on the events of 1926 observes, a 'fertile route' for research 'would be to examine case studies at the level of individual enterprises to explore the impact of the dispute'.[3] This chapter takes up that challenge. Its central concern is to present a study comparing the way the strike affected industrial relations in two large paper and print companies. Histories of trade unionism in that industry indicate that peaceful industrial relations prevailed in the interwar years and that, apart from the action of a few hostile companies which derecognized unions, the General Strike constituted little more than a minor breach in harmonious relationships.[4] Thus little attention has been given to the events of 1926 in this industry, particularly at workplace level. Plant-level studies can broaden and deepen our understanding of the capital–labour relationship in this period and add to our knowledge of the consequences of the General Strike, which remains largely limited to 'its effects on industrial disputes and on the actions of the central organizations of workers and employers'.[5]

This chapter will examine the operation of management authority in John Dickinson and in E. S. and A. Robinson (Robinson), and the experiences of their workforces, before, during and immediately after the General Strike.[6] The skill and gender mix of employees in these organizations were similar; and both employers made a concentrated effort to foster harmonious industrial relations in an industry where print unions have a long history of organizing.[7] Before the First World War, paternalism best describes the employment relationship in each company. This was based on providing welfare benefits and stimulating a sense of economic well-being that fostered self-help rather than discouraged it. It was a relationship that promoted a sense of righteousness and superiority in the companies' owners. Whether their respective workforces held them in such great esteem is open to question, although historians of these companies seemed to think so.[8] The crux of the matter is that the stability of this relationship was dependent on employers delivering secure employment and providing a valuable set of non-wage (welfare) benefits. This was particularly the case in respect to Robinson in its urban setting. Dickinson, on the other hand, was the dominant employer in a rural area and, as such, competition for labour was weaker; there was less pressure to adopt paternalist practices to maintain managerial authority.[9]

Despite the similarities in industrial relations strategy in Dickinson and Robinson, their responses to the General Strike took markedly different forms. The chapter explores why management at Dickinson derecognized trade unions after the General Strike and utilized a house union through which to consult workers on industrial relations issues, while Robinson continued to recognize and bargain with independent unions.[10] In attempting to explain these different responses the changing nature of the character of workplace management–worker relationships is analysed. In both cases, consideration is mainly given to diversity of employers' control strategy; the workplace experiences shaping paper and print workers' thoughts and actions preceding the General Strike; and the impact of the strike itself. Each case study will be presented in turn and the final section draws some conclusions.

Dickinson before the General Strike

John Dickinson established the Hertfordshire company in 1804.[11] Thirty four years later it was producing between four and 5 per cent of the paper made in the UK at four sites (Apsley, Croxley, Nash and Home Park Mills), situated in close proximity to each other in what was, in this period, a rural area.[12] Over the next 60 years growth principally centred on expanding and upgrading existing mills and diversifying into manufacturing stationery. Increasingly, the stationery sector became central and was an important source of employment, especially for women.[13] By 1914 the largest mill, Apsley, where the manufacture of stationery products was centred, employed 2065 production workers and 477 clerical staff, up from 1283 and 209 respectively in 1907.[14] Apsley had grown into an industrial complex utilizing land surrounding Apsley village; workers would have been drawn in from the surrounding villages and the nearby town of Hemel Hempstead.[15]

Dickinson had emerged as a large scale manufacturing company with all the problems that entailed concerning the maintenance of management authority and control at the point of production. A paternalist relationship grew out of, and to a certain extent maintained, the authoritarianism of John Dickinson illustrated by his actions in the dismissal of strikers in 1821.[16] Dickinson had cottages built in close proximity to his paper mills that he let to his workers, binding them to the company. In 1847 he financed the building of a local school in Nash Mills village, near to Apsley village.[17] The company felt, with some justification, that it was providing employment that enabled its workers to enjoy a higher standard of living than rural workers. It was the ability to offer stable relatively well paid employment that John Dickinson felt justified his authoritarian rule.

There is some evidence of workers' resistance from the late nineteenth century. In 1894 the Amalgamated Society of Paper Makers (ASPM) recorded that it enrolled members at Dickinson's mills,[18] although there is no indication that it had recognition rights. In August 1911 Dickinson's envelope and book-printing workers staged a walkout; the source of this demonstration of discontent is unknown although apparently it was resolved within a few hours.[19]

After the outbreak of the First World War in 1914, the company was subjected to pressure from the National Union of Printing and Paper Workers (NUP&PW) to concede recognition to non-craft workers, including women. It strongly resisted this challenge and 700 newly recruited members gave up their union cards.[20] The drain on the labour supply as men left to join the armed forces, the competition for labour from the munitions factories, and the threat of strike action over late working on Saturdays at Croxley and Nash Mills strengthened the union's hand. Dickinson conceded recognition in 1915 despite reservations expressed by half of the company's managers. Reuben Henry Ling, who had originally opposed recognition, persuaded his colleagues to change their minds so that industrial unrest could be averted. Dickinson formally recognized the NUP&PW in July 1915.

After the war the Dickinson family relinquished ownership control. Ling was appointed as a joint managing director with Henry Godfrey[21] in 1918 and, following the latter's death in 1924, he became sole managing director. Under his leadership union membership was encouraged, a development made much of by Dickinson's directors: 'The relations existing with our workers is of a most harmonious character, and the officials of the trade unions are co-operating with our management on a friendly and constructive basis.'[22] This seemed to be the case, for in 1919 Dickinson's managers and print union officials were sharing the platform at meetings to encourage paper and print workers to join their appropriate union and firms to affiliate to their employer organizations.[23] That same year, an agreement, to which Dickinson was party, was made between its Employer' Federation of Paper Makers (EFP) and the unions representing paper workers, the ASPM and the NUP&PW, fixing minimum wages. Moreover, the working week was reduced to 48 hours for day workers and an average 44 hour week for shift workers.[24] Ling, swayed by the government's strategy for resolving industrial disputes through Whitley Councils, enrolled Dickinson in the paper industry's Joint Industrial Council (JIC) on its formation in 1920. [25] Yet the effectiveness of this JIC, from its employer' perspective, was seriously undermined after a dispute at Valleyfield Paper Mill in 1923 when the National Union of Printing, Bookbinding, Machine Ruling, and Paper Workers (NUPBMR&PW)[26] 'emerged victorious' in maintaining a closed shop after a 20 week strike.[27]

The company's apparent enthusiasm with its post war industrial relations strategy quickly evaporated. The threat to strike in support of a national wage claim in May 1920 by the craft union, the Typographical Association (TA), which commanded strong loyalty from its membership, unsettled management.[28] Dickinson was becoming increasingly uneasy with EFP policy, as relationships between its employer' organization and print unions deteriorated in the face of wage reductions, unemployment, and short-time working. The impetus behind Dickinson's acceptance of trade unionism during the First World War was to foster harmonious industrial relations. In the paper and printing industry as a whole during the early 1920s this strategy was in crisis.[29] Dickinson's response was to develop a new employment relationship.

From the early 1920s, welfare policies, both formal and informal, played a large part in Dickinson's industrial relations strategy. For example, in 1920 £50,000 was diverted from company profits to initiate a pension fund. A training programme, mainly in the form of lectures, was introduced at Croxley and Apsley Mills, at a cost of £3000 per year. That same year employees were given the opportunity to buy company shares, a classic tactic used by employers attempting to secure workers' loyalty.[30] Paid holidays were reinstated in 1925 after a three year lapse;

the EFP did not concede this nationally until 1936.[31] When employment security was threatened in the 1921 slump, Dickinson avoided dismissals by introducing short-time working (in operation at Apsley Mill during 1920–21) and temporary shutdowns (Croxley Mill was closed down for a week in January 1921). Some concern for those workers affected is demonstrated by the fact that the company established a small distress fund (£500) for those in the most serious difficulty.[32] In 1922, Dickinson waived the wage cuts that the EFP had squeezed out of the unions nationally. By not exacting wage reductions Dickinson was one of a minority of companies that avoided the TA national strike of 1922.[33]

The General Strike and its aftermath at Dickinson

Despite receiving a raft of welfare benefits, Dickinson's workers in 1926 demonstrated class solidarity rather than loyalty to the company. This was reflected in their overwhelming response to the General Strike call. Dickinson's factories (Apsley, Nash, Croxley and Home Park) were heavily picketed and were forced to close.[34] To reassert and increase managerial authority, Ling seized the opportunity to exploit the vulnerability of his striking workers by derecognizing the unions. Four days into the strike (on 7 May), the company distributed notices to the strikers instructing them to return to work the following day, Saturday 8 May 1926.[35] Management pledged that if there was a return, there would be no reductions in wages or alterations in hours over the ensuing 12 months; and no changes in pay and conditions would be made without full consultation and agreement with the workforce. The company also intended to operate an open house where there would be 'no distinction between union and non-union workers'.[36] The mills reopened on 8 May but only 178 workers crossed picket lines.[37] The failure to attract strike breakers caused the company to adopt a more aggressive strategy. Later that day, it issued a statement to the effect that those unions which had instructed workers to disobey the company's call for a return to work would no longer be recognized and Dickinson would be 'declared an open house'.[38] Ling reasoned that the reassertion of management prerogative could only be assured by sponsoring a house union.[39]

Over the weekend, plans were set in motion to form a house union with its own pension fund. Although additional workers returned to work on Monday 10 May, the company's records do not state how many,[40] and a further notice was circulated to Dickinson's strikers:

Advice to a Trade Unionist
Why you can return to work without breaking your trade unionist principles:–

1. Because the strike is illegal, all who have broken contracts requiring notice to be given, or have incited others to do so, are liable to civil action.
2. Because trade union members cannot be expelled or deprived of benefits for failing to obey the strike order.
3. Because the trade unions were formed for collective industrial bargaining, but the TUC [Trades Union Congress] is today attempting to use its power to force a decision from the Government by a direct attack on the whole community.[41]

By 11 May the management was convinced that the strike was broken and issued a further notice to remaining strikers that they 'must apply for re-engagement before resuming their duties'. [42] By 1.30 pm on Wednesday 12 May, just one and a half hours after the TUC General Council's unconditional surrender to the Baldwin government, significant numbers had returned; 1572 crossed the picket line at Apsley,[43] following which all Dickinson's workers were told that on no account would independent unions be recognized by the company again and that an embargo was placed on employees belonging to an independent union.[44] '[O]wing to' the unions' 'rebellious action' they were to be replaced with a company union, the Union of the House of Dickinson.[45] The next day (13 May), the company claimed that 'virtually all our workers returned to work with the exception of a very few fanatics – numbering about seventeen – with whom reasoning was in vain'.[46] These 17 were not alone. On 13 May nationally the number of strikers actually increased.

On 14 May, Ling sent a statement to the workforce:

Fellow Workers,
We are back at work again after a worrying time. Let us all be thankful that the hum of machines can again be heard in all our Mills. Let us be thankful that there is no ill-will of any kind amongst us and let each one of us show by our good work, our gratitude for these great blessings. I am deeply grateful that I can once again join hands with you in the fellowship of service in our House of Dickinson.[47]

There is little evidence available about the attitude workers took to the collapse of the strike and their employer's behaviour.[48] The threat of dismissal appears to have destroyed any thoughts of resistance, apart from stereotypers who, initially at least, refused to comply with the company's demands.[49] An open letter, dated 14 June 1926, to all typographical workers employed at Apsley Mill, from the Hemel Hempstead TA Branch, suggests that this was the case. It was a response to the communication from members at Apsley Mill, concerning their resignation from the TA to join the Union of the House of Dickinson. The exasperation of its authors, their determination to avoid members signing away their rights, and a reference to those small numbers of stereotypers who had refused to do so, are apparent in these lines:

> Do you really understand what you are doing? Why are the men in the Stereotype department leaving [the company]? Is it because they will not sell their principles for the House of Dickinson [?] ... *We are prepared to stand by all Typographical Workers who refuse to sell their principles by signing the form issued by the Firm. Fourteen days' notice will release you from same.* It is not too late for you to regain your freedom as men, and so keep yourselves free to accept employment outside the House of Dickinson.[50] (original emphasis)

Subscriptions to the Union of the House of Dickinson were set at the same rate as existing union dues. Ling gave long term assurances concerning wages, conditions and benefits whereby they would equal or improve upon those negotiated by unions. Without these Ling realized that his plan to derecognize trade unions and debar membership might well fail. These assurances are reflected in the regulations of the Union of the House of Dickinson. These are reproduced in full in the appendix to this chapter. The most important is the 'objective' of the house union:

> Wages – The wages of all employees of the House of Dickinson will never be below the recognized trade union standards. It will be the definite object of the Union of the House of Dickinson, to secure conditions that will enable all employees to earn higher wages than the minimum trade union rates.
>
> Hours – The hours of work for the members of the Union of the House of Dickinson will never be longer than those operating in the trade generally.

Enrolment of all staff in the house union was completed, according to the company's records, by 17 May 1926.[51] This was not a restoration of the industrial relations practice associated with the paternalism before the First World War. Company growth, the change from personal owner to managerial control and the years of experience of trade unionism, made turning back the clock incompatible with these developments. The company felt that its reassertion of managerial authority was morally legitimized by its endeavour, after the General Strike, to forge a unity of interests by means of company unionism. The character, cost and effectiveness of this strategy will now be examined.

Welfare benefits organized by the house union promoted the principle of self help, but in circumstances where, for all practical purposes, the company laid down the rules of entitlement. On this basis, the company provided financial and administrative assistance. For example, although it gave £100,000 to initiate a new pension scheme in June 1926 this was contributory, workers paying 2.5 per cent of their wages topped up by a contribution from the company based on profit levels.[52] In 1927, an additional unemployment benefit scheme was introduced. For an extra ½*d* (0.2p) per week contribution, workers with six months' service could draw higher unemployment benefits than the standard rate paid by the Union of the House of Dickinson. For a man aged 18 years or over this additional contribution meant a rate of £1 per week for six weeks and 10*s* (50p) per week for another six weeks; the maximum allowed in one full year. Boys under 18 and women over 18 years of age received half of this rate, while girls under 18 could claim only a quarter of the adult male rate.[53]

These rates compare favourably when measured against unemployment benefits paid out by unions; for example, in 1929 the TA was paying out 13*s* per week unemployment pay to its longest serving adult members.[54] Apart from pensions it was company sickness benefits that were in most demand; £2700 was paid out in 1935.[55] This figure could have been higher but for welfare provisions provided directly by the company. A dental clinic was established on site in 1930, and in 1933 a medical practitioner appointed[56] after an influenza epidemic had struck Apsley Mill.[57] Other benefits were assistance in home ownership and a share-ownership scheme; by 1933 the number of employee shareholders exceeded 1400, about 20 per cent of the workforce.[58] Finally, in June 1937, working hours were reduced from 48 to 45 hours for a five day week with no reduction in wages. This preceded by three months the same agreement made between the print unions and the British Federation of Master Printers.[59]

The internalizing of industrial relations accompanied by the exclusion of trade unions did not guarantee a trouble free future for Dickinson. After a period of disarray, in 1927 the Printing and Kindred Trades

Federation (PKTF), covering the print unions collectively, organized a boycott campaign against Dickinson's products, but this failed due to the difficulty of firms in finding alternative unionized suppliers.[60] At the rank-and-file level the Printer's Minority Movement campaigned for more direct intervention, criticizing the craft unions for 'drifting along' but praising the NUPB&PW for 'giving a splendid lead for immediate action', resulting in forcing the PKTF to call 'a meeting of all trade unionists employed at Millingtons... to discuss the whole position'.[61]

In the world economic crisis of 1929–33, Dickinson's profits and dividends fell; Croxley Mill was shut down twice in 1931 as orders dried up. Its industrial relations policy survived this period of depression; but almost nine years after the General Strike rank-and-file opposition to management authority at Dickinson had developed to such a degree that, in the words of a local Labour Party activist, it 'amounted to a challenge to the autocracy of the House Union'.[62] In a high profile case in 1935, 12 stereotypers flagrantly broke the House of Dickinson's rule by joining a trade union, the National Society of Electrotypers and Stereotypers. These stereotypers held out for 16 months before they were finally dismissed.[63] This triggered another protracted effort by unions to gain recognition in Dickinson. Full-time officials from the National Society of Operative Printers and Assistants (NATSOPA) were assigned this task in 1936.[64] Soon afterwards, the PKTF took over responsibility and appointed a full-time official from the NUPB&PW to launch a concerted campaign.[65] By 1937, the NUPB&PW had 85 members out of 280 employees at Croxley Mill.[66] And, in 1939, Dickinson made a significant concession to the print unions; it withdrew the ban, but still maintained workers' compulsory membership of the Union of the House of Dickinson until sometime after the Second World War.[67]

Clearly the unitary approach to industrial relations, although buttressed by company unionism and industrial welfare, could only be sustained with an element of compulsion and the investment of significant managerial time and effort; but it was only stereotypers who offered any real threat to management authority during this period, and they formed only a small minority of the total workforce. Their skills were not firm-specific and increasingly job opportunities for craft print workers in the Hertfordshire area became available during the 1930s.[68] Thus they had superior chances of finding equivalent work with another firm. Undoubtedly this increased their combative and stubborn opposition to management authority. However, as Dickinson was the only paper maker and the only significant manufacturer of stationery in the area, the skills of the majority of the company's workforce were not directly transferable to other forms of available work, such that these workers tended to be more quiescent.

In summary, the company's investment in internal procedures to increase management control and authority after 1926 did not eliminate adversarial relations. This approach only succeeded in containing trade unionism through a pay and rewards system at least as good, if not better, than that achieved by unions in the industry. While workers were given little scope for self activity, paradoxically the company's authority was still subject to indirect collective challenge by unionized labour in the paper and printing industry as a whole.

Robinson before the General Strike

Robinson began trading in 1844 when its founder, Elisha Smith Robinson, exploited a new market supplying ready-made paper bags.[69] In 1848, the firm became known as E. S. & A. Robinson and, by 1856, had become one of the largest suppliers of paper packaging.[70] By 1885, it was employing 600 people at its premises in Redcliffe Street, in the heart of Bristol and, in 1887, a new factory was built in Bedminster, about two miles away. This factory was in close proximity to the tobacco giant W. D. & H. O. Wills which had opened new production facilities in the district the year before. The expansion of Wills and Robinson gave local young women in particular increased employment opportunities; thus there was some competition for female labour. In 1893, Robinson registered as a limited joint stock company and Elisha's son Edward took over as company chairman.[71]

Elisha and Edward Robinson believed strongly in the free market economy and employers' rights to complete managerial authority. They promoted a type of community capitalism in which they saw themselves as among the leading lights.[72] They did not tolerate unions, but were nonetheless regarded as 'good' employers. In 1889, the firm granted one week's paid annual holiday to those workers employed for one year or more, an uncommon occurrence at the time.[73] Almost 20 years later the firm implemented a working week of 50 hours while most print employers were still operating at between 51 and 54 hours per week. Moreover, a profit sharing scheme was introduced in 1912 and the payment of family allowances in 1917. Workers' shares, for those over 21 years of age and with more than two year's service, had been available since 1893[74] to retain employee loyalty.[75] The benevolent paternalism of Robinson was not accompanied by the same degree of authoritarian severity apparent at Dickinson. Robinson's paternalism encompassed laissez-faire principles, which advanced the virtues of thrift and hard work, while in return for the acceptance of these principles the firm offered secure employment, good conditions, fostered a community spirit and some financial involvement in the company.

Robinson readily endorsed the foundation of South West Alliance of Master Printers' Association in 1905. But it was not prepared to join the association until 1917;[76] the company's dominant market position evidently led it to believe that formal links with other printing firms was unnecessary. In response to the growing strength of organized labour, Robinson had granted recognition to the TA in 1910. The Bristol TA had lobbied employers to take on members because it was 'the discipline they [Bristol TA] imposed upon their members which made them the best workmen to employ'.[77] Whether or not this was the deciding factor in winning recognition, by 1915 Robinson employed 60 TA members.[78] Concurrently, NATSOPA was enrolling male semi-skilled workers, and by 1917, as the NUP&PW had done at Dickinson, it had recruited a significant number of the company's female employees.[79] The National Union of Bookbinders and Machine Rulers, which opened its membership to women in 1917, was also successful in recruiting women at Robinson.[80] By the end of the war trade union organization, embracing both men and women, had become firmly established in the company.

The company's labour management strategy was developed around industrial welfare, an approach akin to that at Dickinson.[81] This had much to do with the Robinson family which steadfastly tried to keep the management of the firm under family influence despite being a limited joint stock company.[82] Edward Robinson, company chairman 1893–1929, was a Baptist and an important public figure in the local community. He sat as a Liberal on Bristol City Council between 1906 and 1929 and was Lord Mayor in 1908. He was also a magistrate, vice-chairman of the Bristol Chamber of Commerce, president of the Colston Research Society and president of the Bristol City Mission.[83] His profile was very different from Ling, managing director of Dickinson. While Ling 'had few links with Hertfordshire and played little part in its affairs outside his mills',[84] Edward Robinson's religious and political activity in Bristol brought him increasingly into contact with Labour councillors closely associated with, or members of, trade unions. He was, therefore, aware of the latter's growing power.[85]

In 1919, the company became party to an agreement to negotiate wages and conditions nationally.[86] Concurrently, federated chapels[87] at Robinson secured formal recognition.[88] Soon after, these bodies registered a success by persuading the company to suspend the practice of completing daily timesheets.[89] Union activists in the company were also involved in their city union branch; Fred Ancrum, William Dursley and Emily Hathway were members of the NATSOPA Bristol branch committee. Both Ancrum and Dursley were to serve as branch chair in the early 1930s; Dursley was also active in the local Labour Party and was a delegate to the Bristol Trades Union and Labour Council and Hathway served on NATSOPA's Governing Council for three years.[90]

The company vehemently opposed the printing unions' call for a general reduction of the working week from 48 hours to 44 hours in 1920. Whereas Dickinson took action to avoid official strikes in the early 1920s, Robinson was prepared to support 'any action by Master printers if unions caused trouble'.[91] By 1926 it had become an active member of the Bristol Master Printers' Association which had an accord with the print unions to work towards improving industrial relations.

If there were illusions that employment was secure in Robinson, then the slump of 1921 shattered them. In contrast to Dickinson's strategy of short-time working and temporary closure, in March 1921 the company's directors dismissed 114 workers; 64 men and 50 women out of a workforce of around 3000.[92] Yet Robinson's post war industrial relations strategy included features of the pre-war paternalist system, particularly extensive welfare and social facilities. Its earlier approach was based on fostering employer–worker relationships marked by dependence and philanthropic duty, while now it had to compete with trade unionism for workers' loyalty.[93]

The religious and political views of Edward and Foster Robinson, supported by fellow directors H. G. Tanner, a Quaker, and H. L. Taylor, a Baptist,[94] infused this management strategy with philanthropic and humane principles. Some new positions were introduced to accommodate the change of approach. In 1919, factory managers were installed into three of the firm's Bristol plants to alleviate the work load of directors and to take up responsibilities such as efficiency of production, working conditions, and the hiring and firing of labour. This was an embryonic form of a new professional management hierarchy, though one of the initial three factory managers was a Robinson family member.[95] A welfare officer was appointed in 1920 and, in 1927, J. L. Milligan, formerly an external adviser to Robinson, was engaged initially as a factory manager, but, after Foster Robinson succeeded his father as chairman of Robinson in 1929, Milligan took up the new post of labour manager.[96]

By 1918, as noted earlier, a profit sharing scheme was in operation, family allowances were paid and workers' shares were available.[97] In

1919, a new bonus scheme based on 25 per cent of net profits was introduced.[98] In the previous year, Robinson granted a shorter working week of 40 hours to all men over 60 years of age, all women over 55 years, and all employees with 40 years' service.[99] Benefits available to the company's employees accrued during the 1920s and included additional holidays for workers with 30 years' service, athletic club facilities, a convalescent home, financial assistance to a sick club, and, for a few, low-cost homes.[100]

In 1921, the company introduced rewards for good time-keeping; £1 per year, reduced accordingly by 6*d* (2.5p) for every recorded lateness,[101] but this was discontinued in 1931.[102] More effective schemes that increased workers' dependency on the firm were introduced. One, instituted in 1925, permitted any employee temporarily laid off, and not eligible for state unemployment benefit, to claim 87.5 per cent of his or her day-work rate of pay. For those drawing state benefit the firm topped up their allowance to 87.5 per cent of their day-work rate. Benefits were not payable when the shortage of work was due to an industrial dispute. This scheme was funded by the company but the costs were minimal.[103] Another scheme, introduced after the General Strike, was a mandatory contributory pension for men over 21 and less than 52 years old, which the firm administered and supported by an annual contribution.[104] A plethora of welfare benefits was therefore provided for workers in both Dickinson and Robinson.

The General Strike and after at Robinson

Common to both firms was that the majority of workers observed the call to join the General Strike; 75 per cent came out at Robinson.[105] On 4 May 1926, the local newspaper, the *Bristol Times and Mirror*, commented that the strike was an 'arbitrary ukase of the TUC...We can but hope that a large section of the organised workers will recognise the higher duty of good citizenship'.

This newspaper, together with the *Western Daily Press*, managed to publish a reduced size version throughout the strike and provided some information on the strike at Robinson. On Monday 10 May it was reported that 'apart from clerical staff there are 1100 [out of a workforce of around 3000] at work in the firm's factories. Some hundreds of these are men but the larger number are women and girls'.[106] That day 60 more returned to work; and on Tuesday 11 May it was claimed that 62 per cent of E. S. & A. Robinson's employees were working normally.[107] By contrast, the Bristol General Strike Committee reported that: 'About

500 female and 50 male workers have returned in the printing trades. The reason for this defection seems to be that the firms have approached their people individually and threatened loss of bonus and other benefits. The Printing Trades however up to this morning [11 May 1926] still remain solid.'[108] Even if this was referring solely to Robinson workers, the estimated number returning to work was still considerably less than that reported in the *Bristol Times and Mirror*. The company's lithographic workers were the last to return to work, on 14 May, one day after the official return.

Robinson's directors decided as early as 5 May that 'we could promise workers who were in or who came back that we would not ask them to join a union again'.[109] But it was 10 May before the directors acknowledged recognizing an 'open house'; on 13 May the idea of establishing works councils was mooted.[110] While during the strike Robinson considered a similar 'open house' strategy to Dickinson, once it was over the directors changed their mind. The company did, though, derecognize the federated chapel and established instead departmental works committees;[111] and it paid double wages to employees who worked during the strike.[112]

Despite the drift back to work before the General Strike was officially called off, only 31 semi-skilled workers and four skilled litho-print supervisors at Robinson terminated their union membership because of their opposition to the strike.[113] Efforts to persuade the semi-skilled workers to reverse their decision reduced the number to nine; three of the four supervisors were said to have rejoined the union in December 1927.[114]

There is no evidence to suggest that Robinson had encouraged these workers to remain non-union members or indeed had urged any of its employees to relinquish union membership. Nevertheless, print unions proceeded to demand that the company maintain the closed shop, insisting that the nine non-union workers should be dismissed or rejoin the union. In the aftermath of defeat it is extremely doubtful whether militant action would be forthcoming to support this demand, although the board's minutes recorded that litho printers threatened to strike in 1927 because of the supervisors leaving the union.[115] On the whole, the unions adopted a moderate approach. This precluded any action that might have disturbed this caution, such as the continuation of the inter-union dispute concerning staffing rights, which had been a problem in preceding years.[116] As a result union officialdom strengthened its authority, pursuing its claim for the re-introduction of the closed shop through the external channels of the JIC Conciliation Committee.

This was one of the first cases arising from the General Strike to be heard at the JIC Conciliation Committee. It was called to mediate, through the JIC Bristol District Committee, on the union's demand that the closed shop be maintained. The District Committee succeeded in persuading five of the nine non-unionists to rejoin. The problem of the remaining four was referred to the Conciliation Committee which, on 16 August 1927, recommended that:

Considering the peculiar circumstances of the reference the committee feels that the firm ought not to be asked to assume any responsibility for the present position... [I]t is in the best interests of all concerned that the four men should resume membership of the union.[117]

The unions were dissatisfied and pursued the matter. The district JIC continued to prevaricate:

This Council approves the finding of the [Conciliation] Committee and while recognising the right of either side to take what action they may decide on, the Council emphasise the obligation of both panels and all parties in this dispute to make further efforts to find a solution of the difficulty.[118]

Neither Robinson nor NATSOPA seemed prepared openly to capitulate and appeared content to hope that the dispute would eventually fade away. Significantly, the JIC had been given credence and its authority re-established at a time when rank-and-file union militancy had been curtailed following the TUC's capitulation to Stanley Baldwin's Conservative government that brought an end to the General Strike.

Despite its weakened position, in the early 1930s TA members at Robinson united to repel the unwelcome interest shown by the firm in the Bedaux system, a scientific management scheme.[119] The TA was also the only union which refused to participate in departmental works committees, which were viewed as a method of weakening union representation through incorporation. Simultaneously, relations between the TA and the other unions at Robinson deteriorated as the demarcation disputes, so prevalent in the early 1920s, re-emerged. Despite the negative implications of inter-union disputes, the rivalry challenged the firm's 'right to manage'. In 1934, the Robinson labour manager observed that 'if the printing industry is to obtain the best results from mechanization in the future, there must be some breaking down of the walls which divide these various craft unions',[120] something that the Robinson management had failed to achieve.

Conclusion

While this study of two companies cannot be claimed as representative, it does remind us of the pull which trade union solidarity exerted in 1926 even in workplaces which were far from militant. It demonstrates some of the initiatives, ranging from vigorous to mild, taken by employers to weaken trade unionism in the aftermath of the General Strike. It also suggests the resistance and deep roots of trade unionism in the paper and print industry despite the reverses endured.

The reasons for the contrasting ways in which Robinson and Dickinson dealt with re-establishing influence and authority over their workforces, after the General Strike, are complex. Their roots lie in the changing operational nature of management authority and influence in their respective firms, covering many decades, and the level of union organization and activity in the workplace. While there were many commonalities in management style between the two companies there were some key differences that may well have had a bearing on managing what was seen by many as an unprecedented crisis in British industrial relations. In particular, Robinson family influence in the firm in 1926 was still evident while in Dickinson it was not. The religious values Robinson's directors associated with Methodists, Baptists and particularly Quakers, may also have had some bearing on acknowledging workers' rights to have an independent representative voice. Moreover, religious values in the nineteenth and early twentieth century may well have softened the paternalism practised by Robinson, which seemingly was of a more benevolent nature than that at Dickinson.

In Robinson, union recognition was first conceded among certain classes of employees in the years immediately preceding the First World War and then extended during the war to cover women workers, apparently without resistance. In contrast, Dickinson management succeeded in keeping out unions before 1914, and even after the outbreak of war strongly resisted union organization in its workplaces. This was exemplified by the firm's initial reaction which was to force those employees who joined to renounce their union membership by threatening that they would lose their jobs. When union recognition was finally conceded it was based explicitly on cooperative relationships between the union and the company. Dickinson was one of the few employers who took measures in 1922 to avoid the TA national strike. The General

Strike of 1926 exposed this 'cooperative' relationship and Dickinson took the opportunity to eliminate competition from the trade unions for the loyalty of its workforce.

This was made easier by its being the predominant employer in a rural area. Dickinson's management was never really comfortable with having to deal with unions. It did so only because of the exceptional circumstances of war-time Britain. Robinson's management, on the other hand, legitimized its power and authority by accommodating trade unions, albeit to a limited degree, recognizing that they had certain rights and interests that may have put them at odds with the firm. Of particular significance, print unions at Robinson had in place workplace activists operating collectively in the organizational form of federated chapels, while at Dickinson there is no evidence of a comparative development. Yet Dickinson could only sustain a house union by the guarantee that it would not undercut wages and conditions secured through national collective bargaining by trade unions in the paper and printing industry. So, print unions continued to have a say in determining wages and conditions in Dickinson despite their exclusion from the company.

The General Strike was a critical incident which changed industrial relations in both companies. This study of two large print and paper companies gives us some sense of the importance of 1926 and provides an example of the way in which workers resisted and eventually reversed the immediate consequences of the TUC's capitulation to the Baldwin government. In the years after the General Strike workers in both Dickinson and Robinson regrouped. By the 1930s, workers in Robinson had successfully restored the closed shop, which enabled them to vigorously defend demarcation lines, while at Dickinson workers' demand for independent trade unionism was once more a feature of industrial relations.

Appendix 5.1: Regulations of the Union of the House of Dickinson

- *Membership*:

All employees of the House of Dickinson-including directors, staff and manual workers.

- *Objective*:

Wages— the wages of all employees of the House of Dickinson will never be below the recognized trade union standards. It will be the definite object of the Union of the House of Dickinson to secure conditions that will enable all employees to earn higher wages than the minimum trade union rates.

Hours— the hours of work for the members of the Union of the House of Dickinson will never be longer than those operating in the trade generally.

- *Benefits*:

To secure benefits in the case of sickness, convalescence, and old age.

- *Crafts*:

To secure opportunities for advancement in the various crafts associated with the Union of the House of Dickinson.

- *Recreation*:

To secure through the medium of the House of Dickinson Guild of Sport, the best recreation that can be arranged for all employees of the House of Dickinson.

- *Subscriptions*:

All subscriptions will be for the benefits of the members – none being used for outside propaganda work.

- *Strikes and Lock-outs*:

No strikes or lock-outs by members of the Union of the House of Dickinson will be sanctioned.

- *Federations*:

The House of Dickinson will sever its connection with outside Federations of Employers. The Union of the House of Dickinson will give decisions on all matters coming within the scope of the Union.

- *Funds*:

£50,000 of the special reserves of the House of Dickinson will be appropriated as the starting benefit fund of the Union of the House of Dickinson.

- *Emergency Funds*:

£5000 will be placed at the disposal of the Union of the House of Dickinson, to relieve any special distress that may from time to time occur amongst any of its members.

Source: Extract from the Union of the House of Dickinson, Charter, MSS. 292/7.1/4, MRC; *The British & Colonial Printer*, 27 May 1926, p. 362.1

Notes

1. See J. McIlroy, 'Memory Commemoration and History – 1926 in 2006', *Historical Studies in Industrial Relations* (*HSIR*) 21 (Spring 2006), pp. 65–109; K. Laybourn, 'Revisiting the General Strike', *ibid.*, pp. 109–21; J. McIlroy, A. Campbell, K. Laybourn and Q. Outram, *The General Strike and Mining Lock-Out of 1926: A Select Bibliography*, *ibid.*, pp. 183–207.

2. H. A. Clegg, *Some Consequences of the General Strike* (Manchester Statistical Society, Manchester: 1954), pp. 1–19; G. A. Phillips, *The General Strike: The Politics of Industrial Conflict* (Weidenfeld and Nicholson: 1976); Q. Outram, 'The General Strike and the Development of British Capitalism', *HSIR* 21 (Spring 2006), pp. 121–43.
3. K. Laybourn, 'Revisiting the General Strike', *HSIR* 21 (Spring 2006), p. 118.
4. C. J. Bundock, *The National Union of Printing Bookbinding and Paper Workers* (Oxford University Press: 1959), pp. 337–38; J. Child, *Industrial Relations in the Printing Industry: The Quest for Security* (Allen and Unwin: 1967), pp. 251–53; A. E. Musson, *The Typographical Association* (Oxford University Press: 1954), pp. 362–63; J. Moran, *NATSOPA Seventy Five Years: A History of the National Society of Operative Printers and Assistants (1889–1964)* (Oxford University Press: 1964), pp. 74–84.
5. Clegg, *Some Consequences of the General Strike*, p. 3.
6. Some of the material in this chapter is taken from M. Richardson, 'Industrial Relations in the British Printing Industry between the Wars' (PhD, University of the West of England: 1995), Chapters 4 and 5.
7. Child, *Industrial Relations in the Printing Industry*.
8. J. Evans, *The Endless Web* (Cape: 1955); B. Darwin, *Robinsons of Bristol 1844–1944* (Robinson, Bristol: 1945).
9. For a discussion on the meaning, strengths and limitations of the concept of paternalism see P. Ackers, 'On Paternalism: Seven Observations on the Uses and Abuses of the Concept in Industrial Relations, Past and Present', *HSIR* 5 (Spring 1998), pp. 173–94.
10. John Dickinson was one of a small number of notable employers in the paper and print industry, including the *Manchester Guardian*, which derecognized unions after the General Strike.
11. Evans, *The Endless Web*, pp. 2–3.
12. D. C. Coleman, *The British Paper Industry 1495–1860* (Clarendon Press, Oxford: 1958), p. 237.
13. Evans, *Endless Web*, pp. 237–51.
14. *Ibid.*, p. 172.
15. As late as 1947 Dickinson employed 5500 people out of Hemel Hempstead's working population of 7000 (*New Town Story: Part Three, End for the Line*). Today Hemel Hempstead has a population of over 80,000 and Apsley is a district of the town (http:/www.hemelhempsteadtoday.co.uk; accessed 13 July 2006).
16. Evans, *Endless Web*, pp. 28–29.
17. *Ibid.*, p. 60.
18. Bundock, *The National Union of Printing Bookbinding and Paper Workers*, p. 380.
19. Evans, *Endless Web*, p. 168.
20. 'Personalities: Mrs A. Bridge, Union Organizer, NUP&PW', *The Paperworker*, 1 (October 1940), p. 10.
21. Godfrey was formerly on the Board of Directors of Millington, a competitor company in the stationery business situated in London and acquired by Dickinson in 1918.
22. The Directors' Reports of John Dickinson, 1919, Hertfordshire Archives and Local Studies, D/Ei, County Hall, Hertford (HA).

23. Evans, *Endless Web*, p. 197.
24. *Ibid.*, p. 197; C. J. Bundock, *National Union of Printing Bookbinding and Paper Workers*, p. 413.
25. C. J. Bundock, *National Union of Printing Bookbinding and Paper Workers*, p. 417; The Directors' Reports of John Dickinson, 1919–22, HA.
26. This union was formed in 1921 as a result of a merger between the National Union of Bookbinders and Machine Rulers and the National Union of Printing and Paper Workers. It shortened its name in 1928 to the National Union of Printing, Bookbinding and Paper Workers
27. Bundock, *National Union of Printing Bookbinding and Paper Workers*, p. 224; R. Charles, *The Development of Industrial Relations in Britain 1911–1939* (Hutchinson: 1973), p. 195.
28. Evans *Endless Web*, p. 198.
29. See Child, *Industrial relations in the British Printing Industry*, pp. 233–54.
30. Evans, *Endless Web*, pp. 191–202
31. '500 years of Papermaking in Britain 200 Years of Trade Unionism', *SOGAT Journal*, special souvenir edition (October 1988), p. 19.
32. Evans, *Endless Web*, p. 198.
33. According to Musson, *The Typographical Association*, p. 345, about 7000 TA workers across the country were not called out on strike as their firms did not implement wage cuts in July 1922; seemingly Dickinson was one of them.
34. Apsley Mill's Dairy (1926), 1878–1950, HA.
35. Papers relating to the 1926 General Strike at John Dickinson & Co., HA.
36. *Ibid.*
37. Apsley Mill's Dairy (1926), HA.
38. Papers relating to the history of the 1926 General Strike, HA.
39. The TUC's definition of a 'House Union', given in 1937, says 'an inside organisation confined to a particular employer with the object of separating the employees concerned from the general body of organized labour', MSS 292/7.1/2; TUC ref. 7.25, Modern Records Centre, University of Warwick (MRC).
40. Papers relating to the history of the 1926 General Strike, HA.
41. *Ibid.*
42. *Ibid.*
43. Apsley Mill's Dairy (1926), HA.
44. A TUC survey of House Unions in 1937 revealed only one 'case of a definite prohibition of employment if becoming a member of a Trade Union – the House of Dickinson', MSS 292/7.1/2; TUC ref. 7.25, MRC.
45. Papers relating to the history of the 1926 General Strike, HA.
46. *Ibid.*
47. *Ibid.*
48. This is surprising especially as in 1926 one Labour Party monthly newspaper, *The Worker*, published in Letchworth, Hertfordshire, 'devoted to the cause of all workers', failed to mention the events at Dickinson's mills which were located around five miles distance from Letchworth. The paper did mention that in Letchworth 'over 400 in that industry [printing] struck work in an entirely unselfish effort to support the TUC and help the miners': *The Worker* 3:4, 29 May 1926, p. 4.

49. Despite the stereotypers' stand one can only assume that either they were eventually forced to concede or they were dismissed. Typographical workers at Millington, Dickinson's subsidiary, on refusing to sign away their rights were sanctioned to hold dual membership, that of their own union and the House of Dickinson. The Company reneged on this agreement, dismissed them all on New Year's Eve 1926, and replaced them with non-union staff: *The London Typographical Journal*, April 1927, p. 8, MSS 292/7.1/4, MRC.

50. Correspondence from the Typographical Association, Hemel Hempstead branch to the typographical workers employed at Apsley Mill, 14 June 1926, MSS 292/7.1/4, MRC.

51. Apsley Mill's Dairy (1926), HA.

52. Evans, *Endless Web*, p. 201.

53. Anon., 'Additional Unemployment Benefit Schemes', *International Labour Review* 21 (1930), pp. 379–80.

54. Musson, *Typographical Association*, p. 398.

55. The Directors' Reports for John Dickinson & Co., Ordinary General meeting (OGM) 1936, HA.

56. Evans, *Endless Web*, p. 206; Anon., *International Labour Review*, 1930, p. 379.

57. Apsley Mill's Diary 1937, HA.

58. The Directors' Reports for John Dickinson & Co., OGM 1935, HA.

59. Apsley Mill's Diary 1937, HA.

60. J. Child, *Industrial Relations in the British Printing Industry*, p. 253.

61. *Printers' Pilot*, 1:8 (January 1927). The Minority Movement was closely linked to the Communist Party and comprised organizations and individuals representing various industries.

62. Correspondence from Jesse Hawkes to the Secretary of the TUC Organization Department, 22 August 1937, MSS 292/7.1/2, old TUC ref. 7.2, MRC.

63. *NATSOPA Journal*, November, 1936, p. 24. Interestingly, these stereotypers were refused unemployment benefit until the Court of Referees at the Watford Exchange intervened in their favour ruling that: 'Exercise of the men's right to join their society does not render them less capable of performing their duties to their employers'.

64. *Ibid.*, December 1936, p. 3.

65. Report of the National Executive Council of NUPB&PW for 1938, p. 3, M. Richardson papers; MSS 39/SO, MRC.

66. TUC Memorandum of an interview, 6 December 1937, on the subject of organising workers at Dickinson (present E. W. Spackman (General Secretary of NUPB&PW; H. V. Tewson and E. P. Harries), MSS 292/7.1/4, old TUC ref. 7.23, MRC.

67. *The Paperworker*, August 1940, p. 2.

68. J. Rannard, 'The Location and Economic Growth of the Watford Paper and Printing Industries' (BA Thesis, Department of Geography, University of Bristol: 1963), pp. 24–25.

69. *Bristol Times & Mirror, Bristol's Many Industries* (Bristol, 1922/3), unpaginated.

70. *Ibid.*

71. *Ibid.*

72. C. Harvey and J. Press, 'Industrial Change and the Economic Life of Bristol since 1800', *Studies in the Business History of Bristol*, p. 26.

73. *A Short History of E. S. & A. Robinson Group* (Robinson, Bristol: 1965), p. 4, University of Glasgow Archives and Business Record Centre.

74. *The Robinson Annual 1844–1944* (Robinson, Bristol: 1944), p. 14.

75. See J. Melling 'Employers, Industrial Welfare, and the Struggle for Workplace Control in British Industry, 1880–1920' in H. F. Gospel and C. Littler (eds), *Managerial Strategies and Industrial Relations* (Heinemann: 1983), p. 62.

76. D. Bateman, *The Origins of the Bristol Master Printers' Association* (privately produced: 1992), p. 14, Bristol Records Office (BRO); Robinson's Director's minute book (4 October 1917), BRO.

77. D. Bateman, 'An Examination of the Organisation and Policy of the Bristol Typographical Society in the Second Half of the Nineteenth Century' (MA, Bristol Polytechnic: 1986), p. 87.

78. Bristol Typographical Society, membership lists, BRO.

79. *NATSOPA Journal,* July 1917, p. 7. The Bristol Women's Branch of NATSOPA was 1000 strong by 1917, and Robinson was the second largest employer in the Bristol print and packaging industry.

80. It was a cynical move, and in keeping with the union's past patriarchal practice, to bring this work under the control of men. At Robinson, the first stage to achieving this aim was secured in 1920 when the firm's male bookbinders claimed and won the right to operate and control ruling machine work even though this work had been performed by women for many years: Robinson's Director's minute book, 8 July 1919 and 30 July 1920, BRO. This was achieved against the wishes of the firm whose chairman 'expressed regret at conceding to male control' over this area of work: *ibid.*, 13 September 1920.

81. For an exploration of industrial welfare, see R. Fitzgerald, *British Labour Management and Industrial Welfare* (Croom Helm: 1988).

82. *E. S. & A. Robinson Annual Review* (1935), p. 8, Bristol Reference Library.

83. *Ibid.*, p. 9. The Colston Research Society was founded in 1899 to provide financial support to specific research projects at the University of Bristol.

84. Evans, *Endless Web*, p. 188.

85. During 1922–24, 16 Labour representatives and three aldermen held seats on Bristol City Council. By 1930, Labour representation had doubled. At the 1923 parliamentary elections Labour won its first two seats in Bristol: K. Kelly and M. Richardson, 'The Shaping of the Bristol Labour Movement, 1885–1985' in M. Dresser and P. Ollerenshaw (eds), *The Making of Modern Bristol* (Redcliffe Press, Tiverton: 1996), p. 222.

86. Child, *Industrial Relations in the Printing Industry*, p. 226.

87. *Ibid.*, p. 37, Child defines a print union chapel as 'a democratic workplace institution with authority to legislate on a wide variety of matters connected with the organisation of production and the personal conduct of its members'. A federated chapel is a representative organization of all chapels in one plant. By 1921, Robinson had four factories in Bristol, as well as subsidiaries in England and Scotland.

88. Robinson's Director's minute book, 22 September 1919.

89. Robinson's Director's minute book, 18 February 1920 and 18 March 1920, BRO. By 1921, Robinson had four factories in Bristol, as well as subsidiaries in England and Scotland.

90. *NATSOPA Journal*, June 1932, p. 11.
91. *Ibid.*, 13 January 1920.
92. Robinson's Director's minute book, 23 March 1921.
93. During the slump of 1921, however, Robinson's directors considered pro-posing to print unions that they should take responsibility for paying workers on short time: See Robinson's Director's minute book, 15 February 1921, BRO. There is no evidence that this was acted upon.
94. D. J. Jeremy, *Capitalists and Christians* (Clarendon: 1990), p. 366, records that Taylor was the treasurer of the Baptist Missionary Society.
95. Robinson's Director's minute book, 7 January 1919, BRO. When vacancies occurred, factory managers selected new applicants with the assistance of the 'matron' or her male counterpart, depending on the gender of the can-didates. Dismissals of senior staff were at the behest of the factory manager but had to be authorized by two directors. The dismissal of junior staff was the prerogative of the factory manager usually on the recommendation of the matron or her male counterpart.
96. *E.S&AR. Annual Review*, 1935; Savage, *Histories of Bristol Firms, Vol. 2* (Bristol Reference Library), pp. 3–4; Directors' minute book, 11 August 1927, BRO. Foster Robinson adhered to the principles and ideals of his father. In 1958 he was knighted for his services to the city of Bristol.
97. By 1935, 42 years after its introduction, Robinson's employees held about £75,000 in shares. This sum represented only 4 per cent of the share cap-ital and did not carry voting rights: *Who's Who in Bristol* (Labour Research Department: 1935), p. 17.
98. Robinson's Director's minute book, 27 October 1919, BRO.
99. *Ibid.*, 11 March 1918.
100. In 1923, Robinson set aside £5000 to build houses to sell to its workers in Fishponds, Bristol; ten houses were built and then sold for £430 each: Robinson's Director's minute book, 27 July, 25 September 1923, BRO.
101. *Ibid.*, 17 October 1921.
102. *Ibid.*, 22 May 1931.
103. The average monthly benefit paid in 1925 was £45 6s 1d; in 1926 (exclud-ing June to November as benefit payments were suspended as shortage of work was attributed to the General Strike) £151 18s 9d; in 1927, £255 18s 8d; and in 1928, £150 14s 9d (*The Robinson Annual 1844–1944*, p. 7; International Labour Review, 1930, p. 369; Robinson's Director's minute book, 29 April 1925, BRO.
104. Robinson's Director's minute book, 30 November 1926, BRO.
105. ES&A Robinson, Annual Review, 1969, BRO. Interestingly, one week before the General Strike, Edward Robinson was presented with a Golden Wedding anniversary gift, a gold salver, from Robinson's employees and pensioners: *Bristol Times and Mirror*, 28 April 1926.
106. *Bristol Times and Mirror*, 10 May 1926.
107. *Ibid.*, 11, 12 May 1926.
108. Bristol General Strike Committee report to the TUC Information Department, 11 May 1926, TUC History Online, www.unionhistory.info.
109. Robinson Directors' minute book, 5 May 1926, BRO.
110. *Ibid.*, 10 and 13 May 1926.
111. *Ibid.*, 23 June 1926.

112. *Bristol Times and Mirror,* 14 May 1926.
113. *NATSOPA Journal,* December, 1927, pp. 7–9; Robinson's Director's minute book, 11 August, 1927; TA Bristol Branch, Minutes of a Special Meeting, 19 June 1926, BRO.
114. Robinson's Director's minute book No. 2, 5 January 1928. However, there is evidence from Bristol Typographical Society Minutes, 7 September and 7 December 1929, BRO, that this issue was not finally settled until December 1929 when these defaulters rejoined the union.
115. *Ibid.,* 11 August 1927.
116. Following a development that enabled paper bag machines to perform simple over printing on line, a dispute broke out between NATSOPA and the TA over the rights to operate this machinery: TA Bristol Branch Committee, Minutes, 7 October 1922, BRO.
117. *NATSOPA Journal,* December 1927, p. 7.
118. *Ibid.,* p. 9.
119. TA Bristol Branch Committee, Minutes, 5 March 1932, GPMU Bristol Office. For an in-depth examination of the Bedaux system, see C. R. Littler, *The Development of the Labour Process in Capitalist Societies* (Heinemann: 1982).
120. *NATSOPA Journal,* September 1934, p. 20.

6

Work Relations: Compositors' Experiences in a Family-Owned Printing Company, J. W. Arrowsmith 1918–39

Mike Richardson

In 1918, the printing firm of J. W. Arrowsmith was located in the centre of Bristol. Shares in the company were owned by family members. Thus the divorce of ownership and control had not materialized; a common feature of many small and medium sized firms in Britain.[1] Managerial strategy apropos managerial authority over workers in such firms during this period usually falls somewhere between two ends of a continuum: at one end benevolent paternalism, exemplified by Quaker employers such as Cadbury Brothers of Bourneville, Birmingham, and at the other a harsher traditional form of autocratic management. Here we look at one particular case in order to give some insight into labour management of family-run firms between the wars. With this in mind this chapter examines the key factors shaping industrial relations at Arrowsmith during the interwar years. We begin with a brief outline of the firm's historical development. Next, we summarize the firm's economic circumstances, following which we examine the firm's labour management strategy. Attention is then given to the pace of technological change (mechanization) and the division of labour. Finally, we explore the response of the firm's compositors to changes in the labour process and management strategy in what was a difficult economic environment.

Historical development of the firm

Founded in 1854, the print and stationery firm of J. W. Arrowsmith soon established important connections with railway companies, initially as a printer of railway timetables.[2] By the end of the nineteenth century it had become the leading printer and publisher of popular, economically priced books to the expanding British market of railway station book-stalls, employing around 70 workers, 40 of whom were compositors.[3]

After his father, Isaac, died in 1871, James William Arrowsmith took over the family firm. He was a Liberal supporter wedded to the economic doctrines of *laissez-faire*. Benevolent paternalism underpinned the industrial relations practice under his leadership. Like his father, he was keen to help workers to develop an ideology of self-help. However, he recognized that trade unionism had a role to play in his firm. He supported the benefit purposes of trade unionism where workers made their own insurance arrangements to provide for unemployment, sickness and old age. For instance, when the union superannuation fund ran into difficulties in 1906, James Arrowsmith made a donation of ten guineas indicating that if necessary he would turn this into an annual non-contractual payment in order to keep the scheme running.[4]

Arrowsmith, however, resisted challenges to his managerial authority. A letter to the Bristol Typographical Association (BTA) in 1874 reveals the displeasure and anger he felt at the manner in which the union demanded an increase in overtime rates:

> I cannot too strongly express my disapprobation that the profession of printing in Bristol is descended to the low ebb of requiring an agitator to come amongst them for the purpose of spreading discord.[5]

The BTA was quick to rescind any implied criticism of him acknowledging that his firm was not the target of its discontent and that it regarded his firm as a model employer.[6] Arrowsmith's style of paternalism managed to accommodate the development of trade union representation at the workplace by granting better and more wide-ranging benefits than that demanded by union agreements. For instance, around the turn of the twentieth century a sports club was opened for the sole use of Arrowsmith's workers in a corner of Gloucestershire County Cricket Club's ground in Bristol.[7] More substantially, however, from 1876 all his workers received a week's paid holiday, and by 1894 they were working a 48 hour week. It was 1919 before a 48 hour week was secured for all British print workers. Benevolent paternalism practised by the firm before the First World War minimized conflict and seemed to have been embraced by the workforce. Workers' fears that this relationship would be impaired by the conversion of the firm into a limited company, in 1911, were seemingly put to rest, as the £20,000 of shares were sold to family members only.[8]

Bateman depicts labour relations at Arrowsmith before 1914 as 'deference in exchange for paternalism'.[9] This picture needs to be qualified, however. The skills of compositors, print machine minders and bookbinders were transferable and not confined to one specific firm; thus these workers could seek work with alternative employers. Moreover, workers organized some welfare benefits externally through their trade union further weakening their dependency on the firm. Seemingly, therefore, to obtain the best workers Arrowsmith had to provide pay and conditions above the norm.

J. W. Arrowsmith died in 1913 leaving the business to his nephew, J. A. Arrowsmith-Brown. Within 18 months Arrowsmith-Brown was called up for war duty leaving the firm to be run by his co-director T. H. Davis. By 1914, strong associations with the University of Bristol, the regional railway companies and the Bristol wine merchants, John Harvey and Sons Ltd., had secured valuable and regular business. To accommodate the increase in letterpress work Arrowsmith's premises had to be extended to double its previous size, which was achieved by 1918. More workers were required to execute this expansion. During 1900–18, the workforce increased by over 40 per cent to around a hundred employees.[10] Capital raised in the form of shares from family members was needed to finance this expansion suggesting that funds generated from retained profits were not enough. This brought new problems in that assets in the form of fixed capital increased substantially as new composing and letterpress machines were purchased and housed in larger premises. To avoid a fall in the rate of return on fixed capital, pressure was increased on curtailing other forms of capital outlay, particularly labour costs. Thus by committing investment to plant and machinery, particularly between 1911–18, the firm set in train, even if unintended, the weakening of the paternalistic relationship established in the nineteenth century as employee benefits were less affordable.

Economic performance

By 1921, the assets locked up in fixed capital were an increasing concern to the company. The slump that had come to haunt most firms by the beginning of 1921 had yet to affect the firm; at least so Arrowsmith-Brown reported to his works committee.[11] He recognized, however, that it was only a matter of time before his firm would feel the impact of recession. It had already lost a long standing contract for printing the official publication of the Bristol and Gloucestershire Archaeological

Society, *Transactions*. This business was lost in 1920 because of a price increase of 45 per cent. Its loss is indicative of the problems facing the firm at a time of rising costs.[12]

When the slump did hit the firm the disadvantages of holding large capital assets became apparent. Orders were lost and production curtailed which led to short-time working and reduced output; however, the burden of capital tied up in production plant and machinery remained constant. The drop in output is demonstrated by the fact that no production bonus was paid out in 1922.[13] As examined later, these problems affected labour relations. Nonetheless, the following year trade was reported to be brisker. The opening of a new publishing company in London, in 1923, resulted in an expansion of this side of the business. The annual report of Arrowsmith's Typographical Association (TA) Chapel,[14] for 1923, records that this development 'materially increased the volume of work turned out by both the composing and machine rooms.'

This growth continued into 1924. However, contracts won were invariably obtained on short lead times resulting in the use of excessive overtime followed by periods of low activity which led to workers being laid off.[15] This rush work, as the chapel described it, created large fluctuations in the numbers employed which led to increasing tension. The annual report of the TA in 1924 reveals the instability of employment within the firm. At the start of the year the TA chapel had 34 members, in September it had 44, but by the close of the year membership had fallen to 35. The ebb and flow in the numbers of skilled workers employed by Arrowsmith was due to the liberal use of casual workers, especially around the Christmas period.

It was not until after the 1926 General Strike that the firm once again embarked on a substantial investment programme. By the time the second interwar slump had taken hold in 1930, the firm had spent a considerable amount of capital on upgrading its works in central Bristol. The firm's capital investment over the previous ten years was equivalent to almost half the value of its share capital.[16] Spending on fixed capital included the reorganization of the plant to accommodate new machinery. Equipment in the stereo, bindery and composing rooms was updated. In addition, lighting and heating were improved and an electric lift installed. The composing room was split into two main departments, one of which specialized in work for railway companies, such as timetables. All the old-style wood frame equipment was discarded and replaced by modern dust-proof frames that housed all the essential tools and type used by the compositor.[17] Monotype casting machines were situated on the top floor directly above the Monotype keyboard operators while the printing machines occupied the cellar.[18] The printing plates were transferred from the composing room down to the print room via a small lift.[19] Thus by 1930, Arrowsmith could boast that they had 'one of the most up-to-date composing equipments in the West of England.'[20]

Arrowsmith-Brown's commitment to heavy investment after 1926 may well have been based on the confidence brought about by the pacifying impact that defeat in General Strike had on the workforce. This did not make him complacent; he extolled the Mond-Turner initiative in the belief that demand would expand faster if the talks could provide 'the path to peace in the industry'.[21] His remarks were made in light of the fact that the machine room was once again operating short-time working, and at a time when the British and international economies were about to enter another deep slump. Unsurprisingly, the risks involved in the investment programme during the period 1911–18, and after 1926, stimulated changes in the conduct of labour relations between Arrowsmith-Brown and the workforce.

Labour management

Davis, the director in charge at Arrowsmith, died in the influenza epidemic of 1919. Thus Arrowsmith-Brown returned to head the business. He was faced with a workforce that was showing some signs of discontent (see the section on compositors and collective action below), as industry readjusted to peacetime conditions. This disquiet stemmed largely from internal circumstances, although it reflected in part the general mood of labour unrest in Britain in the immediate post war period. This slight but perceptible change in the disposition of Arrowsmith's workers had no immediate impact, although it was a sign that the long standing authority enjoyed by the Arrowsmith family was beginning to weaken.

In 1919 a national agreement between print employers and trade unions came into operation to which Arrowsmith was a party. This was not a problem for the firm as it was already working a 48 hour week and paying union rates. The relationship between the firm and the print unions, however, was placed on a more formal and distant basis, which was inevitable given that basic pay and conditions were set to satisfy the industry as a whole. Arrowsmith could not ignore the industrial relations' climate prevailing in the industry overall, even though its inclination was to take an insular position. Thus pragmatism seemed to prevail as the firm accepted a more explicit commitment to the externalization of industrial relations.

Arrowsmith's drive to increase output and to expand its market was quickly followed by an attempt to put labour relations on a stable basis. This was of a particular urgency given the heavy investment programme undertaken in the preceding years, especially as it was financed by 'family' capital. The firm adopted a dual industrial relations policy. An internal mechanism was set up to try and improve relationships with employees while negotiations over pay and conditions were left to the central institutions of labour and management; the British Federation of Master Printers (BFMP), the Printing and Kindred Trades Federation (PKTF), and the individual print trade unions and the Joint Industrial Council (JIC). Unlike large scale firms, Arrowsmith could not afford to employ specialist managers to take responsibility for labour relations and the organization of work, therefore, the firm turned to the idea of establishing a works committee.

Arrowsmith, not having experienced war-time shop floor militancy, saw little value before 1920 in taking up a Whitley Committee recommendation to establish works committees (which had been originally put forward to counter the growth of the shop steward movement).[22] However, by 1920 as the workforce began to show signs of dissatisfaction the company somewhat belatedly established a Works Advisory Committee in an attempt to deal with this situation. This committee drew representatives from all sections of the workforce but Arrowsmith-Brown held sway over the proceedings as chairman.

The importance placed upon this initiative is revealed in the published objects of the committee.[23] Principles stressing unity between employer and employee were paramount. For instance, the first stated objective was 'to create a community of interests' and 'a closer intercourse' under the guidance of the committee, which ostensibly had extensive powers but whose decisions were not binding. The idea was that the committee was to be used as a platform to air grievances and suggest ways to improve working relations, working conditions, discipline, technical education, efficiency and anything else that was likely to create harmonious industrial relations. These objectives are little different from the Whitley model view of works committees and, although never cited, there is little doubt that this must have been the source of Arrowsmith's initiative.

The first meeting was held on 20 March 1920, a time when the country was still enjoying an economic boom, and confined itself to social issues by recommending the establishment of a lending library and a cricket team.[24] Both suggestions were implemented and welcomed by most employees, although it is doubtful that these social initiatives would have had much of an impact on improving labour relations. The meeting held on 16 April 1920, just before the end of the boom, cast aside any doubts that the works committee would not deal with more fundamental issues. It was decided that all adult employees with 12 months continuous service were to be given staff status. Moreover, if the volume of business declined, no dismissals of employees with staff status would take place without the consideration of the works committee, which could recommend short-time working as being more appropriate than sackings. These progressive proposals were adopted unanimously.

The final word, of course, fell to Arrowsmith-Brown, but it is perhaps surprising that the firm's 'right' to dismiss workers was allowed to be weakened by this commitment to consultation. Lynden Macassey, writing in 1922, suggests that in some cases this sort of decision was forced on the employer by militants, but there is no evidence to suggest that this was the case at Arrowsmith. [25] A more convincing explanation, as the firm was recruiting skilled labour at this time (see Table 6.1), is that the firm used the commitment to staff status and consultation before sackings as a carrot to retain staff and secure the compliance of its core workers at little cost to the firm. Moreover, this compliance could also have provided immunity from the wave of industrial unrest sweeping the country at this time.

The following month, May 1920, the TA became embroiled in a national dispute that started as a pay claim to keep pace with the cost of living, but escalated into a quarrel over wage differentials and status. The bitterness engendered by this disagreement sent tremors throughout the industry and dragged on throughout the summer. Arrowsmith-Brown thought this was a significant and worrying development and raised the issue at the September meeting of the works committee. Several days later, however, a resolution to the dispute was found. [26]

By January 1921, when it became clear that the British economy was entering a deep recession, objections to the works committee being consulted over short-time working were put forward by two TA members of the committee. It was their view that the matter of short-time working should be dealt with by negotiations between the father of the chapel (FoC) and management. If this counter proposal had been accepted it could have destroyed a key objective of the committee, which was to act as a workplace institution for dealing with in-house labour relations. Arrowsmith-Brown overcame this difficulty by gaining acceptance from the committee that the FoC of the TA chapel should have a place on the works committee by his right of office.[27] The committee did not meet again for two months. At the March meeting it became clear that the FoC of the TA chapel was under the misapprehension that the payment of full weekly wages to those working short-time before 2 March 1921 was due to the firm's generosity. Arrowsmith-Brown dispelled the FoC's illusions by revealing that the money found to make up wages of those on short-time working was taken from the workers' annual bonus.[28]

Initially, the FoC of Arrowsmith's TA chapel had welcomed the establishment of a works committee. He saw it as a vehicle where workers could put forward their ideas to improve output and thereby increase annual bonus payments. This did not happen. There is no evidence of any real enthusiasm for the committee once it had become operative. Moreover, no sorrow was expressed in its sudden passing. The chapel minutes record that following the meeting held on 23 June 1921 the works committee 'died a natural death'.[29] It did not reconvene again until after the 1926 General Strike. The works committee minutes indicated that it was the belated impact of the slump, the question of short-time working and disquiet about unemployment that undermined the effectiveness of the committee. It seems that the potency of *laissez-faire* economic principles during the slump destroyed the credibility of the committee given the unpleasant choices it was faced with concerning lay-offs and short-time working. Thus Arrowsmith-Brown was forced to suspend pursuance of an agenda that seemingly favoured a weak form of workers' participation and the internalization of employment relations. Market forces were seemingly enough to curtail the eruption of any disputes or discontent.

Arrowsmith-Brown, however, even at what was to be the final meeting of the works committee, was still hedging his bets by expressing hopes that the committee would continue once the national coal strike was settled and short-time working within the firm was no longer necessary.[30] That he was reluctant to discontinue the operation of the works committee suggests that he was concerned as to whether workers would accept what Musson describes as the 'appreciation of economic realities or its employer' difficulties'[31] and that he had no alternative strategy. Over the next four years, however, while unemployment in the Bristol printing, publishing and bookbinding sector was relatively high,[32] Arrowsmith-Brown exercised his authority through direct personal control of labour relations without having to resurrect the works committee to legitimize his position or as a mechanism to retain labour. He was supported by the work's manager who had the power to hire and, in consultation with Arrowsmith-Brown, fire labour; but a management structure or hierarchy did not exist.[33]

It took the impact of the 1926 General Strike to instigate the revival of the works committee. Arrowsmith-Brown, as with many other employers, was shaken by the solidarity displayed by his workers in support of the miners, and after the strike sought to create a climate of industrial relations harmony. The defeat of the General Strike gave employers a new opportunity to install mechanisms aimed at sustaining workers' compliance. After 1926 the 'prevention of disaffection and disputes'[34] was probably the main reason behind Arrowsmith-Brown's decision to resurrect the old works advisory committee, which had its first meeting on 18 October 1926. The firm planned to invest heavily, but Arrowsmith-Brown was concerned about the effect on the viability of the firm if they could not maintain continuity of production. The heavier the investment the more vulnerable the firm was to disruption, as it could ill afford to have its plant working below capacity. Therefore, to continue to recognize trade unionism as part of its industrial relations strategy was logical. By re-establishing the works committee, Arrowsmith-Brown created an opportunity to restore his authority, damaged during the 1926 General Strike (see discussion below), by internalizing many issues concerning labour relations and thus keeping outside interference (trade unions and employer organizations) to a minimum.

This period after the General Strike, therefore, saw the consolidation of the reconstructed works committee. A small honorarium was paid to its members in recognition of their support. The 1920 resolution re staff status, dismissals and short-time working, however, was never referred to and therefore probably inoperative. Only modest inducements were necessary to invoke compliance as the failure of the General Strike served to dampen down any overt expressions of discontent among the workforce, which the sharp decline of industrial unrest in Britain after 1926 illustrates. Nonetheless, poor industrial relations were seen to be harmful to the firm, and it was this aspect that helped the TA workers at Arrowsmith to come out of the General Strike without losing face or suffering a serious undermining of the extent of their organizational control.

The works committee seemed to die a second natural death in March 1930, the last recorded meeting, after which there seemed little sign of a coherent labour relations policy. The works committee was no longer functioning, discipline was lax and management was rarely seen on the shop floor.[35] That mechanisms of direct control seemed to lapse by the late 1930s is indicative of the problems that could arise from personal management and the reliance on the entrepreneurship and management skills of the owner. In ownership controlled firms dependence on the initiative and personality of individual owners and the failure to embrace the visible hand of managerial capitalism has been viewed as rather inefficient compared with new forms of management organization and control.[36] It was probably only the relatively favourable market conditions prevailing after 1935 that allowed the firm to trundle along.

Mechanization and the division of labour

The formation of Arrowsmith's workforce had changed significantly by 1919; reflecting the impact that the mechanization of composing had on job opportunities for compositors. In 1900 type was still set by hand which was regarded as the most skilful and important task in the production process. As noted above, Arrowsmith employed 40 compositors in 1900, which represented about 57 per cent of the firm's total workforce. By 1919, the number of compositors employed had fallen to 17 out of 100 employees (see Table 6.1).

Although the ratio of compositors to machine minders employed between 1919 and 1928, (Table 6.1), fluctuates,[37] the transformation

Table 6.1   Numbers of core skilled workers, belonging to the Typographical Association, employed by J. W. Arrowsmith, 1919–28.

Year	Compositors	M/C Minders
1919	17	8
1920	20	10
1921	24	9
1922	24	8
1923	25	10
1924	28	7
1925	23	11
1926	25	10
1927	22	10
1928	21	9

Source: Annual Reports of Arrowsmith's TA Chapel 1919–28.

from hand to machine composition had been completed by 1919 for all but the most specialized work during Arrowsmith's expansion programme.[38] By the interwar years the compositor's main tasks were the operation of Monotype keyboard machines, corrections to Monotype setting by hand, and the fixation of cast type into a letterpress form ready for transferring to the printing press. The TA had almost complete organizational control over this area of production, although one potential obstacle to total control was the division of labour peculiar to Monotype composition. Unlike the Linotype machine, which was designed as a 'slug-casting machine' where it was necessary to have both keyboard and casting integrated into one machine, the Monotype composing process, 'which casts lines of single types and spaces', divorced the composing operation from that of hot metal casting.[39] Thus two machines were used with an operator on each, one for the keyboard and one for casting. This division of labour was the source of national interunion rivalry over who had organizational rights for those involved in the casting process.[40] The result was that almost all the print unions had some Monotype casters in their ranks. It was firmly recognized, however, that the compositor operating the keyboard was skilled and the caster attendant semi-skilled.

By the outbreak of the Second World War, the BTA had secured organizational control over Monotype caster attendants at Arrowsmith.[41] Caster attendants had to serve a five year apprenticeship and regarded themselves as skilled workers. However, before the First World War the TA regarded this work as below craft status and would not admit caster attendants into TA membership.[42] The union's change of heart in 1918 was based on the grounds that the casting machine was part of the composing machine.[43] Moreover, TA control was also linked with the all male environment of composing rooms and to the physical prowess of caster attendants.[44]

Cyril Manfield, who in 1939 began his apprenticeship with Arrowsmith as a Monotype caster attendant, recalled that when he was first interviewed for the job by the firm it expressed concern that he was perhaps too short, as the work required physical strength as well as intelligence. Working conditions were certainly uncomfortable as he recollected: 'Monotype caster attendants employed at Arrowsmith had to operate in very hot conditions, which were the subject of many complaints'. And it was not until the machine (computer) necessitated cooler conditions that the firm introduced any form of air conditioning. Another hazard that he and his colleagues had to contend with was the splash back of molten lead. Damp in particular caused molten lead to spit and splutter. He bore the scars of frequent splash back occurrences. Thus the Monotype caster's job was very much associated with physical endurance which served to underpin the 'masculinity' label attached to hot metal work.[45]

There were no women compositors or Monotype caster attendants working at Arrowsmith between the wars. Apart from printing machine minders, all skilled male print workers were segregated from women workers, as not only did compositors work in enclosed areas, but they also worked on the opposite side of a narrow road from the female staff; only a small bridge connected the two factories.[46] Nonetheless, outside this all male environment other printing and binding processes within Arrowsmith were carried out in a more open atmosphere, although these too were subject to gender divisions. The majority of those engaged in the production process outside the composing room were classified as non-craft workers. Here the production process demanded a more cooperative approach and women workers were organized into rather than excluded from trade unions.[47]

Unfortunately, there is no trace of archives regarding aspects of the labour process such as the pace of work and productivity. Manfield recalled, however, that when he joined the firm skilled workers were paid 'stab' rates (weekly established pay rates) and no compositors or Monotype casters were on piecework. Before the Second World War no counters were attached to Monotype casting machines, thus output per person was not measured to any degree of accuracy. The only incentive to increase productivity was the payment of merit money, which supposedly reflected the quantity and quality of work produced, as well rewarding attendance and punctuality. Work study was not used at Arrowsmith until the 1950s, after which a controversial bonus scheme was introduced.[48]

The strong identification of masculinity with composing work, the compositor's defence of his skill status and the organizational control held by the TA, were the methods used by craft print workers to defend their position, all of which were evident at Arrowsmith. Nonetheless, by 1918 mechanization had reduced the firm's reliance on craft workers considerably. Non-craft workers (including women) outnumbered craft workers. The increase in output made possible by the setting of type at a much greater speeds, whilst reducing the numbers of compositors required, created more printing work and provided more jobs, especially to those engaged on bookbinding tasks. In all aspects of its trade, bookbinding, composing and printing, Arrowsmith mechanized its plant earlier and quicker (before 1918) than most small printing houses in the industry.[49] This explains the greater reduction in the number of compositors than that generally experienced nationally and the increase in non-craft workers.

The demand for compositors, however, increased slightly during 1924, after the firm had opened its London publishing branch, but fell back after the 1926 General Strike (Table 6.1 above). By the mid-1930s, the BTA records show that the aggregate numbers of compositors and machine minders employed by Arrowsmith fell from 28 in September 1934 to 24 in September 1936, thereafter increasing to 30 in 1938.[50] These figures represent a fairly significant decrease in the average number of craft workers employed compared with the 1920s (see Table 6.1), especially since the British economy was pulling out of a slump in 1934. This is probably the outcome of the heavy investment made by Arrowsmith after 1926, which included the reorganization and modernization of the composing room. An alternative explanation, of course, is that Arrowsmith's share of traditional markets was reduced due to increased competition. The firm was able, however, to attract new orders in the late 1930s; for instance it won the contract for producing the staff journal of the Great Western Railway Company and gained some academic printing work from the University of Bristol concerning a social survey of Bristol.[51]

Where it was felt necessary, new processes were introduced such as the use of pantone plates for printing on letterpress machines to improve print quality and reduce the reliance on the skill of the printer.[52] Another factor affecting employment prospects of craft workers was the introduction of new two-revolution letterpress machines, of various sizes. Many of these machines had automatic feed attachments, the operation of which required the machine minder to increase his range of responsibilities while the skills of the machine feeder, a woman, diminished.[53] Surprisingly, the change over from hand to mechanized feeding was not fully completed until after the Second World War. Manfield recollected that in 1938 one or two of the four Meihle letterpress machines were still fed by hand by women feeders.[54] This suggests that changes in the production process were uneven and associated with the availability of capital for investment. Thus there was a long lag in the full implementation of new automatic machinery. The displacement of jobs, deskilling and re-skilling came in short bursts, but the impact of new technology took many years to release its full potential.

Automatic machinery at Arrowsmith had been introduced to cover most tasks in the bookbinding process by 1900.[55] It was in the bindery that most of the female labour was employed. Here, women and/or girl labour operated wire stitching, punching and pasting machines.[56]

Moreover, women operated sewing machines and folding machines but men worked the guillotines, probably because the razor sharp cutting blade was seen to be highly dangerous therefore was classified as men's work. By 1918, employment in this sector of the business had increased substantially to satisfy increasing demand. Mechanization of the composition process lagged behind automation in the bindery. It was after 1911, that the shift from hand to machine composition accelerated curtailing the number of compositors required by the firm. Yet craft identity was still strong, and gender and skill barriers to entry into compositor's work continued to prevail between the wars (and indeed beyond). It is the experience of these Arrowsmith's workers to which we now turn.

Compositors and collective action

Arrowsmith-Brown and at least six of Arrowsmith's compositors temporarily left the firm's employ to serve in the armed forces during the First World War. Just before their return to civilian life, on 30 May 1918, the Arrowsmith's TA chapel sent a letter of congratulation to Arrowsmith-Brown on his award of the Distinguished Service Order for his military endeavours.[57] Rather than a display of deference this was most likely written as a sincere recognition of what was viewed as Arrowsmith-Brown's bravery. This would explain the paradox that only a month previously, on 29 April, the TA chapel had broken from its pre-war passivity by refusing to work overtime unless given 24 hours prior warning or, because of short notice, paid 8d tea money. Trivial though this dispute may appear, it had a considerable impact on the members of the TA chapel. They were proud to have finally plucked up the courage to demonstrate, openly and defiantly, albeit momentarily, a grievance they had against their employer, in whom, until now, they had held great respect.[58]

These deep feelings were revealed in the 1918 annual report of the Arrowsmith TA chapel. In a colourful, commemorative record, of what was a momentous occasion in the chapel's history, the chapel clerk recalled its long and quiescent life. He commented, with a note of embarrassment, that even while the Great War was raging taking the lives of heroic British soldiers 'nothing seemed to disturb our [the chapel's] equanimity'.[59] The day finally came, however, when this was to change, and in a melodramatic style, the chapel clerk described the event thus:

To arms ye comps, Defy I[the] foe. Stand by ye guns. From I[the] enemys' [*sic*] camp we heard I [the] Command-'Work O.T. [overtime] tonight.' 'On our own terms,' we reply. But I [the] enemy wld [would] not yield and I [the] order went forth 'No surrender.' At 5.30 we downed tools, and marched home whistling 'Rule Britannia', 'The Marseillaise', or 'see/ Conquering/hero comes'.[60]

Taking as a model, what they saw as the heroics of the British soldier in the Great War, the Arrowsmith TA chapel members temporarily arose from their passivity to reveal their potential strength but in a distinctly masculine form. As Cockburn comments: 'Second only to warfare, work is the arena in which men wrestle with each other for status and survival'.[61] The firm was quick to channel the dispute along institutional lines, referring the problem to the South West Alliance of Master Printers Association (SWAMPA) and the BTA for a solution. The Arrowsmith's TA chapel was seemingly satisfied with this outcome, agreeing to resume overtime working 'on the written promise of the firm to make good our demands if the case should be in our favour' and happy to have come out of an encounter it had initiated unscathed and with dignity.[62]

It was not long before the Arrowsmith's TA chapel was again to react spontaneously to what it saw as an act of injustice by its employer. This time the firm responded in a different way. On 3 February 1919, the chapel called an emergency meeting 'round the stone'. This was a break from tradition signifying a defiant mood as chapel meetings were not normally held on the firm's premises.[63] The 'emergency' was that the firm had issued a fortnight's notice to two chapel members, taken on during the war years, to make way for six former employees who had just been demobbed from the army and wanted to return to their old occupations under the dilution agreement. Because of the regular amount of overtime being worked, the chapel felt that these sackings were unwarranted. They held a paper ballot which resulted in favour of refusing to work overtime until the dismissal notices had been withdrawn.[64]

This information was conveyed to the works manager, the man responsible for giving out the dismissal notices, who was then allowed to address the meeting. No conciliatory approach was made this time, but rather a direct threat to the workers that if they failed to abide by the instruction to work overtime, other men would be found to perform the task. The manager's intimidating address was enough to panic the chapel into capitulation, as the chapel minutes indicate:

> The members of I [the] chapel looked at I [the] Father, and the poor
> Father looked at I [the] men, and it w [was] felt + [that] we were
> 'between the devil & I [the] deep sea.' It seemed as if our courage of a
> few minutes ago w [was] percolating through our finger tips.[65]

Faced with this new direct coercive strategy, the chapel foundered and
reversed a decision they obviously felt strongly about and had only
made moments before the intervention of the works manager. This time
their courage was found wanting.

This dispute demonstrates the desire of Arrowsmith's TA workers to
resist but with no tradition of militancy they could not hold their position when threatened. They failed to seek external assistance even from
their own organization. Therefore, the dispute was contained within
the internal boundaries of the firm. No doubt Arrowsmith's TA chapel
consoled themselves with the fact that it was a time of relatively low
unemployment, thus the prospects of the two sacked chapel members
finding work were probably fairly good. This does not, however, mask
the reality that the firm was able to exercise authority and subjugate the
will of its employees.

The capitulation of Arrowsmith's TA workers must be put in context,
as any move to undermine the authority of the national union would
inevitably have provoked a backlash. A dispute of a national character was more likely to disrupt production than any internal dispute.
Thus the setback for Arrowsmith TA members in February 1919 was partially offset by the two significant wage increases obtained later in 1919,
through the negotiations between the TA and the BFMP, followed by a
further increase in January 1920, which brought the compositors' wage
level at Arrowsmith, for a 48 hour week, to £3.19.6., the standard local
rate.[66] Moreover, the establishment of a works committee at Arrowsmith
in 1920 reflect that the firm was not totally confident that the authority it held was secure. Therefore, it attempted to forge a labour relations
strategy through internal as well as external means more suitable for
post war conditions. By more subtle means the firm set out to legitimize
its authority by trying to increase the dependency of its core workers in
the firm in the hope of establishing a solid foundation to secure subordination and deference at a time when the labour market was tight.

Marginal though the events of 1918/19 at Arrowsmith may appear, it
is clear that these were times when new forms of authority and resistance were being formed. The onset of slump added a new dimension
to this struggle. The initial signs indicated that slump had weakened
workers' resistance. The staggered imposition of wage cuts, in 1921, by

employers belonging to the BFMP was reluctantly accepted by the TA nationally and very much regretted by Arrowsmith's TA members.[67] Compliance continued but openness to further wage cuts was absent. In July 1922, a national strike was called by the TA against further wage reductions. This strike continued for four weeks. Members of the Arrowsmith TA chapel united behind their union, taking strike action for the first time in their history, illustrating the point made earlier that the focus of resistance had moved on to issues of national importance where the collective power of the union could be released. The strike was lost, however.

On returning to work after the wages dispute had been settled, TA casual workers in Arrowsmith's employ were discharged. Whether this was attributable to a fit of pique by Arrowsmith-Brown or due to orders lost as a result of the strike is open to conjecture. However, following complaints from those casual workers who felt they had been victimized, the TA Bristol Branch protested to Arrowsmith-Brown, but to no avail and the case was allowed to drop.[68] Defeat suffered in the 1922 strike weakened the resolve of the TA to seriously question Arrowsmith-Brown's managerial prerogatives concerning appointing or discharging casual staff.

When the TA's organizational control was threatened, however, its response was a little more forceful. In 1924 a conflict arose over areas of union control after a TA member resigned from the union following a change of job to that of a reader. The TA's Executive Council (EC) refused to accept this member's resignation claiming that his job as a reader[69] was TA work. Arrowsmith's TA chapel supported the EC over this claim but was reluctant to take independent action and recommended that the case should be dealt with through the BFMP and the TA conciliation machinery.[70] While wanting to maintain organizational control, and unhappy about working excessive overtime and the willingness of the firm to hire and fire casual workers, the Arrowsmith's TA chapel was unwilling to take industrial action. An unfavourable industrial relations environment, after the defeat of its union in the 1922 strike, was no doubt partially responsible for the chapel's reticence. However, the timidity displayed by TA workers in matters arising from disputes within the firm since 1918 indicate the predictability of their actions.

The experiences of Arrowsmith's TA chapel in the immediate post First World War period show that its flirtation with independent action in response to the demise of the firm's paternalist authority was confined to specific issues, fought in isolation, and lacked conviction. Although the chapel was weak, the introduction of a national agreement that standardized hours and wages served to shift the struggle over employment conditions to the national arena, as Arrowsmith could no longer claim to offer better rewards to its workers than other employers. Grievances, therefore, were channelled through official union and employer institutions, but, unless they threatened to undermine national agreements or organizational control, were usually dropped. Thus, within certain parameters, Arrowsmith-Brown had ample freedom to assert authority in the workplace. This was the climate at Arrowsmith when the General Strike was declared in 1926.

In response to the General Strike call, on 4 May 1926, the Arrowsmith's TA chapel stopped work and called a special meeting of its members. Two resolutions were considered. The first expressed sympathy for the miners but proposed a return to work, highlighting the fact that by taking immediate strike action contractual agreements would be broken. The second recommended that the chapel abide by the decision of the EC and remain out on strike until 'ordered to return'.[71] The latter proposal was overwhelmingly carried. The leadership given by the Trades Union Congress (TUC) at this juncture was enough to overcome any lack of confidence the print workers may have had arising from the 1922 TA dispute. That Arrowsmith's compositors were supporting the institutions of organized labour, there is little doubt. It was also a profound expression of the demise of the paternalistic industrial relations strategy at Arrowsmith.

The resoluteness of the Arrowsmith TA chapel was soon to be tested. The General Strike was called off on 12 May 1926. Arrowsmith informed the chapel that it would only allow the striking printers back a few at a time. The chapel refused to return to work on these terms. The events that followed are recorded in the annual report of the chapel:

> We decided to await Mr. J. Arrowsmith-Brown and hear what he had to say on the matter. He only confirmed what we already heard, and we flatly refused to commence work. After meeting again at Caxton House the Chapel re-affirmed their decision previously, resolving to stand together whatever decision we came to. The wisdom of this action was revealed at the end of an exciting day when Mr. J. Arrowsmith-Brown met our demands and we started work once more on the old conditions.[72]

The collective spirit of the chapel played a significant part in bringing about a successful and orderly return to work after the General Strike. The chapel's resolve, however, was not fully tested by Arrowsmith-Brown who, under a state of shock at seeing the determined stand of his workers, decided that it was more pragmatic to take a conciliatory attitude rather than pursue the autocratic and coercive strategy practised between 1921–25. This Arrowsmith-Brown demonstrated by conceding to the chapel's conditions for a return to work on the same day of asking. Moreover, within a few days Arrowsmith-Brown offered financial assistance to anyone who found themselves in difficulties as a result of participating in the General Strike.[73]

Conclusion

Short term economic imperatives determined the choice of Arrowsmith's industrial relations strategy to a greater degree than that of the large-scale firms. Although the firm seemed to have been performing reasonably adequately, it depended largely on the family for its finance, as the family held all the shares, which placed constrictions on how the firm was able to operate and expand. This had consequences for the conduct of labour relations. Arrowsmith dropped its strategy of offering wages and benefits above trade union rates. Thus, to retain authority, Arrowsmith, apart from paying an annual bonus related to output and offering a few recreational facilities, tried to gain consent from its workforce by maintaining union recognition to deal with basic pay and conditions, which were the subject of external negotiations on the basis of standardization throughout the industry. The loss of authority associated with this strategy, however, needed to be curtailed. Therefore, apart from wage bargaining, involvement of external organizations (trade unions and employer organizations) in internal affairs was kept to a minimum, and either Arrowsmith-Brown relied on his authority (as owner of the family firm) to secure objectives or, as has been illustrated, the works committee was brought into play. Notably, however, on each occasion the works committee was used, the onset of slump made its operation unnecessary as market forces pacified worker resistance.

Another feature of this case study is that compositors were under severe pressure due to the reduction in the number of available jobs; largely as a result of the introduction of composing machines. Compositors relied heavily on their national union to protect their skilled status and organizational control, but the firm were still able to make significant labour savings. The courage of Arrowsmith's compositors was at times found wanting in defending their interests. This made them vulnerable. Thus, not dissimilar to compositors elsewhere, they focused on sustaining their craft status and extending organizational control by strictly distinguishing themselves from unskilled workers and excluding them from skilled areas of work, such as the example given above concerning the work of a reader. This defensive action also had a gender dimension. Threats to the security of compositors, and deskilling of their work posed by the replacement of hand composition with composing machines, put in jeopardy what identified them as men, their masculinity. Semi-skilled and unskilled print workers were able to place emphasis on the physical prowess of their work to express their masculinity, but for compositors it was their skill, higher earnings, and their position in the hierarchy of labour that defined them as men.[74]

Notes

This chapter has been adapted from a section of work submitted for my thesis: M. J. Richardson 'Industrial Relations in the British Printing Industry between the Wars', unpublished PhD thesis (University of the West of England: 1995).

1. See A. D. Chandler Jr. *Scale and Scope: The Dynamics of Industrial Capitalism* (Cambridge MA: Harvard, 1990)
2. *Our Bulletin*, Journal of the Bristol Master Printers Association, 15 January 1932, p. 29.
3. D. Bateman, 'The Nineteenth Century Printing Trade in Bristol and the role of the Bristol Typographical Society within it', Unpublished PhD thesis (Bristol Polytechnic: 1991), pp. 240–41.
4. *Ibid.* p. 246.
5. *Ibid.* p. 243; Anon, *Arrowsmith, 1854–1954* (Arrowsmith: Bristol, 1955), p. 28.
6. D. Bateman, 'The Nineteenth Century Printing Trade in Bristol', pp. 243–48.
7. *Ibid.* pp. 243–44; Anon, *Arrowsmith, 1854–1954,* pp. 28–29.
8. D. Bateman, 'The Nineteenth Century Printing Trade in Bristol', p. 248.
9. *Ibid.* pp. 238–48.
10. *Our Bulletin*, p. 29; *Western Daily Press*, 24 June 1931; D. Bateman, 'The Growth of the Printing and Packaging Industry in Bristol, 1800–1914' in C. Harvey & J. Press (eds), *Studies in the Business History of Bristol* (Bristol Academic Press: 1988), p. 102.
11. J. W. Arrowsmith's Works Advisory Committee Minutes, 4 January 1921, Bristol Records Office (BRO). We learn from the Arrowsmith's TA chapel minutes, however, that the committee 'died a natural death' in 1921. The works committee was not to reconvene again until after the 1926 General Strike and continued to meet until 31 March 1931. It is not known whether any further meetings took place after this date.
12. P. McGrath and J. Cannon (eds), *Essays in Bristol and Gloucestershire History* (Bristol and Gloucestershire Archaeological Society: 1976), p. 16. Interestingly, in 1923 the president of the Bristol and Gloucestershire Archaeological Society said that the responsibility of higher prices lay with the compositor and not the employer: 'I have gone into the question [high prices] in detail

with three or four leading publishers, and I cannot see that they are sharing to any perceptible extent in the extortionate profits of the compositors; nor is any very heavy proportion of the enhanced book-prices going into the pockets of the master printers', Presidential Address, *Transactions* (Bristol and Gloucestershire Archaeological Society: 1923) p. 63.

13. Minutes of Arrowsmith's TA Chapel AGM, 1923, BRO.
14. The 'chapel' is the printing unions' unit of workplace organization.
15. Special Meeting of Arrowsmith's TA Chapel, 10 October 1924, BRO.
16. *Our Bulletin*, p. 29.
17. *Ibid*, p. 29; J. W. Arrowsmith's Works Advisory Committee Minutes, 1929, 1930, BRO.
18. The Monotype machine reproduces in code form text as a series of perforations on a paper spool. From this spool the Monotype casting machine casts and sets type in single letters or characters using hot metal.
19. Cyril Manfield interviewed by M. J. Richardson, 5 July 1993: Cyril joined Arrowsmith's in 1937 and was apprenticed as a monotype caster in 1939.
20. *Our Bulletin*, p. 29.
21. The quote is taken from J. W. Arrowsmith-Brown's report to the firm's works committee on 16 January 1928. The Mond-Turner conference was an attempt to identify areas of common interest where further discussion could bring about agreement and mutual gains for capital and labour.
22. *Committee on Trade and Industry: Survey of Industrial Relations*, HMSO, 1926, p. 302.
23. J. W. Arrowsmith, *Objects of Works Committee*, BRO.
24. J. W. Arrowsmith, Works Advisory Committee, March 1920:
25. L. Macassey, *Labour Policy-False and True* (Thornton Butterworth: 1922), p. 267.
26. J. W. Arrowsmith, Works Advisory Committee, 3 September 1920: See A. E. Musson, *The Typographical Association* (Oxford University Press: 1954), pp. 342–43; and the *Ministry of Labour Gazette*, 1921, re. details of the TA dispute.
27. J. W. Arrowsmith, Works Advisory Committee, 4 January 1921.
28. J. W. Arrowsmith, Works Advisory Committee, 2 March 1921.
29. 1921 Annual Report of Arrowsmith's TA Chapel, BRO.
30. J. W. Arrowsmith, Works Advisory Committee, 23 June 1921.
31. Musson, *The Typographical Association*, p. 343.
32. Probert, 'An Economic Survey of the Printing Industry in Bristol', unpublished MA (University of Bristol: 1934).
33. Minutes of Arrowsmith's TA Chapel indicate that Grey, the works manager, was responsible for taking on new workers, but probably had to seek the authority of Arrowsmith-Brown to sack workers.
34. J. W. Arrowsmith, *Objects of Works Committee*, BRO.
35. Cyril Manfield interview.
36. See A. D. Chandler Jr., *The Visible Hand: The Managerial Revolution in American Business* (Cambridge MA: Harvard, 1977) and A. D. Chandler Jr., *Scale and Scope: The Dynamics of Industrial Capitalism* (Cambridge MA: Harvard, 1990).
37. The probability is that the Arrowsmith's TA Chapel only recorded permanent workers as full chapel members in their annual reports, and

not those casual workers engaged at various times during the year. This would account for the discrepancy in the annual report of 1924 where in September it was noted that they had 44 members and at the close of the year 35 members, but in the official report only 33 were registered as full chapel members.

38. Cyril Manfield recalled that hand composition was still used for some jobs in the late 1930s. Cyril Manfield interview.
39. H. Whetton, *Practical Printing and Binding* (Odhams Press: 1946), p. 38.
40. Musson, *The Typographical Association*, p. 210.
41. Cyril Manfield joined the Bristol TA in October 1940 one year into his apprenticeship as a monotype caster, suggesting that the TA had by this time secured organizational control over monotype casters in Arrowsmith's.
42. Musson, *The Typographical Association*, p. 210.
43. *Ibid.* pp. 246–47 & pp. 380–82.
44. See C. Cockburn, *Brothers* (Pluto Press: 1983) for a shrewd analysis of masculinity and skill in the printing industry.
45. Cyril Manfield interview
46. *Ibid.*
47. Local wages agreement (male and female employees) between J. W. Arrowsmith and National Union of Printing and Paper Workers (NUP&PW), BRO.
48. Cyril Manfield interview.
49. Bateman, 'The Growth of the Printing and Packaging Industry in Bristol, 1800–1914', pp. 101–03.
50. Bristol Typographical Society-Membership Lists, BRO.
51. Anon., *Arrowsmith 1854–1954*, pp. 15, 19.
52. J. W. Arrowsmith, Works Advisory Committee, November 1926: The difference between the standard relief plate and the pantone plate is that the latter was made in slight relief rather than standing out proudly above the surrounding non-printing area as in the standard plate; H. Whetton, *Practical Printing and Binding*, p. 287.
53. *Our Bulletin*, p. 29.
54. Cyril Manfield interview.
55. Bateman, 'The Nineteenth Century Printing Trade in Bristol' p. 241.
56. J. W. Arrowsmith, Works Advisory Committee Minutes, May 1929.
57. Minutes of Arrowsmith's TA Chapel Meeting, 30 May 1918, BRO.
58. *Ibid.*
59. 1918 Annual Report of Arrowsmith's TA Chapel, BRO.
60. *Ibid.*
61. C. Cockburn, *Brothers*, p. 133.
62. 1918 Annual Report of Arrowsmith's TA Chapel, BRO.
63. Meetings of the chapel were customarily held in the local TA Branch office. See D. Bateman, 'The Nineteenth Century Printing Trade in Bristol' p. 247.
64. Minutes of Arrowsmith's Chapel Meeting, 3 February 1919, BRO.
65. *Ibid.*
66. Minutes of Arrowsmith's Chapel Meeting, 3 February 1919, BRO.
67. Annual Meeting of Arrowsmith's TA Chapel, January 1922, BRO.
68. Minutes of the TA Bristol Branch Committee, 9 September 1922.
69. From a proof pulled from the type a reader checks and where necessary corrects errors in composition such as grammar and punctuation.

70. Minutes of Special Arrowsmith's TA Chapel Meeting, 10 October, 1924, BRO.
71. Minutes of Special Arrowsmith's TA Chapel Meeting, 4 May 1926, BRO.
72. 1926 Annual Report of Arrowsmith's TA Chapel Meeting, 4 May 1926, BRO.
73. A letter dated 26 May 1926, sent from Arrowsmith's TA Chapel to Arrowsmith-Brown says: 'That this Companionship begs Mr. J. Arrowsmith-Brown to accept its hearty thanks for the kindness and forethought displayed in his generous offer to assist any man financially embarrassed during the recent dispute.' (Copy in Chapel Minute Book, 1926.)
74. See Cockburn, *Brothers*, pp. 132–40.

7

Organization, Ideology and Control – Founding Principles: The Case of the BBC

Peter Nicholls

With the constant threats to the future of the licence fee, the regular attacks on editorial control and the strengthening position of the independent sector, it is sometimes surprising to remember that the BBC remains an agency of the State. In this role, the range of discretion and degree of independence appear to walk a tightrope between political convenience and political control.

This chapter provides an analysis of the early formation and development of the BBC as an agency of the State which reveals how this Corporation came to hold such a dominant position in broadcasting. It highlights the existence of an uneasy relationship between itself and the central State as its role emerges in the 1920s and 1930s, where the first Director General set out to secure a degree of independence from the political establishment. It also reveals some of the key features of the style of management control which appeared to recreate many attributes of Edwardian thinking in its forms of paternalistic control. By harnessing the ideal of public service to the business of broadcasting, the early Corporation created a set of coherent logics providing a form of subordination that would appeal, and be acceptable, to a broad class of emerging professional media operatives. In Edwardian Britain, this workforce would be assumed to be compliant and content to exist within a secure form of employment with high status and reasonable levels of pay. The role played by the ideology of public service broadcasting is considered to have contributed in creating a climate for stable industrial relations. This set of principles was to have a fundamental affect upon the attitudes, traditions and working practices of those engaged in producing media outputs of the day. Finally, the chapter will consider the role and influence of the first Director General of the Corporation, who still holds a central place in the history and mythology of the early Corporation. The BBC started life as a private broadcasting company exploiting the newly developed radio technology whose mass market had probably been first considered in the US by David Sarnoff in 1916: 'I have in mind a plan of development which would make radio a "household utility" like the piano or electricity, the idea to bring music into the house by wireless.'[1]

In Britain the technology had been around since the First World War when radio transmission was part of the equipment for communications. In these early days, such a technology was of great interest to the military which played an influential role in trying to maintain a monopoly of control for Marconi who had invented much of the technology at this time:

> With naval vessels, of course, the situation was different, and it was the power of the navy, especially, which led not only to the commandeering of the products of the Marconi Company, but the Admiralty for the duration of the war and for some time after.[2]

Military resources have a long history in supplying the original impetus for conducting research leading to the development and control of new technologies. Their early involvement in radio broadcasting was to provide an important precursor to the developing logic of combining State resources with industrial development. The creation of this Corporation as an agency of the State was also an experiment in using State resources to engage in research and development to produce new broadcasting technologies:

> The formation of the BBC, twenty years before the more considerable measures of the 'Morrisonite' nationalisation, is a blueprint for State financing of products and services which are either essential for, or favourable towards, profitable ventures by private enterprise. In fact, the creation of the BBC is almost contemporary with the setting up of Government organisations to promote research and development in weapons and defence, a move which converted the Government's role from customer of armaments manufacturers to that of inventing, designing, provisioning and contracting for new weapons, tanks, ships, and aircraft, and so laid the foundations of what is now familiar as the 'military-industrial complex'. The creation of the BBC may be seen as marking an equally significant step in the rise of what James O'Connor calls the 'social-industrial complex', by which an increasing proportion of the capital and overhead costs of industry is siphoned off into State-financed ventures and enterprises.[3]

Conventional history usually identifies a breakthrough in technology associated with the idiosyncratic leadership of John Reith as the starting point of the BBC. This contribution is explored beneath, but Burns provides an important reminder for seeing the early Corporation as part of set of changes taking place within the capitalist economy of post-Edwardian Britain.

In the 1920s the unguided transmission of radio signals to radio receivers was still a difficult technology to control. The experience in America had been of massive expansion unchecked by a national licensing system. This often resulted in the jamming of signals as hundreds of radio stations competed on the same frequencies.

Several leading figures in the early industry had travelled to the United States to observe the burgeoning market and provide evidence of the lack of regulation on the development of national radio; Reith had been one such visitor. Such unregulated competition had been noted by the Sykes Committee in 1923 which recommended a blanket licence fee of ten shillings in Britain.

By 1922, there were a hundred applications for radio licences received by the Post Office. This level of demand required some form of control:

> The BBC was formed as an expedient solution to a technical problem. It owes its existence to the scarcity of the airwaves. The Postmaster General solved the problem of radio interference by persuading rival manufacturers to invest in one small and initially speculative broadcasting station: The British Broadcasting Company. John Reith was made its Managing Director.[4]

In management literature much is made of the significance of the impact of early decisions by senior management upon their organization. It is claimed that not only is the structure of the organization shaped by early decisions, but the very nature and character of the corporate culture are established at this time.[5]

In the case of the BBC, authors like Boyle 1972; Briggs 1961; Gielgud 1947; Hood and O'Leary 1990, who deal with its early history,[6] agree that John Reith made a profound impact upon the organization. In explaining this early history of the BBC, it is all too easy to be overwhelmed by the 'great man' version of this early period. The early Corporation does need to be seen within its political and economic context and, therefore, the account of its development needs to be tempered by the realities of labour markets, working conditions, and ideas of public service broadcasting and the conditions of the day, before Reith is credited with forming the BBC single-handed.

Personal capitalism and the impact of war: issues for management control

What cannot be disputed is the fact that this first Managing Director (when it was first established as a private company) and, later, Director General of the British Broadcasting Corporation, as he came to be known, made a profound impact upon the life of the organization. He considered it to be his personal domain, and the achievement of its lasting success the central mission in his life. This was not an exceptional view to take at this time. It conforms to a commonly held belief held within management circles, that ownership or control, bestowed absolute power on executive decision makers. Unlike the US, the growth in scale and size of corporations in the UK had been restrained by the legacy of small and medium sized business which had dominated the nineteenth century.[7] Added to which, family networks and partnerships had served the nineteenth century business class in Britain very effectively. With an expanding market, both national and overseas (resulting in the colonial expansion), firms could retain their original business forms and, with the aid of credit, expand their size without altering their 'regime of control'.

The combination of the tradition of 'absolute control' in senior management, and the small scale of the initial organization, provided two influential determinants of the early Corporation; its operating procedures and its labour relations. With the arrival of the First World War, this sheltered situation would be overtaken as the gathering momentum of international competition challenged the existing order and the war itself was to transform the BBC.

Whether Arthur Marwick[8] is right to portray both world wars as 'total' wars is open to debate, but the State had little choice but to organize the war effort to ensure effective performance of the economy. This would redraw the relationship of the Corporation to the central State. As Marwick correctly emphasizes, this was as much a war of production as it was a war of military campaigns. To achieve a level of production that would outstrip the enemy, nationalization and State control were seen as the most effective methods for co-ordinating the economy and the interests of private capital.

This experience played a major role in changing ideas of the division between the State and private capital. After the experience of extending the power of the State during the war, the possibility of placing the BBC under State control was far more feasible than before the war.[9] The details of this historical juncture are important for understanding how the Corporation could, from the start, benefit from a monopolistic form. Its removal from the pressures of market forces and the belief that its day to day management should reside in the hands of technocrats and experts, was an arrangement that could only have been conceived in this post-war period when disillusionment, borne of the experience of the post-war depression, had spawned alternative forms to conventional capitalist business structures.

Class and the corporation: the influence of Reith

Set within this brief political economy of the Corporation's inception, it was unsurprising that whoever ultimately controlled the organization at this time might see themselves as more than just a civil servant, which would have been the prevailing natural form for such an organization. An extensive literature exists on Reith's contribution to the formation of the BBC and his set of principles which were to embed themselves within the Corporation. As defined by Georgina Born[10]:

> John Reith institutionalised a vision of the BBC as an instrument for social integration, for enhancing democratic functioning and raising cultural and educational standards. Through the trinity of information, education and entertainment, Reith and his peers aimed to foster 'happier homes, broader culture and truer citizenship'.

It can be argued that these 'principles' designed by him, including the idea of public service broadcasting, have survived intact to the present day and reflect many of the ambitions of the central State at that time.

In turn, his concept of 'public service' became part of the ideology of management control. With a strong moral overtone, those who would work for this Corporation would be made well aware that they were not just producing media output, but fulfilling a crucial role in enabling this public service to fulfil its remit for the good of the nation.[11]

While acknowledging that individual managers do not single-handedly design the particular labour process, it is important to understand how management ideas, systems and 'strategies are implemented'.[12] The significance of these early developments in structure and organization of the agency of the State, lies more in the nature of the ideas and definitions he generated to define what was meant by public service broadcasting, the 'public interest' and those ideas and explanations used to legitimate the organization in its particular form.

To pursue these ends, he developed a style of management which contributed to establishing many of the fundamental characteristics of the Corporation and certainly affected the regime of control. Perhaps to underline the degree of influence, Curran and Seaton captured some of the more salient features of his management style:

> How would the BBC have developed if its first director had been a career civil servant, a banker, or a Bloomsbury intellectual? Many features of broadcasting which are taken for granted today would certainly be absent. Reith's domination of the Corporation in its early days was massive, totalitarian, and idiosyncratic, and for many decades the traditions of the BBC seemed to flow directly from his personality. The British Broadcasting Company was set up as a business. Reith turned it into a crusade. 'Scotch engineer, Calvinist by upbringing, harsh and ruthless character', as A. J. P. Taylor has described him, Reith used 'the brute force of monopoly to stamp Christian morality on the British people... This ability to impose his will on staff was helped by his size. Churchill nicknamed him 'Wuthering Heights' and senior staff would stand on stairs to argue with him, 'so I can see you eye to eye, Sir'.[13]

The power of these early ideas lay in their combination of moral imperative alongside the newly emerging concept of 'public service'. By public service broadcasting (PSB) he established the idea that there was a 'public' or rather 'publics' made up of all sections of the community. Perhaps because of his Calvinist beliefs, he saw this audience as capable of growth and development, it could be 'redeemed'. Respecting his audience required the BBC to achieve output of the highest standards with the best programmes available. Part religious zeal, and part the drive to educate, Reith had all the personal traits available to construct an ethos for broadcasting which would make it appear inviolable to the pressures and arguments of external interference. For those who worked with him he insisted on absolute loyalty, and it was not long before the details of 'public sector' broadcasting were to join this moral code as part of the reigning management ideology. In its crudest form Reith, in 1924, opined:

> It is occasionally indicated to us that we are apparently setting out to give the public what we think they need, and not what they want – but few know what they want, and very few what they need.[14]

This paternalist explanation provided a mantel for those looking at the BBC from outside. The Corporation was there to educate, enlighten and set standards for the population at large. Reith went beyond recognizing the early arguments for a public service role for the BBC. Its political and social role was also becoming clearer. The radio could have the effect of 'making one nation as one man'.[15] Paddy Scannell points to the deeper lineage of what is considered to be one of Reith's most fundamental contributions to the emergence of the BBC when he refers to the earlier use of 'service':

> Raymond Williams had identified the idea of service as one of the great achievements of the Victorian middle class, and one that deeply influenced later generations... The Victorian reforming ideal of service was animated by a sense of moral purpose and of social duty on behalf of the community, aimed particularly at the most in need of reform – the lower classes... But it did nothing to change the balance of power in society, and maintained the dominance of the middle classes over the lower ranks.[16]

The attraction of this combination of moral project alongside his complete self-belief, made the ideology of PSB irresistible.

To feed the growing appetite of this expanding medium, a host of educated voices were enlisted to provide relevant material for broadcasting. Those working for it were bound tightly within a strict hierarchy where liberal intellectuals sat at the top of this hierarchy with ambitions to provide a suitable diet of programmes, engineers in the middle and the administration at the bottom. Within this 'cultural institution', Curran and Seaton noted an army of liberal intellectuals: 'Trooped into the studios to educate and inform on every subject from unemployment to the Origin of the Species. Shaw, Wells, the Webb's, Beveridge, Keynes and Huxley, the roll call was endless.' [17]

Reith was able to see the potential for radio to provide the 'cement' of the nation by capturing significant events within the country and transmitting them into a broad audience. He realized that in sharing such events, the listening population was forming a common language of experience. This was an idea that was soon to dawn upon the politicians of the day. To retain this 'voice' to the nation, it was apparent that he would have to ensure that the Corporation would maintain a position of independence from those same politicians. In creating a board of governors to oversee the operations of the Corporation, Reith intended to protect the organization from outside interference, and avoid the charge of being the mouthpiece of politicians.

His awareness of this balancing trick between independence and becoming part of the 'establishment' has remained a tension from that period to the present day and reflects Engels observation that the State serves capital's interests best when it retains a form of relative autonomy.[18] Politicians, especially during war time, had continually complained about the Corporation for its lack of support for the government and its failure to serve the 'national' interest, but it was the General Strike which fundamentally changed the relationship of the Corporation to the State. Up until this strike in 1926, (Reith had been Director General of the BBC from 1926 to 1938), Reith had considered the independence of the newly formed Corporation understood and agreed to by politicians of the day. In the short space of time that the strike lasted, Reith vacillated and compromised in his search to avoid the Corporation being commandeered by the government, which was within its right. Unable or unwilling to allow any trade unionists to represent the strikers' arguments on the radio, and later, the disallowing of the Archbishop of Canterbury to argue for a peaceful resolution to the strike, Reith exposed the weakness of his brainchild. The incident is complex, but it is clear that Reith's motives lay as much in proving to the government (or rather Winston Churchill, who was the then Chancellor of the Exchequer, who was prepared to take control of the Corporation to use as an organ of government propaganda) that it would represent the State's interests at a time of national importance. It was also about protecting a project which he identified as a personal quest, a quest which would not be allowed to fail.

For the first, but not the last time, this Corporation as an agency of the State was exposed to the class system within which it was located. In this, and subsequent moments of crisis in the capitalist dynamic, it was revealed as an agency of the State representing the interests of capital. Ideals of 'impartiality' were compromised by the effect of 'normalizing' the strike and blocking the views and opinions of organized labour.

As Briggs makes clear, at this time, the staff of the BBC was largely ignorant of working class life and there was little appreciation for the hardship inflicted by the mine owners and tolerated by the State.[19] The BBC avoided being taken over by the State to deliver propaganda, but the price had been high and Reith was made acutely aware of the fragility of the Corporation's independence from outside interference.

It also demonstrated for the first time that in an unequal capitalist society, merely 'reporting on the facts of events' could provide a 'calming effect' on the situation.[20] The selection and manner in which events were reported had the effect of 'normalizing' many of the actions taken by the State. To understand the difficulties of creating accurate and 'impartial' news within the Corporation at this time, a number of factors need to be understood within the political economy of the media industry and patterns of ownership that existed.

Due to the pressures of the privately owned, 'traditional' press, the BBC was not allowed to generate its own news items but only utilize material from news agencies. Secondly, it could only broadcast news programmes after seven o'clock in the evening. It was assumed that the selling of newspapers would be complete by this time and hence no competition with the private press would exist. The private sector, which dominated the media industry at this time, effectively defined much of the space granted to the fledgling Corporation.

Reith was clearly committing the Corporation to a role in serving the national interest as defined by the existing status quo. The ability to transmit this news as defined by the national elites was considered to be synonymous with the 'national interest'. Asa Briggs identifies a memo from Reith which clearly sets out his understanding of the Corporation and its relationship to the government:

> ... since the BBC was a national institution and, since the Government in this crisis was acting for the people, apart from any Emergency Powers or clause in our licence, the BBC was for the government in the crisis too; and that we had to assist in maintaining the essential services of the country, the preservation of law and order, and the life and liberty of the individual and the community...had we been commandeered we could do nothing in the nature of impartial news... We felt we might contribute, perhaps decisively, to the attitude of understanding without which goodwill could not be restored.[21]

As Tracey makes clear, Reith was defining the BBC:

> ... as an organisation within the Constitution and thereby effectively defining impartiality- for specific institutional and ideological reasons- in such a way as to make it synonymous not with a particular party line but with a particular political and moral order within which that line rested and which for the duration of the strike was deemed to coexist with the Baldwin government.[22]

As a 'Corporation', the BBC's survival was defined by its position within the machinery of the State even if this was at a distance from it. For most observers this appeared as a degree of independence. The recent episode of the Guiligan report of 'sexing–up the dossier'[23] only serves to demonstrate the continued attempts by politicians and their aides to set an agenda for the BBC, and serves to reinforce its position within the machinery of State.

Uncertainty, hierarchy and paternalism

In 1922 the staff of the BBC (British Broadcasting Company, then existing in the form of a private company and became a Corporation governed by a charter in 1926) had numbered four. In 1924 this had grown to 371 and by 1925, 552; 179 of which were engineers.[24] The organization had been split into three departments, Engineering, Programmes, and Administration. Within each department there were sub-divisions to cater for special requirements. So in the case of Programmes, one of the first sub-divisions was music. Outside London, regions were established for transmitting programmes and this local identity remained strong for many years with each region following its own pattern of broadcasting. Much of the work in these early years was experimental and required a relaxed attitude to job descriptions. Even Reith, as Director General, would sometimes read the news bulletins, act in a radio drama or help in designing a programme. The overall style of management in the period leading up to 1926 could be described as paternalistic.

The attraction for management lay in effecting a consensus of ideas with the intention of achieving high levels of conformity to management objectives. This is usually achieved by drawing upon religious, moral or purely idiosyncratic set of ideas. By providing either a range of resources above and beyond the basic conditions of employment, or by claiming to provide some quality of employment contract that exceeded 'normal' conditions, the employer established a relationship with the individual employee based upon a form of reciprocity belying the reality of the powerful owner forcing the employee into a form of unending dependence. [25]The provision of resources comes with the expectation modelled on the experience a close knit social group, that the 'giving' of resources is recognized by the receiver, who acknowledges this by responding to the requests of the donor.

According to Briggs[26] the BBC had, from its earliest days, been considered a 'good employer' by the standards of the day. Pay at this time was considered good and by the 1930s a medical officer had been appointed and later a surgery. In addition, a 24-hour cafeteria restaurant had been provided in Broadcasting House. As a newly formed 'Corporation' faced with developing a completely novel technology, new employees were made aware of the 'privilege' of working for such an important organization. Reith believed that members of the Corporation had to demonstrate an *espirit de corps*, an ability to behave in a 'gentlemanly' way. Working for the BBC meant 'educating and informing', in his mind this was an onerous task for all the members of the workforce and required commitment and standards of behaviour of the highest order.

The experience of working in the BBC at this time can be inferred from the one of the key staff who managed the engineering department, Tom Eckersley. The arrogance and paternalistic style of management provides a window on the British class system where it is taken for granted that employees will adopt characteristics of the educated middle classes. As Eckersley explains:

> The members of the staff are judged by their character rather than their talents. The typically English idea that all artists are immoral is fostered... The form, content, and influence of the broadcasting service as we know it today is the product of a dominant mind; it represents one man's conception of the role of broadcasting in a modern democracy. No one who is *serving* [my italics] or who has *served* the BBC has had an influence in any way comparable with that exerted by its first chief executive... There was no unkindness in this; it was all part of *duty* [my italics] the *duty* to make a compact loyal and disciplined staff which could cope with the excessive work and complex problems. The great feature of Mr Reith's leadership was that you knew where you stood...The founder of the BBC was basically an organiser and a disciplinarian... It was asked of every applicant for a responsible job in the BBC... Is he a gentleman? ... The term was not meant to describe an easy-going member of the landed aristocracy, but rather someone apt to obey blindly and put behaviourism before intelligence. In these circumstances it was inevitable that broadcasting should have reinforced conformity.[27]

This constant use of the term 'duty' underscores the moral imperative that Reith deployed with the workforce. Alongside the use of 'service', Reith created a management ideology which required strict obedience to his will; an unquestioning adoption of management control. Val Gielgud,[28] who was appointed assistant to the first editor of the

Radio Times in 1928, indicated that in terms of creativity he was out of his depth. Although he was criticized for the atmosphere of 'semi-military discipline', Reith had to allow the 'creative' departments scope to develop entirely new forms of radio programming.

The structure of the organization has been described as loosely bureaucratic in these early years, which is hardly surprising when few alternative forms of organization existed. As stated above, the style of management was paternalistic with a sense of military control leading directly to the top of the hierarchy. To allow him the space to plan the future of the organization, Reith soon installed a layer of senior management which would take responsibility for the day to day operational tasks. This was called the 'Control Board' comprising a senior controller and five assistant Controllers. In Reith's mind it formed his 'management committee', but, like any committee, it did not imply that decisions were made collectively: 'There was never any suggestion however that the Control Board was settling BBC policy by democratic vote.'[29]

Throughout the 1930s the numbers employed rose steadily from 1194 to 5100 by 1939.[30] In 1932, to manage this process of recruitment, an Appointments Board was established which would not only oversee this process, but also pioneer new ideas for training these new staff.[31] Alongside a more systematic approach to recruitment and training, and the provision of health centres and canteens, the Corporation pioneered a large scale pension fund. Aware that people in the creative arts might choose to move on in their careers or, more likely, that the Corporation might wish for them to move on, the scheme allowed departing staff to receive their contributions as well of those made by the Corporation. Payments for 'years served' were also instituted. Both measures, started so early in the history of the organization, reflected an outlook fundamentally at odds with the Civil Service conventions with which many commentators drew comparisons with the BBC. A hard-bitten attitude to achieving a form of planned staff turnover was an early feature of employment in the Corporation. By attracting a constant flow of new staff, the Corporation would have a continuous source of new and fresh ideas for programme making. The provision of good pensions was also considered by senior managers as a method for establishing expectations around the process of redundancy. Where this might take place, or the failure to renew contracts, staff, it was hoped, might be less aggrieved in an industry always searching for new ideas or where staff might fail to deliver after a certain period of time. Whether this was a broadly held view cannot be established, but in this early period it is interesting to note that such sophisticated ideas of the planned redundancy of labour were making an appearance within the Corporation. Identifying this practice is important when so much contemporary research appears to connect its inception with the arrival of the neo-liberal reforms identified with the election of a Conservative government in 1979 under the leadership of Margaret Thatcher.

Consensus, control and labour representation

Behind this period of expansion lay the unshakeable belief that as an organization its success resulted from a continuing consensus of values and attitudes of the entire workforce. This consensus was composed of two elements, a consensus on the value of what the organization was doing as the public service broadcaster, the other consensus was based upon the belief that the direction and ultimate control remained ultimately with one man, John Reith. As an apparatus of the State concerned with cultural production and distribution, such unanimity was important for fulfilling its remit as a voice for the nation and an agency of the central State. This conflation of the two logics would become a device followed by many of the subsequent Director Generals of the Corporation.

By 1933 it had been recognized that the organization was in need of a major redesign to cater for the substantial growth in employees and the extended range of services, including the Empire service of overseas broadcasting, which was to experience massive growth during the Second World War. This first major reorganization achieved a reduction of direct responsibility for the Director General and a consolidation of the role of the 'Controllers'. By separating what was then called 'Output' from 'Administration' in the form of the two new Controllers; it created a distinct change in the operating life of the organization. From an organization which relied upon a degree of informality and flexibility, the reorganization was intended to help it cope with, and respond to, an increasing rate of change and innovation in technology and service provision. This new '1933' structure established sharper lines between the 'creative' output of the organization and the 'administrative' control function. As Briggs observes when he quotes from a memorandum of the time:

> 'The main innovation', it went on, 'is the separation of administrative and creative functions. The purpose of this is to enable creative staff to concentrate on their creative work.' [32]

The break of 'conception from execution' in the design of the organization would have a profound effect upon the working lives of those within it and create a tension and, at times hostility, to the 'Administration', which has survived to the present day.[33]

Burns points to the lack of staff representation as an indicator of the effectiveness of management ideology.[34] In 1935, the staff was asked to vote on the desirability of forming a staff association. Eighty per cent voted against it. As the Director of Staff Administration, W. St. J. Pym commented at the time: 'It probably represented not so much a straight vote on the general principle as a vote of confidence in the present management.'[35]

Pym went on to recommend the formation of such a body to ensure staff had some alternative voice to management. Arguments were put forward that the organization was composed of so many different forms of work and occupations that no single body would be able to encompass the entire workforce. Reith believed that the 'consensus' of the Corporation had been sustained by management which distrusted the development of a staff association or trade union. Such apparent continuing support for management and the lack of interest by the employees in any form of representation needs to be understood within the context of the period. Following the depression of the late 1920s, the following decade continued to experience high levels of unemployment. Anyone with a job with reasonable pay in an organization that had continued to buck the trends of that decade, and continue to grow in size, was hardly likely to risk such a secure job. Employees were certainly not prevented from joining trade unions, but the impetus to join was weak in such circumstances. It would take the experience of the Second World War and the necessity of an expansion in State planning and involvement in industry, as well as the direct control of the Corporation by the Ministry of Information, to encourage staff to develop two new staff associations, one for the engineers and one for the creative and administrative staff. At the end of the war these two merged into the BBC Staff Association. This arrangement remained in place until the arrival of commercial television as late as 1975.

The details as outlined suggest a set of understandings, rationalizations, traditions and practices which made a significant contribution to shaping the labour process of media production within the BBC, firstly in radio and, subsequently, in television. From a position of complete autocratic control over labour, senior management and the State saw their power checked by the growing influence of organized labour. In control of an ever increasing range of advanced technological skills, labour was to see an improvement in its bargaining position with increasing levels of job security.

The cosy duopoly, work organization and the development of television

In the aftermath of the Second World War, the reputation of the BBC had risen significantly. After a difficult stage at the beginning of the war, where its role in supporting the war effort was argued and debated, the BBC enjoyed an enlarged role with overseas broadcasts playing an ever more important role in informing, sending messages and codes, and raising morale across a growing number of countries.[36]

The size, scale and influence of the Corporation had expanded dramatically to cater for this enlarged role. News had become the byword for its reputation. Overseas its standing worldwide for accurate news had further strengthened its position within the machinery of the State. In this context, William Beveridge[37] had been asked to consider the affairs of the Corporation. It was assumed that he would be sympathetic to continuing with its well established role. He was increasingly sceptical of its patrician approach to broadcasting, but in the end he endorsed the continuation of its licence probably because the alternative of American style commercial broadcasting appeared worse. Beveridge also commented on the absence of trade unions and the failure of the staff association to provide an independent stance against the Corporation. In this respect there was no modification to the status quo, but it was recommended that the BBC should recognize any union which could claim more than 40 per cent of employees in the relevant occupational class.[38] The idea of working for public service still pervaded all aspects of the employment relationship.[39]

When the Conservatives came to power in 1951, the recommendations of Beveridge were largely forgotten. The new Conservative government were eager to modernize the media industry with the creation of a commercial broadcasting company alongside the threat to introduce sponsorship and advertising into public sector broadcasting. With a powerfully funded campaign, backed by the entertainment industry, advertising organizations, and with the aid of the ex-director of the Light Programme and controller of BBC Television, Norman Collins, the commercial lobby were well placed to argue for the new service. They also had influential supporters within the Conservative party (Lord Woolton and Winston Churchill) who could see a valuable role for this new provider. A commercial network would in itself represent and articulate the very principles of the free market, it would help the Conservative party to modernize and introduce new ideas about industry and commerce. Not surprising then that the new provider should be called 'Independent Television' (ITV).

It was Selwyn Lloyd, a Conservative MP who had been part of the Beveridge committee, who had been the only dissenter to Beveridge's report and had written a minority report where he had argued strongly for the introduction of commercial radio and television.[40] Commercial television arrived in 1954 and provided the BBC with a major challenge. ITV would provide a range of popular programmes as an alternative to the elitist programmes of the BBC. Like so many areas of change, however, people's imaginations were restricted by the experience of what they knew. The Conservative White Paper of 1953 which foreshadowed the Television Act of 1954 that established commercial television, made it plain that commercial television would need to be regulated and that responsibility would rest with a new public body , the ITA (Independent Television Authority). The desire to open up broadcasting to commercial funding was circumscribed by the continuing belief that the controller of commercial television should pursue public service principles. It would be a public corporation. The 1950s decade saw the rapid expansion of television from both providers. The BBC, progressively moving to compete in more popular forms of entertainment, saw steady expansion in its workforce. The Pilkington Report of 1962 had the effect of checking the progress of commercial broadcasting. He was concerned that the quality of ITV programmes was being jeopardized by triviality, and he argued commercial programmes should still remain within the standards set by Reith for PSB. In essence, commercial television in the post-war period up to the 1980s was moulded in the shadow of the BBC. The public service duopoly was the outcome.

Once commercial television had become established, the Corporation could no longer cling to the fiction that its staff association represented its staff interests. Just as soon as commercial television received approval it started to outbid the BBC for its technicians and producers. This was the moment when the unions could move to control employment in commercial broadcasting. The Association of Cinemagraphic Television and Allied Technicians (ACTT) moved quickly to negotiate agreements and, in time, create a model of employment similar to that of the BBC where jobs were relatively stable, careers were available and pensions could be expected. This was a time when demand completely outstripped supply. With the sustained pressure of a tight labour market, the BBC changed its staff association to Association of Broadcasting Staff (ABS) with the intention of making it easier for staff to return to employment in the Corporation. Outside unions were also increasing membership. The National Union of Journalists (NUJ) joined forces with the Staff Association and subsequently the Electrical

Trades Union (ETU); finally the National Association of Theatrical, Television, and Kine Employees (NATTKE) gained recognition by the Corporation. Most of the impetus for such recognition agreements within the Corporation resulted from the awareness that these unions were gaining dominant positions within independent television and they needed to keep up with these developments or face a declining ability to recruit and retain staff.

By the mid-1960s, the Corporation had finally lost its 'Reithian' institutional logic where staff 'belonged' to the corporate identity of this organization, thereby denying an organizing logic for independent trade unions. The impact of union recognition was to remove the final vestiges of the ethos of consensus.[41] The presence of trade unions had undermined the mask of loyalty that senior management had been so eager to maintain. With a traditional lack of experience in dealing with trade unions and collective bargaining, BBC management often hid behind walls of administrative procedure before acknowledging that workers should have the right to good information and participate in areas of change and development which would directly affect them.

The BBC continued to expand into new genres and, during the sixties and seventies, the success of these ventures resulted in a rapid increase in overseas sales. This provided a strong argument for the continuation of the licence fee and freedom from commercial constraints. What was less certain was, within the decade that saw a major change in ideas of civil liberties and the rights of minorities, that either broadcaster was accurately reflecting this more complex and fragmented society. The Left in Britain had continued to attack the duopoly for its elitism and its failure to reflect the working class culture and interests.[42]

The Annan Report of 1977, like Pilkington before it, sought to enquire about the state of broadcasting with the prospect of establishing a fourth channel. Like Pilkington, it endorsed the principle of PSB, but unlike Pilkington, it questioned what were 'good' programmes when, in a more divided society, there was little agreement about what was 'good'. The answer for Annan was to establish an Open Broadcasting Authority (OBA). This body would act as a publishing house commissioning programmes from a wide range of sources to reflect the growing diversity within Society. Initially rejected, the ideas were modified by a new Conservative government of 1979 that gave the fourth channel to IBA (Independent Broadcasting Authority). The concept of a publisher, however, remained with the birth of Channel Four that was established in January 1981 as Channel Four Television Company.

The battleground

The title above is taken from one of the chapters from Barnett and Curry's book '*The Battle for the BBC. A British Broadcasting Conspiracy*'. On page one they claim that the ten years from 1984 to 1994 were 'extraordinary':

> As an institution at the heart of British public life, the BBC has been embroiled in conflict before, but never so often and never for such a sustained period. Those ten years have raised some fascinating questions which go beyond the BBC itself: about organisational change, the conduct of journalism, issues of management, the concept of public service, and the survival of public institutions in a hostile political environment.[43]

They might also have mentioned the fundamental restructuring of the labour process of television workers. From whatever the perspective adopted, this period is clearly considered to be a watershed in the development and form of the Corporation. It is interesting that so many of these accounts of change within broadcasting and the BBC are concerned to unravel the micro-politics of pressure groups and cabals which had arranged themselves around the Thatcher government. So much of the analysis dwells on the individuals identified with this turbulent time and the associated political intrigue.[44] Such accounts have a tendency to point the analysis of change to one driven by competing careers of individuals representing different factions within the broadcasting community. There is little discussion of the changes in the structure of the economy and even less on the experience of those working in the middle off this industry. Barnett and Curry go on to say that: 'The BBC of the mid-1980s was in most respects similar to the BBC of the late 1950s.'[45]

However, while acknowledging this period of change, Burns emphasizes that change in the structure and the conduct of the organization to achieve greater levels of financial control had already been implemented in the 1970s.[46] These reforms were as much to do with achieving higher levels of accountability as in proving to outside bodies that it was managing its resources efficiently. The fashion for devising and monitoring corporate strategy was as advanced in the Corporation as any large organization in industry. In addition, advanced computer systems were in place to ensure greater control over budgetary processes.

Interestingly, the Conservatives saw little merit in disturbing the broadcasting duopoly when their interests, broadly speaking, had been well represented by this arrangement.[47] This approach changed dramatically with the arrival of the Annan Report which finally forced the Conservatives to become involved in the debates about the future of broadcasting. Their plans for the future of broadcasting were encapsulated in the 1980 Broadcasting Act which contained their modifications to Annan, namely a Channel Four controlled by IBA, and, in more detail, a sustained public service responsibility on the IBA which now meant catering for tastes previously unrepresented in the duopoly. By adopting the role as 'publisher/ broadcaster' it also had the effect of establishing the independent sector: 'In 1984/5, for example, Channel Four made payments to 313 independent production companies, the vast majority of which had simply not existed before the creation of the channel.'[48]

The landscape for the reform of the media was starting to take shape. The Independents Programme Association (IPA) was putting pressure on the Peacock Committee, set up by the Conservative government to scrutinize the financing of PSB, to establish a 40 per cent quota of independent production for both ITV and the BBC output.[49] The role of broadcasting for Conservative politicians had moved from a simple polarity between public and private funding, to one that saw the media as an 'industry'. This 'new independent' industry was also providing the first signs of potential competition to the existing duopoly. For Thatcher it provided a force for challenging the labour process of television production in these two vertically integrated producers. It held the potential to challenge the trade unions and their working practices which had appeared inviolable up to this time. Inadvertently, Whitelaw's support and ideas of funding for the new channel were providing the seeds for neo-liberal reforms that were to arrive in the 1991 Broadcasting Act.

Notwithstanding these developments, it was clear that the Corporation of the seventies was much more vertically integrated than horizontally. It was segmented into fiefdoms where 'prestige-poker' created additional tensions. Throughout this period staff numbers increased from 15,886 in 1960 to 24,779 by 1975. By 1975 the bulk of these were working in television. Increases in staff costs were a product of numbers as well as pay rates: 'Financial pressures on the BBC between 1960 and 1975 was almost continuously accelerating rate of increase in staff costs, the larger element in which is not larger numbers but higher pay.'[50]

The reorganization of the 1970s was to create three conventional divisions, Television, Radio and External Services. Budgets were attached to each and, henceforth, programmes would be made within set budgets where all in-house resources used were to be costed. As Tom O'Malley highlights:

> The state relinquished some power over broadcasting to capitalists, intensified other forms of control and tried to maintain elements of the previous system. On matters of broadcasting policy the state in the 1980s was not monolithic. It was made up of a series of competing centres of power and influence, all seeking changes of a different order and import.[51]

In 1979, with the election of the Thatcher government, the main concern was to press ahead with the implementation of what became the 1981 Broadcasting Act and the installation of Channel Four. In the background, a number of right wing think-tanks were starting to confront the development of longer term policies. The Centre for Policy Studies, The Conservative Philosophy Group, The Institute of Economic Affairs (IEA), The Adam Smith Institute, and the Advertising Association all engaged in policy development with the aim of shaping the government's agenda for broadcasting in the future. Of these, the IEA was to provide the intellectual base for the neo-liberal policies; providing several key staff for the Peacock Committee to review the financing of the BBC.[52] The findings of this committee then shaped the 1990 Broadcasting Act introducing the neo-liberal reforms, albeit, in a more restrained form.

Neo-liberal reforms?

Between 1979 and 1987 the relationship between the government and the BBC began to deteriorate dramatically. From 1979 onwards the BBC became embroiled with the government over a whole series of programmes which had caused offence; from the reporting of the Falklands war, the issues surrounding the Westland Affair, and the reporting on Northern Ireland culminated in a concerted campaign against the Corporation. With Thatcher's own hatred for the trade unions and the closed shop operating in much of the duopoly, and an inherent distaste for its elitism and anti-commercialism, a sustained campaign emerged which was to provide an important space for the ideas and fledgling policies forming in the think-tanks identified above. Perhaps it was the Corporation's campaign around the renewal and increase of the licence fee in 1984 which triggered the final onslaught. This took the form of a vitriolic press campaign where particular newspapers (owned by Rupert Murdoch) provided a daily campaign attacking the BBC for its privileged position. As O'Malley indicates: 'The section which was most vociferous in supporting the attack on the BBC was the Murdoch-owned press. This organization was close to Mrs. Thatcher and was strategically placed which would open the UK system to more commercial pressures.'[53]

The Peacock Committee reflected the government's bias towards introducing commercialism into broadcasting both in its membership and the speed in which it worked. There were no Labour party members and no trade unionists on the committee. The government wanted the committee to report within one year and, as a result, decisions were made in haste; as O'Malley reports on one of the committee member's observations of the deliberations over the future of radio: 'Along with the Committee's other thoughts on radio were the outcome of no research, little consultation and half a day's discussion, at the end of which Professor Hetherington and Judith Chalmers dissented.'[54]

By the launch of the Peacock Report, in July 1986, the idea of introducing advertising into the BBC had been dropped. Peacock himself as a neo-liberal economist had had to look beyond the immediacy of ideological ambition and assess the impact of advertising on the whole sector. As a position on broadcasting, it embraced the industry as a whole; the resultant policies emphasized the 'business' of broadcasting and, as a result, pushed the attack on the BBC to the periphery. The impact of changing the whole financial map of broadcasting would have the effect of fundamentally altering the assumptions about the role and position of the BBC. By introducing a whole raft of neoclassical reforms into the broadcasting industry as a whole: 'This meant laying the economic and managerial foundations for restructuring the BBC, deregulating ITV and ILR (Independent Local Radio) and creating new openings for market-driven cable and satellite delivered services.'[55]

The government took two and half years to respond to the report as tensions mounted between the Home Office and the Department of Trade and Industry (DTI),. Its final response was published in the White Paper, 'Broadcasting in the 90s', which focused primarily on the commercial broadcasters. The direction of the White Paper was seen by many as a compromise between the different factions of the State. The BBC was left to deal with a fixed income resulting from cuts in the licence fee introduced by Samuel Brittan in 1983 and Douglas Hurd in 1987, (where the licence fee was set three per cent below RPI (Retail Price Index).

By the time the 1990 Broadcasting Act arrived, other means of effecting change within the Corporation had been identified. Although the 1990 Broadcasting Act required a 25 per cent quota of production to be sourced from the independents for both channels, the Corporation had largely escaped from major internal reforms as set down by the Act. Instead, the process of charter renewal would provide the government with ample opportunity to put pressure on the Corporation, in a sense, leaving the Corporation to undertake its own restructuring as a result of a constant reduction in its budget.

The imposition of 'Producer Choice', where programme making had to establish the financial case for making programmes in-house, a series of financial and budgeting procedures would subsequently accelerate the pace of change. As Goodwin signals:

> So, much of the authority and adaptability of the BBC central management was, from the mid 80s onwards, deployed to further the market mechanism in television generally favoured by the Tories. When the BBC actually came to make policy, as it increasingly did in the 90s, with initiatives like Producer Choice and BBC Worldwide (were the BBC initiatives, not direct government suggestions), these were along lines in keeping with the Tories pro-market drive. But there was an important limit to this. However much the BBC's management might endorse and promote aspects of the market after 1986, the Corporation was still firmly involved in adaptation for its own institutional survival still meant survival as a public Corporation, with substantial public funding. In adapting to protect its institutional base, the BBC was considerably more successful than many of its continental cousins, not least because it started from an altogether more resilient base.[56]

Introducing neo-liberal reforms into the Corporation had produced a series of contradictory outcomes. The 1990 Broadcasting Act was not well received in most sections of the media industry. The BBC had avoided the worst excesses of the original plans for commercialization but Producer Choice had reduced staffing levels and been associated with the growth of non standard employment. By continuing to adhere to their general policy of not expanding public sector funding, the government had unleashed an internal pressure within the Corporation which would have a significant impact upon its working practices. The industry, within which the BBC was now located, had changed dramatically. To survive in this competitive environment it would require major changes to its structure and operations.

Conclusion

This chapter has located the emergence, development and current structure of the BBC within a political economy of British capitalism. The intention has been to reduce the traditional significance attached to individuals, technological change or government legislation as central levers of change to the Corporation. Though all of these factors remain significant, they can mask the constant pressure for change as the class nature of British society had continually shifted the boundaries between the interests of capital and labour. Representing that dynamic, the emergence, consolidation and expansion of management had reflected fundamental changes in this shifting balance of power.

As an agency of the State, the BBC continued to reflect the contradictions of supplying the central State with a process for explaining and rationalizing the status quo while at other times losing control to the critical accounts broadcast in the name of editorial independence.

At the level of the labour process, the relationship of labour to management freed itself from a more imposed personal relationship as depicted in the earlier forms of paternalist management. With a long tradition of staff associations, trade unions appeared late in the day when, in one sense, the Corporation had no choice but to embrace their emergence to avoid losing staff to the new commercial sector.

The survival of the public service ethic and other elements of the management ideology had remained as powerful systems of meaning within the Corporation, and continue to exert an influence over attitudes to work to this day.

Notes

1. J. Curran and J. Seaton, *Power without Responsibility: The Press and Broadcasting in Britain* (Routledge: 1981, 4th edition), p. 31.
2. T. Burns, *The BBC – Public Institution and Private World* (Macmillan: 1977), p. 2)
3. *Ibid.*, p. 11.
4. M. Eckersley, *Prospero's Wireless: A Biography of P. P. Eckersley* (Myles Books) quoted in Curran and Seaton, *Power without Responsibility*, p. 132.
5. T. E. Deal and A. A. Kennedy, *Organisational Cultures: The Rites and Rituals of Company Organisational Life* (Addison-Wesley Co.: 1982); E. H. Shein, *Organisational Culture and Leadership* (San Francisco: Jossey Bass).
6. A. Boyle, *Only the Wind will Listen: Reith on the BBC* (Hutchinson: 1972); A. Briggs *The History of Broadcasting in the United Kingdom Vol. 1: The Birth Of Broadcasting* (Oxford University Press: 1961); V. Gielgud, *Years of the Locust* (Nicholson and Watson: 1947); S. Hood and G. O'Leary, *Questions of Broadcasting* (Methuen: 1990).

7. A.D. Chandler, *Scale and Scope: The Dynamics of Industrial Capitalism*, (Harvard: 1990).
8. A. Marwick, *War and Social Change in the Twentieth Century* (Macmillan: 1974).
9. Curran and Seaton, *Power without Responsibility*, p. 134.
10. G. Born, 'Reflexivity and Ambivalence: Culture, Creativity and Government in the BBC', *Cultural Values* 6:1&2 (2002), p. 68. [AQ: Please provide year.]
11. Boyle, *Only the Wind will Listen*; Burns, *The BBC – Public Institution and Private World*; Curran and Seaton, *Power without Responsibility*.
12. T. Elger, 'Braverman, Capital Accumulation and Deskilling,' in S. Wood (ed.), *The Degradation of Work? Skill, Deskilling and the Labour Process* (Hutchinson: 1982), p. 29.
13. Curran and Seaton, *Power without Responsibility*, p. 132.
14. Quoted in Briggs, *The History of Broadcasting in the United Kingdom Vol. 1* 1961, p. 238.
15. J. Reith, *Into the Wind* (Hodder and Stoughton: 1949) p. 4.
16. P. Scannell, 'Public Service Broadcasting: The History of a Concept' in E. Buscombe, (ed.), *British Television: A Reader* (Clarendon Press: 2000), p. 55.
17. Curran and Seaton, *Power without Responsibility*, p. 138.
18. F. Engels, 'The Origin of the Family, Private Property, and the State' in K. Marx and F. Engels *Selected Works*, Volume Three (Lawrence and Wishart: 1969)
19. Briggs, *The History of Broadcasting in the United Kingdom Vol. 1* 1961,
20. P. Goodwin, *Television under the Tories: Broadcasting Policy 1979–1997* (British Film Institute Publishing: 1998).
21. Briggs, *The History of Broadcasting in The United Kingdom: Vol. 1*, p. 365.
22. M. Tracey 'The BBC and the General Strike: May 1926' in E. Buscombe (ed.), *British Television: A Reader* (Clarendon Press: 2000), p. 37.
23. G. Dyke, *Inside Story* (Harper Collins: 2004), p. 258.
24. Briggs *The History of Broadcasting in the United Kingdom Vol. 1*, p. 200.
25. R. Bendix, *Work and Authority in Industry: Ideologies of Management in the course of Industrialisation* (University of California Press: 1974); S. Pollard, *The Genesis of Modern Management* (Penguin: 1958).
26. A. Briggs *The History of Broadcasting, Vol. 11: The Golden Age of the Wireless* (Oxford University Press).
27. M. Eckersley, *Prospero's Wireless: A Biography of P. P. Eckersley* (Myles Books: 1998), p. 46.
28. Gielgud, *Years of the Locust*, p. 47.
29. Burns, *The BBC – Public Institution and Private World*, p. 24.
30. Briggs *The History of Broadcasting, Vol. 11: The Golden Age of the Wireless*, p. 450.
31. Burns, *The BBC – Public Institution and Private World*, p. 449.
32. Briggs *The History of Broadcasting, Vol. 11: The Golden Age of the Wireless*, p. 444.
33. See H. Braverman, *Labour and Monopoly Capital*, (Monthly Review Press: 1974).
34. Burns, *The BBC – Public Institution and Private World*.
35. Quoted in Burns, *The BBC – Public Institution and Private World*, p. 60.

36. L. Kung-Shankleman, *Inside the BBC and CNN: Managing Media Organisations* (Routledge: 2000), p. 69.
37. William Beveridge was leader of the Liberals in the House of Lords following the Second World War.
38. Burns, *The BBC – Public Institution and Private World*, p. 55.
39. *Ibid.*, p. 62.
40. J. McDonnell (ed.), *Public Service Broadcasting: A Reader* (Routledge: 1991)
41. Burns, *The BBC – Public Institution and Private World*, p. 67.
42. Goodwin, *Television under the Tories: Broadcasting Policy 1979–1997.*
43. S. Barnett and A. Curry, *The Battle for the BBC: A British Broadcasting Conspiracy* (Aurum Press: 1994), p. 1.
44. *Ibid.;* S. Hood and G. O'Leary, *Questions of Broadcasting;* R. Collins and C. Murroni, *New Media New Policies* (Polity Press: 1996)
45. Barnett and Curry, *The Battle for the BBC*, p. 12.
46. Burns, *The BBC – Public Institution and Private World.*
47. Goodwin, *Television under the Tories*, p. 22.
48. *Ibid.*, p. 3.
49. The Peacock Committee reported on the financing of public service broadcasting to the Conservative Government in May 1986. See T. O'Malley and J. Jones (eds) *The Peacock Committee and UK Broadcasting Policy* (Palgrave Macmillan: 2009).
50. Burns, *The BBC – Public Institution and Private World*, p. 228.
51. T. O'Malley, *Closedown? The BBC and Government Broadcasting Policy, 1979–92* (Pluto Press: 1994), p. X11.
52. See O'Malley and Jones (eds) *The Peacock Committee and UK Broadcasting Policy.*
53. *Ibid.*, p.31.
54. *Ibid.*, p. 96.
55. *Ibid.*, p. 117.
56. Goodwin, *Television under the Tories*, p. 168.

8
Taylorism in the Mines? Technology, Work Organization and Management in British Coalmining before Nationalization

Stephanie Tailby

Taylorism, and the scientific management movement that emerged initially in the United States from the end of the nineteenth century, grew out of the trend towards 'systematic management' of the 1880s and 1890s. Investment in larger and more technically complex factories generated new management problems of coordination and control that prompted, in turn, innovations in cost accounting, inventory control and production scheduling.[1] Frederick Winslow Taylor applied and refined a number of these techniques and added new ones. His 'system of scientific management' can be interpreted as a system of labour control based on work study that addressed the management of production as a whole.[2] In addition to time-and-motion studies and rate-fixing, it embraced 'the routing of materials, tools, etc., and the planning of production, the running and maintenance of machinery, a series of functional foremen, and, in overall control, a central Planning Department'.[3] As such, it entailed changes in management's own organization and procedures, the insertion of new management functions, and a new division of responsibilities that stripped powers from the traditional supervisor on the shop floor.

General accounts of the development of 'modern management' rarely understate Taylorism's influence. Nevertheless, historians and social scientists have offered a range of assessments of its impact on management organization and practice in Britain in the first half of the twentieth century. Many have concluded that British employers remained sceptical of the benefits to be gained, opted to pursue alternatives, or were constrained from embracing Taylorism because of product market considerations or by worker resistance to intensified management

155

control.[4] By contrast, Craig Littler suggests that Taylorism was significant and that it came to exert an extensive influence on job design and technology design from the interwar years. However, this influence derived principally from employers' greater receptivity to neo-Taylorist systems – in particular, the system fashioned by Charles Bedaux – that fused Taylorism with First World War fatigue studies and early industrial psychology.[5]

Kevin Whitston elaborates a third position. Taylor's 'system' was rarely adopted in its entirety in Britain (or, indeed, in the United States). It nonetheless came to be absorbed into the 'mainstream of management development', principally in the form of time study and production engineering. This was because 'in some senses, Taylor simply offered an extreme formulation of what was happening independently of any particular prescriptions for management'. More specifically, the separation of the conception and execution of work, 'central to the management of mechanization implicit in the scientific-technical revolution, was developing independently in British engineering workshops from the turn of the century'.[6]

Whitston concludes that Taylorism's influence in Britain was more common in, although not confined to, large scale manufacturing and the new industries such as cars and chemicals. This chapter explores its impact in British coalmining in the interwar years. Mines were dark, their layouts were often complex, and mineworkers had to contend with the unpredictable movement of the coal seams and overlying strata of rock. These special features, and the social relations at work that they fostered, have been highlighted as particular constraints on any management attempt to exert control over labour through the detailed prescription of the task to be achieved by the worker. In the 1950s, Trist and Bamforth of the Tavistock Institute of Human Relations developed a version of this argument in a critique of the work systems and production control regimes that had been installed, during the interwar years, in mines equipped with mechanical coal-cutters and face-conveyors.[7]

This chapter is divided into four parts. The first sketches details of work organization and management in British coalmining at the start of the twentieth century, when hand coal-getting remained the predominant technology at the coalface. The second is concerned with the mechanized 'longwall' system, or 'unit system of intensive machine mining' as it was termed by mining engineers in the 1920s. It considers the system from the perspective of the engineers and managers who prescribed it as best practice at the time in the application of coalface machinery. In their papers and presentations to their professional associations, these exponents of the unit system defined its core features as production planning by management, and worker execution of tasks made routine in accordance with a prearranged schedule. Some urged a more complete reconstruction on Taylorist lines, and prominent among these were owners of the firms that manufactured coalface equipment, who prescribed the application of work study to bring work organization in the mines to approximate more closely with that in the then 'modern' factory. Prescription obviously needs to be evaluated against practice. The third part of the chapter considers the changes in work organization and management that were effected in mechanized mines in the interwar years. It suggests some of the factors that constrained the transformation that had been envisaged by exponents of the unit system in the 1920s. The fourth and final part draws together the analysis in an evaluation of the impact of Taylorism in coalmining during the interwar years.

Work organization and mine management before the onset of mechanization

Coalmining in Britain was a labour intensive process at the beginning of the twentieth century. Some mechanization had taken place, but this had been confined largely to surface operations[8] and to the construction of mine shafts. The process of coal extraction remained broadly unchanged, with hand coal-getting being the predominant technology at the coalface. The social organization of production, however, was far from uniform or static. The British coal industry was geographically fragmented and diverse in a range of respects, including its structures of work organization below ground.[9] These differences were in part a function of divergent geological conditions across the British coalfields, but they also reflected the outcome of struggles between employers and workers.

Coal-getting remained a complete operation performed on a single shift or consecutive shifts by colliers (or hewers) working with a day-wage assistant, or in pairs, or as part of a larger coalface team of six or eight men. The work involved the following processes: undercutting the base of the exposed coalface with an iron pick or, from the 1880s, a 'patent pick' or 'mandril'; ripping, or 'getting the coal down', possibly with the aid of explosives; and filling the coal into tubs, which were brought to the face by haulage workers. Additional 'deadwork' (preparatory and maintenance) jobs might be part of the colliers' task or allocated to other specialist grades. Coal-getting was physically demanding work, performed in conditions that constantly threatened health and safety. It required years of experience if it was to be performed skilfully and with attention to safety, although the length of the collier's 'apprenticeship' and its content – the path of promotion to the face – varied from coalfield to coalfield.

Colliers decided how best to work their 'stall', or place at the face, and in which sequence to perform the various operations of coal-getting. Paid on a piece-wage basis, they retained immediate control over the pace of work. Providing a measure of the intensity of labour and the quality of the work performed, the piece-wage enabled employers to circumvent the difficulties of intensive management supervision in the underground environment and to minimize expenditure on 'oncost' supervisory employees.[10] It buttressed colliers' commitment to self-regulation at work while allowing employers to delegate aspects of supervision.

Various forms of subcontracting, labour subletting, and internal contracting have been identified in nineteenth century British coalmining, and several forms persisted well into the twentieth century. A great deal has been written about the 'butty' system. In its truncated form, this involved a senior worker (a 'butty') contracting with the mine manager or pit under-official to work a stall, or a length of coalface, at a piece-rate that included some allowance for the wages of the other members of the coalface work team. Goffee's study of the operation of the butty system in the Kent coalfields in the 1920s and 1930s highlights the diverse ways in which relations between the butty and his co-workers could develop.[11] The division of the contract earnings might be a decision made by the group as a whole or by the butty alone. There could be substantial equity in the distribution of the contract earnings or no equity at all; at the extreme, the butty could contribute little effort and take the lion's share of the reward. Relations between the butty-man and colliery under-officials varied. Mine managers were apt to use their control over the allocation of working places to reward favoured men and nurture cooperation. Goffee's study shows how the diversity of workers' experiences under this 'little butty' system, and the influence of the butty-men in the local miners' union, could inhibit any united workers' opposition to the system's continuation. As Colin Griffin's account of industrial conflict in the Leicestershire coalfields in the early twentieth century illustrates, however, where the butty-men's ability to maintain their earnings was threatened they could present the front line of resistance to employers' work reorganization initiatives.[12]

Durham and Northumberland were the oldest English coalfields. Bord-and-pillar working (see below), or modifications of this system, continued at many pits well into the twentieth century. Pairs of hewers worked a stall at the coalface, although on consecutive shifts. Teams were self selecting and shared equally the earnings from the stall over the two shifts. Hewers enjoyed the right to 'cavil'; that is to draw lots (each quarter) for a working place at the face and hence to equalize, over the hewer group as a whole, the chances of gaining access to a good or bad place. Cavilling was underwritten by the agreements that had been secured by the hewers, through their collective organization, with mine owners at local and county level.[13] Nevertheless, the system had to be defended against employer attempts to extend management control at the face.

The hewers in the North East were equals in their coalface teams and enjoyed more autonomy in their work than many of their counterparts in British industry. These work arrangements coexisted in the nineteenth century with a relatively elaborate hierarchy of directly employed managerial and supervisory staff. 'Viewers' in the North East had emerged as an influential elite by the beginning of the century.[14] Their influence had derived from their role as coal-land surveyors and consultants to the landowners – who, under the law, owned the coal seams beneath their property – and to the mine owners, who had to negotiate the terms for working coal and the royalty payments to be made to landowners. Viewers combined a range of expertise; in surveying and developing coal lands, and in colliery cost accounting and record keeping. Through their commissions and consultancy activities, they disseminated views of 'best practice' in shaft construction, the layout of underground workings and work organization. A similar function was performed by the professional mining engineers from the late nineteenth century through the transactions of their professional associations.

By the early nineteenth century, at larger pits in the North East, the viewer's comprehensive job role had been subdivided between grades of resident viewers and under viewers. Such an advanced management hierarchy was uncommon elsewhere in the industry before the mid-nineteenth century.[15] In other mining districts, the pits might be managed through some combination of directly employed officials and subcontractors. The 'big butty', for example, was a contractor or chief worker who worked a whole pit on a contract or piecework basis, and who engaged and paid the labour necessary to complete the task. This system, which could amount to 'sweating', was denigrated as 'worst practice' by the northern viewers, who were represented among the staff of the government's Mines Inspectorate, established in 1850. As it transpired, it required workers' agitation and the stimulus of parliamentary intervention both to curtail the worst abuses of labour practised in directly managed as well as butty-operated pits and, also, to extend the northern model of direct mine management elsewhere in the industry.

A series of safety statutes from the 1870s obliged owners to place their mines under the control and daily supervision of qualified managers, prescribed the nature of the qualifications, and required the appointment of 'competent persons' to complete safety inspections below ground prior to the commencement of each working shift. Legislation in 1911 ostensibly restricted these latter officials – variously known as 'firemen', 'examiners' or 'deputies' – to safety duties, and limited the size of the underground district that they were required to inspect. The safety legislation applicable to coalmines provided an 'impetus towards centralization of managerial control'[16] and standardization of the job titles and functions of colliery underground staffs.[17] Most of the legislation had been passed in the face of strenuous opposition from the mine owners, whose local associations had united to form a national body, the Mining Association of Great Britain, for the purpose of resisting the imposition of standardized (industry wide) 'restrictions' on their activities.[18] The statutory prescription of duties fostered the colliery deputies' sense of their distinct identity and interests. Their efforts from the late nineteenth century to organize in unions, separate from those of the mineworkers and independent of the mine owners, also reflected the conflicting pressures to which they were increasingly exposed. Mine owners demanded their services – and loyalty – as production officials. Mineworkers and their unions were concerned to ensure that the deputies adhered to their statutory, safety officer role.[19]

Much of the engineering effort in mining in the nineteenth century had centred on improvements to coal access technology.[20] Better techniques of boring, shaft construction and sinking, and the application of steam power to winding and pumping, facilitated the industry's expansion to deeper lying coal seams. Mine size generally increased with depth, as owners sought to recoup by economies of scale the outlay on shaft construction, and these developments also encouraged innovation in management structures and procedures and the refinement of management information control systems. There were changes, too, in the layout of the underground workings, although these were adopted gradually and unevenly, as between different coalfields and pits within them. Longwall mining progressively displaced the bord-and-pillar system and similar earlier methods of coal extraction, with the pace of the transition to the longwall system accelerating from the 1860s. Church *et al.* estimate that three quarters of British coal output was won from longwall faces by 1900, with bord-and-pillar working retained on any scale only in a few regions, including the North East.[21]

With the earlier methods, mentioned above, the coal was worked in two operations. A series of parallel roads were driven through the coal to the pit boundary and connected at intervals by roads driven at right angles ('working the whole'). The isolated pillars that had been left to support the roof were subsequently cut away ('working the broken'). This extensive grid layout of stalls was displaced by the longwall method, which involved working the whole face simultaneously, either outwards from the pit bottom (longwall advancing) or backwards from the boundary (longwall retreating).

The merits of the longwall method were initially defined in relation to the high oncosts of road building incurred in pits working thin seams. Subsequently it was recommended more broadly as the method that would normally yield the largest extraction of coal from a given area and the highest percentage of 'round' or 'large' coal. Longwall advancing, which emerged as the dominant method of extraction in British coalmining, also had the great merit for owners of allowing profitable mining to commence with the minimum of delay once the shaft had been constructed.[22] It is, however, the potential that the longwall system afforded for the imposition of a new management regime of intensified (factory type) labour supervision at the coalface that has captured the attention of social historians and sociologists.

Longwall mining permitted a greater concentration of coal-getting operations below ground, along a length of working face; indeed, in its 'advancing' form, it was almost defined by this. Management's ability to observe workers was enhanced. Wellisz argued in 1953 that the extension of longwall mining also involved the subdivision and specialization of labour and the aggrandizement of the under-official's role to that of overseer of coalface operations.[23] And there is evidence that longwall mining in some mining districts did indeed involve some of these features. Bulman and Redmayne, leading mining engineers of the late nineteenth and early twentieth centuries, urged that if the 'full benefits' of the longwall system were to be realized, 'the face should be carried forward as regularly as possible' and 'kirving should be continuous along a good length of face, before coal is allowed to fall'. They concluded that it was in recognition of 'this truth' that 'some managers have adopted the division of labour which is common in Derbyshire and elsewhere – namely, that of holers, getters and fillers – thus dividing the hewers' work into three classes of labour'.[24] But longwall mining had been known in Derbyshire long before the 1850s and it is not clear that its use in this coalfield had involved a more active role for pit officials, so much as the delegation of supervisory functions to a 'chief worker' or 'contracting collier'.[25]

What the available evidence makes clear is that there was no single longwall system in late nineteenth century British coalmining, and no single system of work organization associated with it. Longwall face layouts varied enormously between coalfields, and even between pits operating within them. Although the whole of the face was worked, it was divided into stalls either side of the roadways and the length of these stalls varied from a few yards to 50 yards or more. These formed the working places for a collier and his helper, two colliers sharing, or a larger face-team of eight or more men. There might be some specialization within the group, as to who cut, ripped and filled, or a more flexible arrangement. In some instances the pit officials assumed a more interventionist role – in particular, where longwall mining was accompanied by the extension of shift working, so that the operations of cutting and filling were separated in time as well as between members of the work group.[26] Elsewhere, as contemporary commentators noted and social historians have since reported, established work arrangements were reimposed with the introduction of the longwall system.[27]

These differences were in part a function of geology; individual mine managements adapted the longwall system to the nature of the coal seams worked.[28] They also reflected the outcomes of the conflicts and compromises struck between miners and managers over the work arrangements to be employed. Mine owners and managers were inclined to attribute their failure to establish longwall mining to labour resistance. They reported colliers' efforts to 'maintain under the new conditions the rights, customs and traditions which had grown up under the old conditions, but which were singularly inapplicable to the new ones'.[29] Yet in practice a variety of factors could favour the retention of bord-and-pillar working, such as geological conditions and improvements to that system of working. And a range of considerations including workplace relations, the state of underground workings, and the potential for innovation afforded under the terms of the mineral lease negotiated with the landowner, could combine to favour modest rather than radical change with the transition to longwall working. Thus, Rhodes and Rhodes, mining engineers writing in the early 1920s, suggested that longwall face layouts with large stalls and large coalface work teams were more likely to be installed successfully at 'greenfield' sites than at pits that 'have gradually evolved longwall from some earlier method'.[30]

Coal-cutters, conveyors and the 'unit system'

Nineteenth century longwall mining was in practice enormously varied and very often did not conform with the best practice prescribed by mining engineers. Yet, the application of mechanical coal-cutters and face-conveyors, from the beginning of the twentieth century, brought about some standardization. Coal-cutting machinery was developed initially in Britain principally for longwall applications. The advantages of face-conveyors were also seen at first in terms of allowing the working of longer faces. Through the various trials of the equipment, and the exchange of practical experiences, mining engineers by the 1920s were generally agreed on the arrangement and management of labour required to reap the maximum gains from coalface machinery in longwall advancing 'installations'. This 'unit system' of mechanical coal-cutting embraced a rigid horizontal division of labour at the coalface. It was Taylorist in its imposition on coalface workers of a production schedule predetermined by management. Some exponents of the unit system urged its further development through 'scientific management' as espoused by Taylor, and recommended the use of work study to further 'standardize' job performance and cut job times.

Reliance on the physical strength of a collier to undercut the coal had limited the rate of advance at the coalface and the amount of coal that could be extracted by the labour employed on a shift. Consequently, much mental energy had been applied to the means of mechanizing the task of undercutting. Innovations in the generation of power and its transmission below ground assisted. The use of compressed air below ground, from the 1850s, and of electricity from the 1880s, stimulated the design and development of commercial coal-cutters.[31] The machines developed were of two broad types, percussive and rotary. The former reproduced mechanically the action of the miner using a hand pick, while the more powerful rotary machines were designed to undercut the base of the exposed coalface.[32]

The coal-cutting machines in use by the beginning of the twentieth century could undercut at a rate some two or three times faster than a collier using a hand pick, and considerable improvements in machine capacity were made over the interwar period.[33] But the cut coal had still to be blasted off the face and filled, by hand, into tubs brought to the face by haulage workers. Efforts to maximize machine potential diverted attention to the operations of filling and transporting coal from the face. Mechanical face-conveyors were developed from the late nineteenth century, although their use was limited before the 1920s. Mining companies had initially viewed such conveyors as reinforcing and extending the advantages of the longwall method – that is, in terms of reducing the number of gate-roads that had to be built to give access to and from the face.[34] But the merits of the conveyors quickly became defined in terms of supporting the accelerated rate of advance of the face, made possible through the application of the mechanical coal-cutters, in other words, in terms of speeding up the operation of filling.[35] Thus the 'application of power to the conveying of coal at and in the vicinity of the face' came to be vaunted as 'technically and economically essential to intensive machine mining in which the productive effort is concentrated and large outputs are obtained from comparatively small areas'.[36]

By the 1920s, mining companies investing in coalface equipment were tending to use the chain type coal-cutter and belt face-conveyor (where conveyors were installed). These technologies had been applied in conjunction with, or to extend, face and underground layouts occurring with the longwall advancing method. Mining engineers had settled on a view of what constituted best practice in the arrangement of labour and machinery in such longwall systems; the merits of the unit system were proposed in terms of 'standardisation of method' and 'specialisation of labour'.[37] These were elaborated through contrasts with other possible arrangements.

For example, while the adoption of coal-cutters had facilitated the division of coal-getting into discrete operations, and many of the mining companies installing the new equipment had formalized the division through the insertion of a new grade of 'machine operator', a number had sought to maximize machine use through the 'long face' system. This involved minimal change to existing longwall face layouts, but considerable encouragement to machine operators to undercut the maximum possible length of face during their working shift. This relatively 'flexible' system had come to be disparaged by the early 1920s as 'mechanical coal-cutting' as distinct from 'machine mining'; the latter being a concept used to signify 'systematic working' or, more specifically, 'the application of machinery in systematic conformity with a predetermined mining policy'.[38]

Among the most ardent exponents of 'machine mining' on the unit system were firms that manufactured the coal-cutting equipment. Their designers had an 'engineering model' of how work could be organized, and their owners had a material interest in the extended use of coalface machinery built to standard design. Sam Mavor, of Mavor & Coulson, in particular spent much of his time proselytizing the unit system as the means for extending 'factory methods' to the mines.[39] His prescriptions, nevertheless, built upon the work reorganization initiatives that mining companies had tried during their early experiments with the application of coal-cutters and conveyors at the face.

Advocates of the unit system discussed it as a 'cut and strip' operation, organized over three shifts in a 24-hour cycle of coal-getting.[40] It carried further the development towards 'intensive' mining that had been evident in the longwall layouts of 'modern' pits sunk in the late nineteenth century; and it involved the displacement of the small work group, of earlier longwall and bord-and-pillar installations, through the subdivision of the coal-getting operation and the allocation of component tasks among workers now grouped into much larger production units. The system's core features, as identified by its exponents, were production planning by management, and worker execution of tasks made routine in accordance with a prearranged schedule.[41] In these respects the unit system was essentially Taylorist.

The literature prescribing the benefits of 'intensive mining on the unit system' placed central emphasis on the need for managers to plan 'every detail of the scheme of operation in advance' so that 'organisation is built up once and for all' and thereafter 'has only to be maintained on established lines' by subordinate officials.[42] At that time, planning centred on the reorganization of the face layout and of face-workers into teams of the size and composition required to extract a specified quantity of coal each day. The working face had to be divided into 'units' of a length that could 'with certainty' be undercut to a specified depth by a single coal-cutting machine within the limits of a single working shift. The length and depth of the cut to be achieved by each machine crew in its shift specified the daily output target for the production unit as a whole and for its constituent occupational groups. In other words, a 'well-organised coal face set a definite pace of the cycle of operations which must follow in its sequence'.[43]

A single face-unit would be between 100 and 150 yards in length, depending on the thickness of the seam, with a three foot seam undercut to a depth of, perhaps, five feet. The anticipated yield of a double face-unit, comprising a pair of faces created either side of a central loading road, would be 200 to 250 tons per day. To obtain this output, however, effort had to be 'concentrated'. Each machine crew was now assigned a 'definitely specified task to be performed within specified limits of time and to be repeated at regular intervals', or once in every 24-hour or, in some instances, 48-hour cycle. Similarly, all other tasks involved in the extraction of coal – drilling, shotfiring, filling out the coal, ripping the roadways, timbering and packing – had to be 'so organised that they too [could] be regularly completed in a given time' and the face advanced each day a distance equal to the depth of the cut.[44]

In place of the collier and his assistant, or small work team of hand coal-getting, a production unit of upwards of 40 men (in a double face-unit) was created; the members of which were divided by time, working on three separate shifts in a 24-hour period, and by task. An array of specialized job roles was thus created. Some of these were new and introduced with the use of machinery (cutting-machine attendants, conveyor-belt breakers and builders); others were traditional specialisms (timbering) or the disaggregated elements of the collier's complete job. Fillers, confined to 'clearing' the coal from a length of the face-unit, formed the largest single occupational group; around one half of the production unit. All job roles and specialisms were arranged in sequence over the three shifts of a cycle, with the idea that they would be performed in accordance with management's 'prearranged timetable'.[45]

Target setting and production scheduling alone were insufficient to realize the objectives of intensive mining. Interwar commentators noted that mechanization had created the need for a 'far more intensive and continuous supervision over the progress of work in each district than was required in hand mining'.[46] Mining engineers similarly urged that 'outputs, such as thoroughly justify the use of mechanical conveyors, can be obtained only by the most carefully thought out organization and skilled and constant supervision'.[47] For if a 'well organised machine face set a definite pace of the cycle of operations that must follow in its sequence',[48] equally it demanded the 'rigid adherence to timetable'.[49] Labour functions had been divided, but tasks and shifts were interdependent and no shift could begin until work on the preceding one had been completed. The creation of a large scale, differentiated and rigidly sequenced work system, as researchers from the Tavistock Institute of Human Relations were later to emphasize, had created the potential for large scale disruption and failure in production.[50]

Prescriptions varied on the ways and means of motivating face-workers to keep pace with the 'machine system'. Much emphasis was given to the need for 'careful selection of sets of men' working conveyor-faces[51] and to the selection of superintending officials who could generate team spirit.[52] Mavor, among others, urged the merits of Taylor's own methods. He argued that the term 'supervision' should:

> not be used in the sense of policing but of planning and organising the work and guiding and instructing the men in the methods and manner of carrying it out, of the tuning up of the organisation so that coal cutters and their crews shall be enabled to be actually at work during the largest possible proportion of the cutting shift, and so that during the stripping shift the filling of coal on to the conveyors shall be a continuous process, uninterrupted by periods of idleness imposed on the men by eccentricities of the tram traffic or other causes.[53]

In short, Mavor proposed work study, 'the systematic observation and recording throughout a shift of minute to minute time intervals in relation to work done', as the means of perpetually 'refining' and intensifying the performance of work. Towards this end, he urged mine managers to give particular attention to the underground transport of coal. 'Inadequacy of transport facilities', he observed, was 'the most common cause of restriction of output from conveyor faces' and the 'rock on which ambitious schemes of face conveying have not infrequently been wrecked'. Attention should be given, he maintained, to the 'optimal' size of coal tubs as well as to the layout of underground haulage routes, and a specialized manager should be appointed in overall charge of the traffic 'department'.[54]

Mavor prescribed the appointment of 'coal-cutting supervisors'[55] and, at each colliery, a production engineer who would 'concentrate in the study of the problems of direct application of labour' and 'acquire skill in the conduct of investigations having for their object the raising of effectiveness of the human effort'.[56] Job analysis and the standardization of procedures and tasks, in his scheme, paved the way for the 'scientific calculation' of the 'incentive wage'.[57]

Mavor was not alone in his efforts to promote 'scientific management' in the mines. The editors of the *Colliery Guardian* professed a good deal of scepticism, but continued to publish articles on the subject. A translation of a paper on 'Taylorism in the Mine' by Langrogne, then Director of the Mines Service in Alsace-Lorraine, was published over three issues at the end of 1919. Designed 'exclusively to French conditions', the proposals were for the creation of a planning department, or *bureau d'études*, in each mine, the application of work study, and the institution of a payments system that tied bonuses 'strictly... to the work actually done'.[58] Boyns suggests that this contribution failed to stimulate any major debate in the British coal industry, possibly because attention had been diverted by 'more pressing problems, such as trade depression'.[59]

But discussion of best practice in the application of coalface machinery continued among mining engineers and managers. The transactions of their professional associations incorporated papers prescribing the regular completion of 'time studies' as of 'great use in furthering the efficiency of the [machine mining] system' and as 'the only sound way of determining where efficiency is lost'.[60] And there was some developing interest too in the work of industrial psychologists.[61]

The experiments conducted by the Industrial Fatigue Research Board into the 'psychology of hewing' (noted by Whitston), which seemed to consist of tests of the use of different types of shovel for coal filling, were reported at length by the *Colliery Guardian,* whose editors drew the comparison with Taylor's experiments on workers shovelling iron ore at the Bethlehem Steel Company.[62] Industry sponsored university professors of mining disseminated the results of their experiments in, for example, ergonomics and the 'physiological cost of muscular work measured by the expiratory discharge of CO_2',[63] and those same professors discussed the results of time studies of coalface workers conducted to establish the 'optimal' length of rest periods.[64]

Such experiments were conducted in mechanized and in unmechanized mines, with, and sometimes without, the knowledge of the mineworkers under observation. The results were presented in elaborate statistical detail. Mining engineers and managers could be equally attentive to detail in recording the outputs that they had obtained in experiments with different configurations of labour and coal-cutting equipment. There is certainly evidence that some mining companies intensified and systematized their monitoring practices, although principally in the form of more elaborate cost control systems.[65] There is also much evidence of the intensification of management supervision at machine-cut faces. What is less in evidence is any development of time study as a management practice. Since there is much to suggest that employers continued to rely on 'traditional' modes of labour control, in particular the piece-wage mechanism, in mechanized and unmechanized mines alike, an early conclusion would be that Taylorism did not reach very far in the mines. Practices developed at some large companies towards the end of the interwar years counsel a more open ended verdict.

Colliery mechanization in the interwar period

The conversion to mechanized coal-cutting in Britain as a whole was slow in comparison with the pace of change in most other major coal producing countries. Only 59 per cent of aggregate British coal output was undercut mechanically in 1938. Progress toward mechanization was a highly uneven process in the British coal industry, however, and at the end of the interwar period the proportion of coal cut mechanically ranged from 91 per cent in the Northumberland coalfield to 26 per cent in South Wales and Monmouthshire.[66] Similarly, while the concentration of investment on large scale mines progressed in some districts, and notably in the more recently developed coalfields of the east Midlands, the overall structure of coal production in Britain remained fragmented. A large number of small scale mines remained in operation at the end of the 1930s.

Explanations for the British industry's inability to reconstruct, even in the face of intensified international competition, have been proposed in terms of adverse geological conditions,[67] poor managerial or poor entrepreneurial performance,[68] and labour resistance to technological change.[69] A detailed review and discussion of the debates is not possible here. It can, however, be suggested that geology and industrial relations, as well as the provisions of the mineral lease negotiated with the landowner,[70] combined in different ways to shape each company's 'investment options'. Differences of circumstance were in turn of profound significance in the mine owners' collective response to the demands of the Miners' Federation of Great Britain (MFGB). Some brief illustrations can be given.

The early lead in the application of coal-cutting equipment established by the Scottish coalfields (over 50 per cent of output was cut mechanically by 1927) is generally attributed to the rising production costs incurred as mining progressed to deeper and thinner seams. Melling emphasizes also, as a force for change, the growing strength of the Scottish miners' unions in the period before the First World War.[71] Pits nevertheless remained relatively small, even at the end of the interwar period. In the years before the First World War, the Scottish coal masters had sought to mechanize coal-cutting and impose a regime of 'driving supervision' by using subcontractors. Union policies in relation to mechanization were forged in this context. Alan Campbell's study shows that union leaders identified the broad range of threats posed; to jobs, skills, earnings and, crucially, miners' safety.[72] That they opted to accept mechanization and to mobilize action to regulate use of the new equipment can be understood in relation to the available alternatives (worsening conditions in thin seams worked by hand, or mechanization under a butty regime). Many pit level disputes connected with the introduction of machinery arose, but these focused largely on the miners' efforts to enforce union policies, particularly in relation to the abolition of subcontracting and the standardization of piecework price lists across mechanized pits.

Miners in South Wales, as in Scotland, had achieved a greater unity, displayed in more assertive union policies, from the end of the nineteenth century. The age of pits, the geological conditions of mining, and the extant systems of work organization nevertheless differed in the two regions. Mine owners in South Wales were under less pressure than their Scottish counterparts to invest in coal-cutting machinery. Coal-getting required limited undercutting and the condition of the coal seams presented technical obstacles to the use of cutting equipment. A number of owners introduced face-conveyors. In 1921, South Wales accounted for 40 per cent of all conveyors in use in the British coal industry, although only around 14 per cent of pits in the coalfield used the technology at this time.[73] The reduction in the length of the working day sanctioned by the Sankey Commission in 1919 had built up pressure on the owners to achieve an intensification of working hours, and efforts to install face-conveyors became more widespread in the early 1920s.[74]

Worker resistance was galvanized by the mine companies' attempts to renegotiate piecework price lists and to use contractors for conveyor-belt 'turning', and also by the safety hazards introduced with the use of conveyors on longer working faces. A series of pit based disputes centred on such issues.[75] The South Wales Miners' Federation attempted to negotiate a framework agreement with the mine owners' association that would regulate the use of conveyor technology. A sub-committee of the Joint Standing Disputes Committee was established for the purposes and met regularly from 1923. No agreement was reached, however, and on the eve of the 1926 miners' lockout the owners' announced their withdrawal from all joint agreements relating to working methods and use of coalface machinery.[76]

British mineworkers were divided by grading structures, forms of payment, structures of work organization and systems of labour management. They nevertheless achieved a growing unity, from the late nineteenth century onwards, around the demands for national wage bargaining, the reduction of working hours, and higher safety standards enforced through legislation. The mine owners' resistance to these demands served to rally workers in support of the MFGB's campaign for nationalization of the mines. Mine owners were divided by the geological conditions in which they organized coal extraction, by the types of coal that their pits produced, by the markets in which they operated, and by their relations with labour and with the owners of coal lands. Geological conditions and the interplay of local economic and social relations shaped the potential gains to be derived from investment in scale and in the mechanization of mines. For example, the terms of the mineral lease and share of the productivity gains to be appropriated by a landowner could encourage or inhibit investment in technical change.[77] By virtue of the divergent conditions in which they organized coal production, mine owners found their common position only in the defence of local autonomy. Faced by the miners' increased solidarity around demands for industry wide improvements in terms and conditions of employment, they strengthened their own national organization to mount a yet more vigorous defence of the freedom to exploit labour by the means 'dictated' locally.

The miners' defeat in the 1926 lockout, and large scale unemployment in the coalfields thereafter, weakened labour resistance to mechanization under the terms sought by employers. Use of coal-cutting equipment accelerated in a number of coalfields.[78] The broad trend was one of an increased use of machinery in mechanized mines, however, and marked regional differences persisted in the percentage of coal cut and conveyed mechanically.[79] The wage reductions and extension of working hours achieved by mine owners in 1926–27 allowed many small mines and many unmechanized pits to remain in competition. Only modest change was achieved in the structure of coal production; the British coal industry comprised 2861 mines in 1927 and 2125 in 1938, by which latter time only 45 per cent of the total number of mines used coal-cutting equipment.[80] Coalface machinery was installed in many mines without the comprehensive reorganization of underground layouts and investment in new haulage techniques that had been prescribed by Mavor, among others, in the early 1920s.[81] The annual level of capital investment (in plant and machinery) in the British industry in the 1930s fell to 60 per cent below that of 1919–25.[82]

'Machine mining', and accompanying regimes of more intensive managerial supervision, served to intensify labour effort at the coalface. In the Scottish coalfields in particular, there were marked increases in output per man-shift at the face. And the speed up of work was by no means confined to mechanized pits. Even so, the overall productivity growth achieved by the British coal industry in the interwar period was modest by international standards. Output per man-shift rose by a mere 13 per cent during the 25-year period between 1913 and 1938. In contrast, in the German Ruhr, Belgian, Polish and United States' coal industries in the same period the recorded increases were 64 per cent, 40 per cent, 59 per cent and 36 per cent respectively.[83]

Mechanized longwall advancing emerged as the dominant, although not the only, system of 'machine mining' in Britain in the 1930s. In their evidence to the Royal Commission on Safety in Coal Mines in the late 1930s, divisional inspectors of mines summarized the changes in working methods effected with mechanization in the term 'concentration': 'the getting of a large output from a comparatively short working face divided into units of suitable length, each of which must produce a definite quantity of coal daily'.[84] Specified output targets and the institution of a daily cycle of operations had generated the requirement for intensified management supervision at the face in order to maintain the continuity of production. Tighter supervision was also required in the interests of safety. Much of the evidence presented to the Royal Commission was of the subordination of the latter interest as managements fashioned regimes that relied to a large extent on coercion to achieve output and cost control objectives. The cycle of operations, one divisional inspector noted, had tended 'to more hurry, and the taking of greater risks which otherwise would not be taken'.[85]

The Coal Mines Act 1911, fashioned in an era in which hand coal-getting remained the dominant technology at the coalface, remained in force throughout the interwar period. Nominally, it confined colliery deputies, the front line supervisors, primarily to the performance of safety related functions. The deputies' representative organizations had campaigned at the end of the First World War for Civil Service status for their members, on the basis that pressure, from piece working colliers as well as from managers, had obliged deputies to neglect their safety duties.[86] After the 1926 lockout, however, membership of the deputies' associations fell and mining employers invigorated their efforts to organize colliery officials into company schemes. The deputies' grievance, articulated by officials of their independent unions in the late 1930s, was of 'being forced onto output' in order to meet employers' priorities. They were 'more speeded up in their production than they ever have been' so that they were not 'spending the time that they should be on safety'.[87]

The deputies complained of 'interference' from other underground officials and in particular from colliery overmen. Occupying a position in the underground supervisory hierarchy between the deputies and the under manager, the overman's duties were not prescribed in the safety legislation because the mine owners' insistence that these were exclusively 'production officials' had prevailed. Available statistical evidence suggests that, in the British coal industry as a whole, the increase in the proportion of supervisory staff to all employed below ground had tailed off in the early 1920s. There is some evidence, however, of a continuing expansion of the overman's rank among larger, mechanized mines, in the late 1920s and 1930s.[88] Earlier in the century, Jevons had reported that larger collieries were using centralized cost accounting techniques and 'cash incentives' to place overmen in competition to maximize output and minimize costs in their respective underground districts.[89] Frowen, the colliery deputies' representative, argued before the Royal Commission on Safety in the late 1930s that overmen were 'officers of economy' who 'get their paper from head office of the costs and that kind of thing, and their whole time seems to be taken up with that side of mining'.[90]

Overmen might have been able to be 'incentivized' by those in the higher echelons of colliery management to achieve output and expenditure targets. In mechanized mines, however, they had to contend with frequent delays occasioned by breakdowns of machinery and disruptions in the supply of tubs to and from the face. These conditions militated against the 'standardization' of tasks and work rules. 'Forceful' supervision could be applied, and there is considerable evidence in the literature of the period to suggest that it was,[91] but constant supervision was prohibited by underground conditions and by managers' cost objectives. Employers and their supervisory staffs continued to rely heavily on the 'self-acting stimulus' of the piece-wage to extract effort from miners and to secure their cooperation in the resolution of production bottlenecks. The negotiation of piece-rates remained the miners' immediate means of exerting an influence on anticipated effort levels. In this struggle for control, colliery managers experimented with different schemes of group or individual piecework on the coal-filling shift (payment by the tonnage raised from a 'unit' or by the yardage of face 'cleared').[92]

In summary, mechanization was accompanied by an intensification of management supervision below ground in the mines. There were changes in the structure of production management in larger, mechanized pits. Yet there was continuity, too, in the range of labour management techniques deployed. Unemployment in the coalfields amplified the force of established management methods in the mines, even as the ideas of the 'management movement' were being aired in the transactions of mine managers' professional associations. Nevertheless, Boyns's study of the more radical overhaul of production and labour management attempted by the Powell Duffryn company in South Wales at the end of the 1930s (see below) indicates that prescription and evolving practice did on occasion intersect more precisely.[93]

As one of the largest employers in the South Wales steam coalfield, Powell Duffryn had pursued a fairly consistent 'growth strategy' in the interwar years. This entailed the acquisition of other colliery firms operating in a geographically proximate area of the coalfield, the 'rationalization' of productive capacity and the re-equipment of remaining pits with coal-cutting and conveying technologies.[94] With the acquisition of the Welsh Associated Collieries in 1935, Powell Duffryn doubled in size. Boyns describes how senior management proceeded to group operations under the control of three area general managers, who reported to a director of production, who was, in turn, responsible to the main sub-committee of the board of directors. It was this committee that 'took important decisions regarding matters of output and techniques' and that, in the late 1930s, decided to adopt 'panel mining', a form of 'retreat' mining. The system was 'particularly suited to development along Taylorist lines'.[95] The area of coal to be worked could be explored in advance and a production plan devised, prior to the commencement of mining operations, that detailed the number of machines and miners to be employed, the rate of advance of the face, and the tonnage of coal to be extracted. Powell Duffryn developed the system at a number of pits, and used 'process' men and boys to time how long work took and to recommend ways in which delays could be obviated.[96] Efforts to translate the specified work rates into revised piecework price lists nevertheless met with fairly forceful worker opposition.

Conclusions and postscript

The Powell Duffryn company's initiatives in the late 1930s can be interpreted as an exception to the broad rule of production management organization and practice in interwar British coalmining. Certainly, there is little available evidence to suggest that other coal companies, even the most modern at that time, attempted to embrace 'scientific management' as comprehensively. The Powell Duffryn example nevertheless can be situated at the extreme of the changes in work organization and management that had been adopted more widely in the British coal industry by the 1930s. The unit system of mechanized longwall mining was Taylorist in work design. Mining engineers in the 1920s had attempted to 'theorize' its advantages for management, in relation to other work arrangements at machine-cut faces, in terms of production scheduling by management and worker execution of routine tasks. Prescriptions for a more comprehensive overhaul of underground layouts and haulage systems, and for the institution of centralized production planning and use of work study techniques, were taken up more rarely.

This situation can be explained partly by the fragmented structure of coal production in Britain. Coalface machinery was often introduced into mines where the existing underground layouts prohibited innovation in haulage techniques. Much labour effort was expended in the grinding task of navigating tubs to and from the face. Established haulage techniques, however, set limits on the productivity increases that could be secured through further investment at the face and constrained management attempts to achieve a fast throughput, 'flow line' production system. The machine manufacturer Mavor, an arch exponent of 'scientific management' in the mines, had made the point in the 1920s.

The same point was reiterated in the report of the Reid Committee, established in the 1940s to investigate the 'technical condition' of the British coal industry. The committee comprised managers and engineers selected from the staffs of the coal industry's most 'innovative' companies. As such, it distilled prevailing technical and managerial conceptions of best practice in the use of technology, in work organization and in production management. It prescribed bord-and-pillar or 'retreat' mining as the basis for the subsequent development of mechanization, in preference to the method of longwall advancing that had been developed in the British coal industry and extended more widely in the interwar years with the application of coal-cutting equipment. Under the retreat system, the coalface was constantly being advanced into 'unproven' mining conditions. This militated against standardization of work tasks and procedures. It fell to production supervisors and workers at the coalface to resolve the delays frequently occasioned by unanticipated geological conditions and machine breakdowns.

What constrained consolidation of the structure of coal production in Britain? The analysis made by Fine *et al.* gives particular attention to the private ownership of coal royalties. Landowners controlled access to the coal seams lying beneath their property. Through the terms of the mineral lease they could attempt to confine the development of mining to the perimeters of their property. They could also seek to appropriate a share of the gains secured through any investment in the expanded scale or mechanization of mining operations. Such conflicts of economic interest between the landowner and the mine owner were resolved locally in different ways. In combination with the mine owners' ability to impose wage reductions (in 1921) and an extension of working hours (after 1926), the broad effect was to dampen forces for a 'radical' (capitalist) restructuring of production. In the light of this analysis, it is relevant to note that the Powell Duffryn company was one of the colliery concerns that bought up the freehold to the minerals that it worked.

Coal royalties were nationalized in 1938. The centrality of an adequate coal supply, and hence of coalmining labour relations, during the Second World War and for post war reconstruction encouraged support for the nationalization of the mines, which was effected in January 1947. Coal production was brought under a more unified management structure. In the years immediately after the industry' nationalization, the pressure on management was to achieve output maximization with existing resources.[97] Piecework rates and 'additional payments' remained a focus for workplace disputes.

The National Coal Board's scheme for the reconstruction of production, developed from the 1950s, centred on the 'rationalization' of capacity and the application of the new production technologies of power-loading and hydraulic face props. It was these technologies that afforded the potential for continuous mining on the longwall retreat system. It was also the scale of the capital investment entailed that prompted NCB management to attempt the introduction of work study. The National Power Loading Agreement, negotiated with the National Union of Mineworkers in 1966, replaced piecework by a form of measured day work. As such, it delivered a long term objective for the miners' national union and helped to build solidarity at local level. For management, however, the benefits of work study were offset by the intensified difficulties of supervision in the absence of individual or group piecework incentives.

Notes

1. D. Nelson, 'Scientific Management, Systematic Management, and Labor, 1880–1915', *Business History Review* 48:4 (1974), pp. 480–1; M. Jelinek, 'Toward Systematic Management: Alexander Hamilton Church', *Business. History Review* 54:1 (1980), pp. 63–69.
2. K. Whitston, 'Scientific Management and Production Management Practice in Britain between the Wars', *Historical Studies in Industrial Relations (HSIR)* I (March 1996), pp. 50–51.
3. J. E. Kelly, *Scientific Management, Job Redesign and Work Performance* (Academic Press: 1982), p. 12.

4. For example, H. F. Gospel, *Markets, Firms and the Management of Labour in Modern Britain* (Cambridge University Press: 1992); J. Zeitlin, 'Labour Strategies of British Engineering Employers, 1890–1922' in H. F. Gospel and C. R. Littler (eds), *Managerial Strategies and Industrial Relations* (Heinemann: 1983); S. Tolliday and J. Zeitlin, 'National Models and International Variations in Labour Management and Employer Organization' in S. Tolliday and J. Zeitlin (eds), *The Power to Manage? Employers and Industrial Relations in Comparative-historical Perspective* (Routledge: 1991).

5. C. Littler, 'Taylorism, Fordism and Job Design' in D. Knights, H. Willmott and D. Collinson (eds), *Job Redesign: Critical Perspectives on the Labour Process* (Gower, Aldershot: 1985), p. 13.

6. K. Whitston, 'Scientific Management between the Wars', *HSIR*, pp. 50–51.

7. E. L. Trist and K. W Bamforth, 'Some Social and Psychological Consequences of the Longwall Method of Coal-Getting. An Examination of the Psychological Situation and Defences of a Work Group in Relation to the Social Structure and Technological Content of the Work System', *Human Relations (HR)* 4:1 (1951), pp. 3–38.

8. For example, the use of mechanical screens in 'coal preparation' operations which facilitated the imposition on surface workers of a 'factory regime' of close supervision. See A. John, *By the Sweat of Their Brow* (Routledge and Kegan Paul: 1984).

9. See, for example, M. J. Daunton, 'Down the Pit: Work in the Great Northern and South Wales Coalfields, 1870–1914', *Economic History Review* 34:4 (1981), pp. 578–97.

10. K. Marx, *Capital. A Critique of Political Economy, Vol. 1* (Penguin, Harmondsworth: 1976), pp. 696–98.

11. R. Goffee, 'Incorporation and Conflict. A Case Study of Subcontracting in the Coal Industry', *Sociological Review* 29:3 (1981), pp. 475–97.

12. C. Griffin, 'Shovel or Fork? The Coal-filling Question in the Leicestershire Coalfield, *c.* 1870–1940', *HSIR* 4 (September 1997).

13. See M. J. Daunton. 'Down the Pit', *Economic. History Review;* H. Beynon and T. Austrin, *Masters and Servants: Class and Patronage in the Making of a Labour Organisation: The Durham Miners and the English Political Tradition* (Rivers Oram Press: 1994).

14. M. Flinn with D. Stoker, *The History of the British Coal Industry, Vol. 2: 1700–1830: The Industrial Revolution* (Oxford University Press: 1984), pp. 57–68.

15. *Ibid.;* R. Church with A. Hall and J. Kanefsky, *The History of the British Coal Industry, Vol. 3: 1830–1913: Victorian Pre-eminence* (Oxford University Press: 1986), pp. 409–21.

16. Church *et al.*, *The History of the British Coal Industry, Vol. 3*, p. 420.

17. P. Ackers, 'Colliery Deputies in the British Coal Industry before Nationalization', *International Review of Social History (IRSH) 39:3* (1994), pp. 390–95.

18. R. P. Arnot, *The Miners: Years of Struggle* (Allen and Unwin: 1953), p. 30.

19. Ackers, 'Colliery Deputies', *IRSH;* S. Tailby, 'Labour Utilization and Labour Management in the British Coalmining Industry, 1900–1940' (PhD, University of Warwick: 1990), pp. 271–345.

20. Church *et al.*, *The History of the British Coal Industry, Vol. 3*, p. 420.

21. *Ibid.*, pp. 336–37.

22. Ministry of Fuel and Power, Technical Advisory Committee, *Report* (Reid), Cmd. 6610 (1944), p. 42; B. Supple, *The History of the British Coal Industry, Vol. 4: 1913–46: The Political Economy of Decline* (Oxford: 1987), p. 30. The Reid Committee estimated that 74 per cent of British collieries employed the longwall system. Supple's analysis suggests that, by the end of the Second World War, 90 per cent of British coal output was obtained from longwall faces advancing from the shaft.
23. S. Wellisz, 'Strikes in Coal-Mining', *British Journal of Sociology (BJS)* 4 (1953), pp. 346–66.
24. H. F. Bulman and R. A. S. Redmayne, *Colliery Working and Management* (5th ed., Technical Press: 1951), p. 227.
25. H. Rhodes and M. Rhodes, 'Methods of Working the Barnsley Seam of the South Yorkshire Coalfield', *Colliery Guardian (CG)*, 23 June 1923, pp. 1555–56.
26. R. Church and Q. Outram. *Strikes and Solidarity: Coalfield Conflict in Britain 1889–1966* (Cambridge University Press), p. 30.
27. Bulman and Redmayne, *Colliery Working and Management;* J. W. F. Rowe, *Wages in the Coal Industry* (P. S. King: 1923), pp. 60–61; A. Campbell and F. Reid, 'The Independent Collier in Scotland' in R. Harrison (ed.), *The Coal Miner as Archetypal Proletarian Reconsidered* (Harvester Press, Hassocks: 1978); D. Douglass, 'Pit Life in County Durham' in R. Samuel (ed.), *Miners, Quarrymen and Salt Workers* (Routledge and Kegan Paul: 1977), pp. 218–20.
28. *CG*, 2 May 1919, p. 1034. This report on new methods of extracting thick coal seams at the Earl of Dudley's Baggeridge Colliery, Warwickshire, noted that the innovation was 'practically an adaptation of what is known as the "Longwall System"' and was to be commended for securing the 'complete extraction of coal'.
29. *CG*, 5 June 1925, p. 1381. See also H. Rhodes and M. Rhodes, 'Methods of Working the Barnsley Seam', *CG*, 23 June 1923, p. 1555.
30. H. Rhodes and M. Rhodes, 'Methods of Working the Barnsley Seam', *CG*, 23 June 1923, p. 1556.
31. R. Nelson, 'Electricity in Coal Mines: A Retrospect and A Forecast' *Institution of Electrical Engineers* 84:510, pp. 597–609.
32. R. Shepherd and A. G. Withers, *Mechanised Cutting and Loading of Coal (1960)* Long Acre, London.
33. Church *et al.*, *The History of the British Coal Industry, Vol. 3*, p. 348. Royal Commission on Safety in Coal Mines, *Report*, Cmd. 5890 (1938–9).
34. Departmental Committee Appointed to Inquire into the Probable Economic Effects of a Limit of 8 Hours to the Working Day of Coal Miners, *Minutes of Evidence*, Cd. 3505 (1907), Q. 17,050.
35. J. S. Carson, 'A System of Mechanical Coal Mining, Combined with the Adoption of Systematic Timbering Using Composite Steel Props', *CG*, 1 January 1926, pp. 35–36.
36. S. Mavor, 'The Application of Machinery at the Coalface', *CG*, 16 April 1926, pp. 901–3.
37. 'Longwall Machine Mining: The Unit System', *CG*, 31 August 1923, p. 525.
38. *Ibid.*

39. 'The Limitations of Coal Cutters', *CG*, 10 December 1921, reported that Mavor & Coulson Ltd had established a monthly magazine entitled *Machine Mining*.
40. See, for example, 'Longwall Machine Mining', *CG*, 31 August 1923, p. 525.
41. S. Mavor, 'Problems of Mechanical Coal Mining', *CG*, 13 June 1924.
42. 'Longwall Machine Mining', *CG*, 31 August 1923, p. 525.
43. I. W. Cumberbatch, 'Coal Face Machinery', paper read before North Staffordshire Branch of the National Association of Colliery Managers (NACM), *CG*, 9 February 1923, p. 346.
44. 'Longwall Machine Mining', *CG*, 31 August 1923.
45. For fuller detail, see J. H. Mitchell, 'The Worker's Point of View: The Mechanization of the Miner', *Human Factor* 7:4 (April 1933), pp. 139–50; E. R. Manley, *Meet the Miner* (Lofthouse: 1947); Trist and . Bamforth, 'Some Social and Psychological Consequences of the Longwall Method'; J. Goldthorpe, 'Technical Organization as a Factor in Supervisor-Worker Conflict', *BJS* 10:3 (1959), pp. 213–30.
46. Royal Commission on Safety in Coal Mines, *Report*, p. 48.
47. R. Clive, 'Abstract of the Report on an Investigation of the Underground Conveying and Loading of Coal by Mechanical Means', *Transactions of the Institution of Mining Engineers* 78 (1929–30), pp. 305–38.
48. 'Longwall Machine Mining', *CG*, 31 August 1923.
49. A. C. Moonie, 'Machine Mining in Northumberland and Durham', *Transactions of the Institution of Mining* Engineers 92 (1936–37), pp. 244–63.
50. Trist and . Bamforth, 'Some Social and Psychological Consequences of the Longwall Method'.
51. H. E. Tyson, 'Some Mechanical Conveyor Systems', *CG*, 5 December 1930, p. 2068.
52. L. J. Barraclough, 'Some General Considerations of Machine-Mining Practice', *Transactions of the Institution of Mining Engineers* 74 (1927–28), pp. 177–98; D. S. Newey, 'The Introduction of Machine Mining at Newdigate Colliery', *Transactions of the Institution of Mining Engineers* 78 (1929–30), pp. 372–402.
53. S. Mavor, 'Problems of Mechanical Coal Mining', paper read before the Empire Mining and Metallurgical Congress and reproduced in *CG*, 13 and 20 June 1924.
54. *Ibid.*, 20 June 1924, p. 1591.
55. 'The Limitations of Coal Cutters', *CG*, 10 December 1921, p. 1607.
56. Mavor, 'Problems of Mechanical Coal Mining', *CG*, 20 June 1924, p. 1591.
57. *Ibid.*
58. M. Langrogne, 'Taylorism in the Mine: Efficiency Methods below Ground', *CG*, 28 November 1919, pp. 1429–30; *CG*, 12 December 1919, p. 1574; *CG*, 24 December 1919, p. 1714.
59. T. Boyns, 'Powell Duffryn: The Use of Machine and Production Planning Techniques in the South Wales Coalfield', in K. Tenfelde (ed.), *Socialgeschichte des Bergbaus im 19. und 20. Jahrundert* (C. H. Beck. Munich: 1992), p. 373.
60. Barraclough, 'Some General Considerations of Machine-Mining Practice'. *Transactions of the Institution of Mining Engineers*, p. 177.

61. G. Wightman, 'The Psychology of Management', *The National Association of Colliery Managers' Transactions* 30 (1933), pp. 479–98. The author prescribed that 'management should learn the art of directing the individuality of the working forces under its supervision to the most desirable end'. The practices to be used were listed as the 'functionalisation' of work, namely that of miners and managers, work study, and use of an incentive scheme that tied bonus payments to defined output standards, thereby 'enticing the worker to strive to do better work'.

62. 'Psychology in the Mine: Rhythm in Coal-getting', *CG*, 27 October 1922, p. 1201; 'The Psychology of Hewing', *CG*, 3 November 1922, pp. 1093–94; 'Psychology in Relation to Coal Mining', *CG*, 9 February 1923, p. 332: 'A Psychological Investigation of a Coal Mine', *CG*, 21 September 1923, p. 716; 'The Inter-Connection between Economics and Psychology in Industry', *CG*, 28 September 1923, p. 777.

63. For example, 'The Measurement of Work', *CG*, 20 May 1921, p. 1466.

64. K. Neville Moss, 'A Time Study of Coalface Workers', *Transactions of the Institution of Mining Engineers* 90 (1935–36), pp. 62–66.

65. See, for example, 'Underground Costing at Collieries', *CG*, 27 June 1919, p. 1550.

66. *Annual Report of the Secretary for Mines*, Mines Department, Board of Trade, 1938. According to the International Labour Organization (ILO), *The World Coal-Mining Industry* (ILO: Geneva: 1938), p. 196, mechanized coal-cutting in 1935 accounted for 97 per cent of output in the German coal industry; 95 per cent in Belgium 88 per cent in France; and 79 per cent in the United States.

67. N. K. Buxton, 'Entrepreneurial Efficiency in the British Coal Industry between the Wars', *Economic History Review* 23 (1970), pp. 476–97.

68. A. J. Taylor, 'The Coal Industry' in D. H. Aldcroft (ed.), *The Development of British Industry and Foreign Competition, 1875–1914* (Allen and Unwin: 1968), pp. 37–70; M. Dintenfass, 'Entrepreneurial Failure Reconsidered: The Case of the Interwar British Coal Industry', *Business. History. Review* 62 (1988), pp. 1–34.

69. Taylor, 'The Coal Industry'.

70. See B. Fine, with K. O'Donnell and M. Prevezer, 'Coal Before Nationalization' in B. Fine and L. Harris (eds.), *The Peculiarities of the British Economy* (Lawrence and Wishart: 1985), pp. 285–323.

71. J. Melling, 'Safety, Supervision and the Politics of Productivity in the British Coalmining Industry, 1900–1960' in J. Melling and A. McKinlay (eds), *Management, Labour and Industrial Politics in Modern Europe* (Edward Eigar, Cheltenham: 1996).

72. A. Campbell, 'Colliery Mechanisation and the Lanarkshire Miners', *Bulletin of the Society for the Study of Labour History* 49 (1984), pp. 37–43.

73. *CG*, 7 December 1923, pp. 1433–44.

74. T. Boyns, 'Of Machines and Men in the 1920s', *Llafur* 5:2 (1989).

75. *Ibid.*, pp. 3–7; *CG*, 9 February 1923, p. 344; *CG*, 17 July 1923, p. 406.

76. *CG*, 3 July 1925, p. 30.

77. Fine *et al.*, 'Coal Before Nationalisation'.

78. 'Although machine mining has been practised for 25 years or more by some collieries, there has been a remarkable extension of the system during the last seven years during which the percentage of the national output of

machine-coal has been doubled and the percentage of coal conveyed tre-
bled': Institute of Mining Engineers, in evidence to the Royal Commission
on Safety in Coal Mines (1938), *Minutes of Evidence*, p. 1339.

79. Supple, *The History of the British Coal Industry, Vol.* 4, p. 383.
80. *Annual Report of the Secretary for Mines* (1927 and 1938).
81. Reid *Report*, p. 65.
82. Supple, *The History of the British Coal Industry, Vol.* 4, p. 388.
83. *Ibid.*, pp. 318–87.
84. E. Rowley, Inspector of the Midland and Southern Division, Royal
Commission on Safety in Coal Mines (1938), *Minutes of Evidence*. p. 188.
85. *Ibid.*
86. J. W. England, *A Short History of the National Association of Colliery Overmen,
Deputies and Shotfirers, Midland Area, 1908–1962* (R. K. Rudd, Hindley: 1963).
See also Royal Commission on the Coal Industry (Sankey) (1919), *Minutes of
Evidence*, Q. 4,854.
87. Royal Commission on Safety in Coal Mines, *Minutes of Evidence*, QQ.
15,701–2.
88. Melling, 'Safety and Supervision in British Coalmining', p. 157. See also
Newey, 'The Introduction of Machine Mining at Newdigate Colliery',
Transactions of the Institution of Mining Engineers
89. H. S. Jevons, *The British Coal Trade* (Kegan Paul, Trench, Trubner and Co.:
1920), p. 528.
90. Royal Commission on Safety in Coal Mines, *Minutes of Evidence*, Q. 15,511.
91. Frowen, on behalf of the colliery deputies, reported the 'harassing conditions' under which his members worked in 'nearly all coalfields' and
emphasized: 'In some pits the overmen harass the deputy very much';
Royal Commission on Safety in Coal Mines, *Minutes of Evidence*, QQ. 15,512
and 15,547. Accounts by miners or their representatives highlighted the
'immense speeding up of the work underground' that was forced by supervisory staff who had 'to carry out the owners' policy of maximum effort at
minimum cost': J. Jones, *The Coal Scuttle* (Faber: 1936), p. 20.
92. For example, see Newey, 'Machine Mining at Newdigate Colliery'; Boyns,
'Of Machines and Men'.
93. T. Boyns, 'Powell Duffryn: The Use of Machinery and Production Planning
Techniques in the South Wales Coalfield' in K. Tenfelde (ed.), *Towards a
Social History of Mining in the 19th and 20th Centuries* (C. H. Beck, Munich:
1992).
94. E. M. Hann, *Brief History of the Powell Duffryn Steam Coal Co.,* 1864–1921
(1922); T. Boyns, 'Rationalisation in the Inter-war Period: The Case of the
South Wales Steam Coal Industry', *Business History* 29:3 (1987), pp. 282–303.
95. Boyns, 'Powell Duffryn', p. 376.
96. *Ibid.*, p. 377.
97. W. Ashworth with M. Pegg, *The History of the British Coal Industry, Vol.* 5,
1946–1982: The Nationalized Industry (Clarendon Press: 1986), pp. 213–20.

9
Shop-Floor Bargaining and the Struggle for Job Control in the British Automobile and Aerospace Industries, 1950–82

Mike Richardson, Paul Stewart and Andy Danford

Introduction

In the UK automobile and aerospace industries, the struggle over job control and rewards for labour expended in the production process was particularly intense in the period of steady economic growth, high and stable employment, and low inflation following the Second World War. This struggle reached its zenith during a phase of increasing output in the 1950s and early 1960s. By the late 1960s, however, as wages and unemployment began to rise and the rate of growth slowed there was a discernible shift in management industrial relations strategy and efforts by government to curb the authority and influence of shop stewards. Despite disparities both between and within these respective industries, particularly the higher skill levels required by the aerospace sector, common experiences of the transformation of labour conditions of work are noticeable. In mapping some key historical struggles of automobile and aerospace workers against management forms of authority and control, it should be possible to distinguish the critical dynamics prevalent in both industries. Knowledge of the trajectory of labour relations, and the pattern and character of conflict, is critical to understanding and accounting for continuity and change in the social relations of production.

What interests us here is the differing form and content of the antagonistic relationship between capital and labour at particular times in order to enhance our understanding of specific processes of change. These are necessarily bounded by prevailing geographical, social, economic, and political climatic factors as well as industry specific characteristics such

as skill levels; the latter impacting on unions' ability to hold some lever-
age over the regulation of labour supply. Although much has been written on industrial relations in the UK motor industry, to shed more light
on the dynamics of shop-floor bargaining between 1950 and 1982 comparisons are made with experiences in the aerospace industry, which
has received little academic attention. This chapter, therefore, seeks
to highlight the similarities and differences in these two industries in
the shift from the predominance of piecework in the post war period
– typified by the growth of shop-floor organization that strengthened
workers' bargaining position over piece-rates, ensuring mutuality was
real rather than theoretical – to a regime of direct control as witnessed
by the implementation of measured day work (MDW). Moreover, while
this period in general terms can be characterized in two phases (from
mutuality to increasing managerial control) this trajectory was uneven
and by no means unambiguous. Even with the introduction of MDW
across the sectors, worker resistance was still evident.

The critical issues here are to link the various phases of the tensions,
conflicts and accommodations over the capital–labour relationship in
two emblematic sectors - one characterized by British-owned motor
companies' pursuit of Fordist ideals[1] and the other characterized by
high skill and heavy reliance on the State in financing research and
development, and in awarding government contracts for aircraft and
weapons for Britain's military.[2] While all these issues cannot be covered
in full here, this chapter attempts to begin to highlight the contours
of change, stressing the divergent as well as the related experiences
between the two industries.

Informality and localism: regulation and control on the shop floor

By the late 1950s there emerged two principle characteristics, informality and localism, in the automobile and aerospace industries that,
in combination, came to determine management-labour relations
throughout the 1960s and most of the 1970s. The effect of this development of informality and localism, bargaining processes that had broken free of the formal industry wide negotiating arrangements, was to
weaken the influence of and central role played by the trade unions'
national organizations. Moreover, this development could be seen to
occur not just at plant level but also inside the plants themselves.[3] Since
shop stewards depended upon area support within a particular plant,
improving the remuneration and situation of workers in a specific area

often led to individual stewards holding differing attitudes which, at times, placed them at odds with leading shop stewards.[4] This was particularly the case in the motor industry and led to considerable conflict over wage levels both within and between plants and across companies, where national agreements were either ignored or seen to be ineffectual in their implementation. Localism was also apparent in the aerospace industry: 'The workers in the aircraft industry have built up a good trade union organization which produces useful shop-floor representation on questions of wages, work allocation, labour load etc.' to the extent that '[t]he management have to consult and co-operate with the shop-floor workers in order to maintain production.'[5] The result of informality and localism was that for all intents and purposes the management of discontent was appropriated from national union officialdom, which is reflected in the increase in unofficial strikes in both the automobile and aerospace industries.

The Labour government that came to power in 1964 set its store in modernizing British industry. Part of this process included the attempt to improve industrial relations. Concerned about the increase in unofficial strikes and restrictive practices, the government set up a Royal Commission under the direction of Lord Donovan to 'examine the relationships between management and employees, and the work of employers' associations.'[6] To better understand the causes of strikes in manufacturing, the Commission decided to examine the automobile industry in more depth because of its strike proneness. As a result of this examination the Commission pronounced that:

> We attach more importance to the industry's wage structure as a cause of strikes. It is plain that employees' actual earnings are not determined by the negotiations conducted at industry level…. Two major manufacturers (Ford and Vauxhall) are not in any case in the Engineering Employers' Federation, which is one of the parties to such negotiations. In the other remaining companies earnings are a long way in advance of the rates so settled at industry level, and a crucial part is therefore played by workplace negotiations.[7]

That the workplace was the site of real industry negotiations reflected the strength of the power-base built by shop stewards and the readiness of workers to take industrial action in the favourable economic climate of the early 1960s. As Donovan noted, this informal domain, where actual decision making occurred, was inherently unstable deriving from a highly competitive pattern of remuneration. Yet this competitive facet of the employment relationship reinforced steward power within and between plants and different companies.[8] How was it possible for stewards to attain such a high degree of knowledge of the micro conditions of other plants not just within their own companies but those of other firms as well? This became possible as a result of the growth of what were known as 'combine committees' or 'parallel unionism'.[9] These materialized in the automobile industry in the post-war era as organized labour was much strengthened by the war-time accommodation between trade unions and government. In the aircraft industry these first emerged as a *tour de force* in 1935 when union activists formed the Aircraft Shop Stewards National Council to coordinate solidarity work.[10] Combine committees were effectively an unrecognized system of union organization running parallel to the recognized one as defined by the Donovan Commission. Despite being frowned upon by trade union centres, the emergence of these shop-floor networks (the combine committees) between shop stewards in different plants allowed stewards to get to grips with the minutiae of the industry, probably making them better informed, and usually more articulate about processes, than plant management.

While a sector combine committee was stymied in the automobile industry, they nevertheless flourished for a considerable period within companies, despite the downturn in the economy that began in the late 1960s and continued throughout most of the 1970s. In aerospace, combine committees continued to thrive both within and across manufacturing plants and companies throughout the period. For instance at British Aircraft Corporation (BAC) Guided Weapons division in the late 1960s, the plant's Electrical, Electronic, Telecommunications and Plumbing Union (EETPU) shop steward recalled 'we had our own shop stewards committee with the fitters, the coppersmiths and the transport and general, which was about 18 stewards at Dynamics [BAC Guided Weapons].'[11] Eventually, in the early 1970s, BAC Guided Weapons set up their own shop stewards committee: 'so we had a few disputes and sit-ins and we ended up with our own autonomy where we negotiated for Dynamics [BAC Guided Weapons] and they negotiated for the rest of aerospace, although we did work closely together.'[12]

In the post-war period it was axiomatic that whomever 'called' local agreements determined local power.[13] In this situation while industry wide agreements existed they were only ever as good as the local industrial relations environments in which they were introduced. A well organized plant could, and often did, secure significant advances on national agreements.[14] Piecework, which served employers so well in the interwar years when trade union organization was weak, provided shop stewards in the post war years with the means to bargain effectively. In the post war boom, union membership increased and shop stewards were able to take advantage of the drive for increased production, and a tight labour market, to demand higher piece-rates knowing that employers were under pressure to keep their plants running for fear of losing business to their rivals.

This was the view of the Donovan Commission, which famously attributed the absence of national level control over workplace institutions as the prime cause for the inchoate nature of industrial relations in the auto industry and elsewhere.[15] The consequent fragmentation of bargaining which allowed, in the view of the Commission, undue scope for local determination of, *inter alia*, pay and conditions was the principal reason for the high level of disputes over pay related issues.[16] Yet informality was crucial for managers who needed to resolve local difficulties speedily, and crucial for stewards who needed to hold the line against management in defence of the 'gang', or work group in their shop-floor area.[17] The Donovan Commission lamented the demise in the influence of full-time union officials:

> There is no doubt in our view, that the unions have not had sufficient influence on the workplace situation. There are a number of reasons for this, one of which is the readiness of management to deal directly with shop stewards to the exclusion of full-time officials.[18]

With the growing importance of local bargaining the ambiguity of the informal system emerged. On the one hand, the establishment of local bargaining units provided shop stewards with the mechanism to resist or challenge managerial authority. This enabled them to take advantage, in those plants that operated piecework payment systems, to negotiate increases in the wages of pieceworkers. This resulted in rapidly increasing wages and wage drift.

On the other hand, the ability to generalize this local power along national lines proved largely elusive. For instance, at this time unions in the Coventry car industry 'appear not to have developed a company or even plant wide view of industrial relations'.[19] Stewards, however, had to prove themselves by providing leadership and addressing the concerns of their members. This was not easy. For example, in 1951 at the Rolls-Royce aero-engine plant in Hillington, Glasgow, shop stewards complained that their members frequently took unauthorized action to bring about a resolution of their grievances, which stewards seemed powerless to prevent. Department identities undermined the stewards' efforts to pursue factory-wide negotiations.[20] Thus localism in union-management orientation inevitably recreated, at the same time as it reinforced, local steward propensity to settle things at source. Inevitably this allowed for competitive wage bargaining; whatever the other disadvantages, labour could be a relatively powerful player. Given that it was the wage and remuneration system which encouraged this process, the following section looks at some examples to shed some light on its workings.

Aerospace industry: piecework to measured day work (MDW)

A pieceworker's pay, wholly or in part, is directly linked to work measurement: the time taken to produce work of the appropriate quality. In the aerospace industry of the 1960s and 1970s, in essence the pieceworker's wage comprised a basic rate that varied with skill and an incentive bonus that was usually premised on a standard time allowance to complete a specific job and applied to individuals or groups (gangs) of workers. By contrast, MDW is a payment system that provides a regular weekly wage, negotiated between management and the appropriate union, for which workers are expected to meet standard times for each job set by work study engineers.[21] In the 1950s and 1960s, a period of tight labour markets in engineering, aircraft workers exerted increasing upward pressure on piece-rates. Managerial control over piecework systems weakened as workers combined to resist the imposition of demanding time values by rate-fixers. The rate-fixers determined the level of effort required to produce a new or altered job. Ostensibly, piecework wage determination involved a process of continuous bargaining between the rate-fixer and the operator. But 'custom and practice' demanded that once set piece-rates could not be altered unless changes occurred in the product or productive method. Defence against rate cutting depended on union strength at the workplace. Organized resistance from gang workers to 'adjust' the effort bargain often occurred if piece-rates were deemed to be unfair. Shop stewards, however, were frequently called upon to act on their members' behalf in respect to individual piecework bargains, a time-consuming process, which gave reason for some shop stewards to favour time-work over piecework.[22] However, one Rolls-Royce (Coventry) convenor representing aircraft workers argued that in well organized union shops piecework could lead to higher earnings and give workers greater control over the labour process, as the operator had direct control over the pace of production. Moreover:

The continual battle over rates makes the workers very militant, for when the rate-fixer comes out to argue with you, you're immediately faced with the basic element of class struggle: exploitation, potential or actual. [23]

On the deficit side, piecework could generate inequities and weaken shop-floor solidarity based on egalitarian principles.[24] As reported at one Rolls-Royce negotiating committee meeting: 'members come into piecework areas and can't get into the "brotherhood"' [25] which resulted in pay inequality. And differentials between operators on piecework could be substantial; often the cause of much tension among workers because some earned substantially more than others. A retired British Aircraft Corporation (BAC) convenor observed: 'I mean, say the average was one hundred pounds with shop average, I mean, you'd get guys on one hundred and forty, one hundred and fifty pounds.'[26]

This convenor recalled how rate-fixing disputes were continuous. Rate-fixers were described as some 'of the most obnoxious people you could ever come across'. A retired shop-floor worker in the same company likened rate-fixers with the 'Gestapo'.[27] If workers were the least bit timid, some rate-fixers would try to take advantage and cut the rate, and in so doing bring down the shop average. This was important to all concerned because when a job value was in dispute, which was an everyday occurrence, affected workers were paid the average earnings of the shop. So the shop steward's role was to contest those rate-fixer values that fell below that deemed to be fair. The BAC convenor recalled that, on those occasions, he would take the case to the senior rate-fixer and either reach a compromise or place the job in dispute. Once in dispute operators, under the national engineering agreement, had to be given another job until the dispute was resolved. Non-compliance with this agreement resulted in a stoppage of work by the gang or section affected.[28]

These types of disputes were common across the aerospace industry and in some plants were incessant. For instance, at Rolls-Royce Bristol engine plant the frequency of disputes was of serious concern to the company. In 1970, Rolls-Royce management protested: 'We cannot allow the "argy bargy" of the existing system to carry on where there are daily argument[s] in every detail.'[29]

The following year, 4 February 1971, the company was forced into receivership. The Conservative government bailed out the company by taking it into State ownership with the intention of turning the company around and returning it to the private sector. Nationalization was not the policy of a Conservative government. State ownership did not bring with it a resolution to labour relations problems. Disputes over piece-rates continued reaching crisis proportions again in 1974. Increasingly concerned by this state of affairs on 29 January 1975, R. Whitfield, managing director of Rolls-Royce, wrote to union representatives:

I regret that in 1974 we continued to suffer industrial disputes, each with its own deadly effect on our performance. We have not been free from some form of industrial action on any working day since I was appointed your Managing Director. The vast majority of these industrial disputes involved manual employees at Bristol. It is vitally important for our future that a new wage structure should be agreed for the Bristol factories – one which is felt to be fair, which achieves constructive relationships and working practices, and which drastically reduces the amount of industrial action we have suffered.[30]

Although Bristol was opposed to MDW, most other plants in the Rolls-Royce combine committee had accepted its introduction and Bristol workers found that as a result their wages, relative to other Rolls-Royce workers in the UK, were falling behind. Moreover, the company was preparing the ground for the introduction of MDW without union involvement. Thus the decision was taken 'to take the bull by the horns and get involved in the new scheme'. After lengthy negotiations in the spring of 1975 an agreement was reached on a Bristol wage structure that included the replacement of piecework, which directly affected around one sixth of the workforce, with MDW. The new structure comprised six grades of labour with wages ranging from £40 per week on the lowest grade to £57 on the highest. This lifted Bristol workers back into second place in the wages league behind Coventry.[31]

Around the same time, just before nationalization of the industry in 1977, an agreement was reached between the engineering unions and management at BAC Guided Weapons in Bristol to abolish piecework. The strong bargaining position of labour on the shop floor had resulted in wage drift. This was in part a consequence of the rise in 'non-negotiated' shop-floor wages, primarily fragmented piecework bargaining.[32] As the plant's retired EETPU convenor put it: 'I think the Company had a problem ... because the shop-floor wages were escalating out of control really ... quality control, the clerical people ... the planners and engineers, really were being placed relative to the shop-floor, whose wages were the highest.'[33]

The carrot offered by BAC, to unions and their members, to replace piecework with MDW was full sick pay; increased holidays; improved pension scheme; guaranteed regular and predictable earnings; and the discontinuance of the weekly confrontation with the rate-fixer.[34] Ostensibly, control over the pace of production shifted from mutuality between the rate-fixer and the operator to the foreman. In reality workers were still able to assert some informal control by working at the same pace as before (under the piecework system). Knowledge of production was still to a certain degree in workers' hands and thus foremen were not always able to fully assert their authority. The retired BAC convenor explained:

> Well they put it [control] back to the foremen, but I don't think the foremen or really the system was adequate. I mean people were so used to working in a certain way by that time that the supervisor would give you a job and the job ensured that you were really working and that was it.[35]

Nonetheless, the replacement of piecework with MDW was a qualitative change in that 'by separating negotiations over pay and work, change can be introduced with less resistance'.[36] This, together with collapse of the post war consensus; rising unemployment; nationalization of BAC in 1977, re-privatization in 1979; and the emergence of Thatcherism, raised the stakes and put increased pressure on shop stewards and convenors. At the once State owned British Aerospace (BAe):

> The collective strength of the shop-floor unions was now central to the bargaining machinery, and more effectively controlled the rate of exploitation than the traditional control battles between the individual rate-fixer and individual operator.[37]

At Westland Helicopters, in 1975, management abolished piecework by decree. This provocative action was met by a strike on 16 May which lasted several weeks. On 23 June, a back-to-work agreement was reached that, except for the pension scheme, secured staff conditions for manual workers including a new sick pay scheme, and an ex gratia payment of £50 to skilled employees and pro rata payments to other grades in exchange for withdrawing resistance to the introduction of MDW.[38]

At Rolls-Royce, company strategy to eliminate piecework was first initiated in 1968. It took a decade to achieve, and the end was bitter. In 1978, a small pocket of workers employed at Parkside, Coventry, was still paid by the piece. Thus, the elimination of piecework for these remaining 330 manual workers still paid by that system was, in the company's eyes, critical as the Rolls-Royce workforce looked to these pieceworkers 'as the pace-setters for the whole pay structure'.[39] In early April 1978, 2600 manual workers were suspended without pay after refusing to work 'normally' following the breakdown of pay negotiations. The company demanded that an agreement over the elimination of piecework for the remaining 330 manual workers must be part of any wage settlement. The union insisted that the two issues (wage claim and the elimination of piecework) be dealt with independently citing that: 'every other section of Rolls-Royce Ltd throughout the country has been paid the 10% in full'.[40] Union members started a work-in. The Company cut off the power, so the workers occupied the plant. The occupation lasted four weeks before a settlement was reached that included shop stewards acceding to the elimination of piecework 'provided that they [members] do not lose money from the change over'.[41]

Thus, by the late 1970s, piecework had been vanquished and MDW well established. Yet, despite the establishment of MDW, control over the pace of production was still contested. For instance, the launching of the Rolls-Royce Bristol Survival Plan in 1982 revealed that restrictive practices were still evident in the company despite the introduction of MDW. This plan set out the problems faced by the organization, objectives and scope, and a detailed point by point diagnosis of the effect of restrictive work practices. A remedy or a requirement crowned each point. The problem:

- Excessively high indirect-to direct support in all departments;
- Low overall productivity;
- Poor response to Engineering and Manufacturing Programmes;
- An atmosphere of conflict and narrow-mindedness between groups.[42]

Two examples out of 59 of changes required in working practices (see Table 9.1) are suffice to reveal that the implementation of MDW at Rolls-Royce may have enhanced managerial control but it did not eliminate all forms of shop-floor control and resistance:

Clearly, despite the universality of MDW in the early 1980s, at Rolls-Royce job times were not always recognized and work study did not have the run of the factory.

Table 9.1   **Bristol Survival Plan (1982).** Standby agreements and other established working practices. Items for review

Subject	Areas affected	Current effect	Management requirement
48 Toolroom: recognition of estimated time standards	No. 2 Toolroom	Refusal to recognize work estimates times for jobs and to permit monitoring of work to these estimates results in: high tool costs due to excessive time taken. inability to investigate causes of excess time and hence to eliminate problems faced by the toolmaker. Difficulties in performance and cost monitoring	Toolmaker should be accountable for work produced and time taken
49 Tool manufacture: restriction applied to Planner/ Estimator	No. 2 Toolroom	Refusal to allow Planner/ Estimator on the shop-floor to discuss job requirements causes loading of foreman with excessive duties that need not involve him	Planner/ Estimator to discuss job requirement with Toolmaker

Automobile industry: piecework to measured day work

It is important to note that employers adopted piecework to stimulate greater productive effort from their workforce. In many instances, especially where organized labour was weak, workers' experience of piecework was one of self-exploitation as they strove to produce more and more in order to achieve a living wage. The strength of piecework in the post war boom, however, was that 'negotiations for increases can take place on the time for the job whenever a change takes place in the means, method or material involved.'[43] Eschewing central bargaining arrangements and establishing the dominance of local pay bargaining and job regulation were particularly apparent in the motor industry. The Donovan report was especially concerned to remedy the disorder resulting from conflict between formal and informal systems of industrial relations:

> At Morris Motors Ltd., Cowley, for instance, the Council found that in 1965, 256 out of 297 stoppages of work had occurred before the senior shop steward had even a chance to put the grievance into procedure.

In the first half of 1966, again 128 stoppages out of 142 took place before the senior shop steward had time to act on them....[44]

In effect the Donovan report saw part of the solution resting on the introduction of factory-wide MDW agreements.[45] The most bitterly fought struggle against the introduction of MDW took place at British Leyland's Cowley plant in Oxford. Thus, despite many ready examples we have taken this plant as an exemplar of this invariant relationship across the sector in Britain.

The history of the Cowley plant (or complex of plants as it was) is an instructive one. For our purposes we focus upon the reason and consequence of the introduction of MDW in 1971 (although, it did not achieve complete coverage in British Leyland (BL) until 1975 with nationalization). Why was the 'piece-rate system' the defining social and political face of industrial relations both at BL and across the automobile industry? And why was its successor, MDW, so central to management between the 1970s to the late 1980s?

By the mid-1960s, the pay of 72 per cent of the Cowley workforce was either directly or indirectly based on piecework payment systems.[46] The number of shop stewards had increased by 280 per cent between 1959 and 1966.[47] Originally piecework, when it was introduced in the 1920s, had been an effective tool of management control in an era of weak trade union organization. This was the case until the 1950s by which time unions had achieved a strong workplace presence, represented by determined shop stewards, and 'control'; or at least a significant degree of regulation of the piecework system:

> [Management] rightly...saw piecework as one of the pillars of the shop steward movement in the car industry and they knew that to attack it was to attack the shop stewards.

> Our stance [the union, the TGWU, at plant level] was the outright defence of the piecework system despite the fact that the piecework system was originally brought in by [the owner] when his plants were non-union as the most effective way to maximise profitably.[48]

However, Hyman and Elger in recalling this period argued that one should be cautious 'against over-romantic conceptions of the efficacy of workers' job controls...Frequently they operated within limits acceptable to employers'.[49] For example piece-rate systems 'cushioned the company [BMC, Cowley] against production losses, for the basic principle of "no work, no pay" meant that workers, rather than the company, bore the cost of "idle time" or "shut outs".[50]

Nonetheless, the description above is really an account of the balance of power in the plant at the level of the assembly track itself. The level of earnings of 40 per cent of the workforce 'was dependent not on their own production but on the earnings of pieceworkers' mainly employed on assembly.[51] Thus, outcomes from the struggle over piecework rates and job controls during this period were fundamental to both the company and its employees. It is clear that by the mid-1960s the piece-rate system had led to the erosion of management control, declining productivity and wage drift.[52] As elsewhere, the Morris management at Cowley chose to ignore these developments as it was, along with other motor manufacturers, too preoccupied with output while demand for cars was buoyant in the 1950s and early 1960s.[53] Managers of specific work areas were usually quite desperate to forge local deals with the stewards, who were recognized by management as the negotiators on behalf of workers in particular areas. In the 1970s, however, as the market situation further deteriorated, a pattern of increasing management frustration with shop steward autonomy emerged.[54] 'Once management had lost control of the piecework system, they no longer wanted it, and sought to replace it by an alternative system...'[55]

The alternative system, MDW, was forcibly introduced in December 1971 after a long and bitter struggle. Cowley shop stewards did secure an important concession, however, in that mutual agreement had to be reached before the results of work study could be implemented. In the event of a failure to agree a temporary arrangement to maintain production involving 'fair effort' would operate until a final agreement was concluded.[56] That shop stewards were able to secure a mutuality clause slowed the company's capacity to reassert management control and obtain the full benefit of MDW. However, the company had secured a platform enabling it to move towards intensifying the work effort and reducing comparative wage levels.[57]

The idea behind MDW[58] was to attempt to centralize decision making, first at the factory level and then at the level of the firm. This was why at Cowley, and at BL's other sites, although with varying degrees of conflict, the unions opposed the introduction of MDW. MDW was a means by which management could set wage rates at plant level and later, company level.

The centralizing drive behind MDW also goes some way towards accounting for the fact that the union centres (outside the plants and nationally) were lukewarm in opposition. Negotiations and decisions on remuneration would be completely taken out of the plants and out of the hands of the shop stewards. At Cowley, after a six week strike in 1970, the workforce was forced to accept MDW on the new Marina model assembly line but without agreement from the local union branch. However, the company was unable to achieve the productivity increases that it required because Cowley workers refused to strike an agreement to allow work study experts on to the production line. The company attempted to force the issue but this prompted a walkout. Acknowledging the unfavourable climate management decided to bide its time and conceded the principle of mutuality, and an agreement with the unions was struck.[59] This agreement re-introduced an element of *in situ* control by the stewards. Basically 'mutuality' meant that any change to the line-speed had to be negotiated with the shop steward in his or her particular area. The 'mutuality' agreement was management's concession to get MDW through. Nevertheless, while the 'mutuality' deal returned a significant element of steward negotiating power the beginning of the end for shop-floor autonomy had been signalled with the introduction of MDW.

In 1974, the company attempted to circumvent the mutuality agreement by imposing new schedules on the Marina line without union agreement. A full-scale stoppage in April followed. A letter was sent by the plant director to striking workers demanding that they work the Marina line under new conditions without union agreement:

> ... report for work, tell your foreman you will give your assignment a fair effort at a line-speed of 30 per hour. To those who refuse, I must ask the question – do you wish to remain in our employment? If you won't work we must assume you wish to leave us and we will respond accordingly.[60]

Three days after this letter was sent the workers voted to accept the company's terms and return to work. 'Management opened the plant the following day and the industrial engineers commenced their studies on their own terms.'[61] The company finally accomplished what it had set out to do in 1971.

The period after this was marked by the corporatist engagement between the unions and the Labour government and the establishment of the National Enterprise Board (NEB); a vehicle for holding controlling stakes in manufacturing firms 'as a way of injecting public money into private companies, and exercising some control over the use of the funds, while encouraging competition'.[62] This government control was exercised to encourage company restructuring and rationalization, as British Leyland workers experienced after the NEB took over the company helm in 1975. This is crucial for making sense of the historical import of MDW. The automotive industry was but one of a number of sectors where the Labour government and official unions struggled to contain shop-floor power. While often exaggerated, on sporadic occasions this local strength, nonetheless, significantly undermined national trade union and Labour government industrial and economic strategy. The introduction of MDW (1970–73) at British Leyland Motor Company (BLMC), followed by the formation in 1975 of British Leyland under State control, may have cleared the way for the Company to bring about the centralization of bargaining on remuneration and other conditions 'but it was to prove a long-drawn-out and conflict-prone operation'.[63] This was both cause and effect of the diminution of shop steward power, a long sought goal of both trade unions outside both plant and firm, and of government, as codified in the Donovan Commission from as early as 1965–68.

This diminution of shop steward power was reflected in the unions' acceptance of the Ryder plan which included the approval of the executive 'right to manage' without union interference and endorsement of a worker participation scheme. Leading Communist Party convenors, Derek Robinson, Peter Nicholas and Tom Steward gave credence to the scheme by enthusiastically taking up places on the BL Cars Council. Together with other council members, and union national secretaries Jack Jones (TGWU) and Hugh Scanlon (AUEW), they supported a strategy of company survival at all costs even though this meant accepting redundancies, plant closures and opposing strikes.[64] Senior stewards became 'dangerously detached from their membership'.[65] Their actions, however unwittingly, paved the way for the appointment of Michael Edwardes as Chair of British Leyland (1977–82) who was to preside over reducing the workforce by half; significantly intensifying the pace of production; cutting real wages; and sacking leading shop stewards including Derek Robinson.

Edwardes, by jettisoning recent commitments to worker participation, as defined by the Ryder plan, was able to break union solidarity on the basis that it had no alternative strategy. As Edwardes himself put it, his aim was to 're-establish management authority'.[66] According to him, the Ryder report reinforced bureaucratic decision making. It would have to go. It was 'a bureaucratic paper chase dissipating management resources and effort. Some management decisions were delayed by months while the joint consultative machinery tried unsuccessfully to grind out a consensus'.[67]

Edwardes' hard line approach was signalled by his determination to tear up existing agreements and sweep away the remnants of mutuality. His aim was essentially to destroy traditional job controls and rationalize production. Plant closures followed, first the Speke Triumph TR7 factory and then plants at Canley, Abingdon, Castle Bromwich, Liverpool and Park Royal in London. Edwardes' final triumph came, in November 1981, when the TGWU acceded to take international levels of competition as 'the bench mark for all future negotiations on pay, conditions and manning'. Automotive workers across the globe were increasingly subjected to 'chasing each other's effort under the watchful eye of bankers and managers intent only on the preservation of their profits and the capitalist system'.[68]

Conclusion

In the 1950s and 60s, informal localized bargaining came to characterize union-management negotiations in both the automobile and aerospace industries. The importance of shop stewards directly representing their members in these industries, as indeed elsewhere in manufacturing, increased to the extent that this development became the subject of a major inquiry, the Donovan Commission. By the time the Donovan report was published, however, the intensification of international competition had already compelled car producers to put in place plans to reassert management authority; piecework was to be eliminated and replaced by MDW. The ending of piecework was strenuously opposed and took over a decade to achieve. Only management concessions such as *ex gratia* payments and the shift to harmonization in the conditions of employment in aerospace and mutuality in automobiles, in conjunction with an increasingly hostile economic climate, cleared the way for employers to establish MDW. This major reform was buttressed by State intervention, particularly in the automobile industry. By taking control of British Leyland the State set in train an extensive restructuring and rationalization programme in the context of increasing international competition and a history of low capital investment. That this was undertaken under a Labour administration served to heighten expectations among union leaders and most, but not all, leading shop stewards that this was to be the salvation for the company and indeed the British car industry. Instead it opened the door for Edwardes, on his appointment as Chair of British Leyland, to carry out a further rationalization of the company and reassert managerial authority.

The reassertion of managerial authority did not happen to the same degree in the aerospace industry. Unlike the car industry, aerospace, at least the military arm, had access to a captive market, the State. While this point should not be exaggerated, as increasingly during this period the industry became dependent on export-related products, it should not be ignored.[69] Another important difference between the industries, as highlighted in the introduction, is that aerospace products are not mass produced and require more highly skilled workers than the car industry. Therefore the influence of craft unions has been greater and employers' dependence on skills heavier, which has enabled stewards to sustain influence at the workplace to a greater extent than their counterparts in the car industry.

Notes

1. See A. Mair, 'From British Leyland Motor Corporation to Rover Group: The Search for a Viable British Model' in M. Freyssenet, A. Mair, K. Shimizu, and G. Volpato (eds), *One Best Way? Trajectories and Industrial Models of the World's Automobile Producers* (Oxford University Press: 1998), p. 399.
2. See A. Rooney, 'The Aircraft Industry' in K. Coates (ed.), *Can the Workers Run Industry?* (The Institute for Workers' Control, Speare Books: 1968); J. Lovering, 'Military Expenditure and the Restructuring of Capitalism: The Military Industry in Britain', *Cambridge Journal of Economics*, 14 (1990), pp. 453–67.
3. See Rooney, 'The Aircraft Industry' in H. A. Turner, G. Clack and G. Roberts, *Labour Relations in the Motor Industry* (George Allen and Unwin: 1967).
4. Turner *et al.*, *Labour Relations in the Motor Industry*, p. 222.
5. Rooney, 'The Aircraft Industry', p. 209.
6. *Royal Commission on Trade Unions and Employers' Associations 1965–1968* (Donovan), *Report*, Cmnd 3623 (HMSO: 1968), p. 6.
7. *Ibid.*, p. 104.
8. Turner *et al.*, *Labour Relations in the Motor Industry*.
9. *Ibid.*, pp. 216–223.
10. N. Fishman, *The British Communist Party and the Trade Unions, 1933–45* (Scholar Press: 1995).
11. Frank Tamlyn, retired BAC (EETPU) shop steward, interview, November, 2003.
12. *Ibid.*
13. Turner *et al.*, *Labour Relations in the Motor Industry*; P. Higgs, 'The Convenor' in R. Fraser (ed.) *Work: Twenty Personal Accounts* (Penguin: 1969); A. Friedman, *Industry and Labour. Class Struggle at Work and Monopoly Capitalism* (Macmillan: 1977); R. Church, *The Rise and Decline of the British Motor Industry* (Macmillan: 1994).
14. Higgs, 'The Convenor', p. 124.
15. *Royal Commission on Trade Unions and Employers' Associations 1965–1968.*

16. Notably the government was not convinced that formalization of industrial relations as recommended by Donovan was enough. While Barbara Castle, Secretary of State at the Department of Employment and Productivity (after April 1968), was concerned about the increase in unofficial strikes she was not convinced that to formalize industrial relations procedures at company and plant level would resolve this problem. The Ford Motor Company, for instance, had procedural agreements in place and eschewed piecework but was still far from strike free (R. Croucher, 'The Coventry Toolroom Agreement, 1941–1972, Part 2: abolition', *Historical Studies in Industrial Relations* 9:38 (Spring 2000), pp. 37–71).

17. T. Donnelly and D. Thoms, 'Trade Unions, Management and the search for production in the Coventry Motor Car Industry', *Business History* 31:2 (1989), pp. 98–113.

18. *Royal Commission on Trade Unions and Employers' Associations 1965–1968*, p. 104.

19. Donnelly and Thoms, 'Trade Unions, Management and the search for production in the Coventry Motor Car Industry', p. 107.

20. A. McKinlay, and J. Melling, 'The Shop Floor Politics of Productivity: Work, Power and Authority Relations in British Engineering, c. 1945–57' in A. Campell, N. Fishman and J. McIlroy (eds), *British Trade Unions and Industrial Politics, Vol.1: The Post-War Compromise, 1945–64* (Ashgate: 1999), p. 234. For similar examples in the automobile industry see D. Lyddon, 'The Car Industry, 1945–79: Shop Stewards and Workplace Unionism' in C. Wrigley (ed.), *a History of British Industrial Relations 1939–1979: Industrial Relations in a Declining Economy* (Edward Elgar: 1996), pp. 203–04.

21. T. Lupton and D. Gowler, 'Selecting a Wage Payment System' in T. Lupton (ed.) *Payment Systems* (Penguin: 1969), pp. 239–77.

22. B. Brown, *Piecework Bargaining* (Heinemann: 1973), p. 125.

23. Higgs, 'The Convenor', p. 163.

24. Brown, *Piecework Bargaining*, p. 147.

25. Rolls-Royce Negotiating Committee, Modern Record Centre, University of Warwick (MRC), MSS 390/1/1/2, 12 December 1969.

26. Frank Tamlyn, interview.

27. Bert Yeandle, retired BAC employee, interview November 2002.

28. Frank Tamlyn, interview.

29. Rolls-Royce Negotiating Committee, MRC, MSS 390/1/1/3, 15 July 1970.

30. Parkside Bulletin (Rolls-Royce) Issue 58, Feb/March 1975, MRC, MSS 390/4/1/48.

31. J. Blackley, AUEW, Convenor Rolls-Royce 'Rolls-Royce New Pay Structure' *Bristol Socialist*, July/August 1975; *Parkside Bulletin* (Rolls-Royce) Issue 60 April/May 1975, MRC, MSS 390/4/1/50.

32. Brown, *Piecework Bargaining*, p. 26.

33. Frank Tamlyn, interview.

34. *Ibid.*

35. *Ibid.*

36. A. Flanders, 'Measured Daywork and Collective Bargaining', *British Journal of Industrial Relations* 11:3 (1973), p. 388.

37. C. Smith, *Technical Workers: Class, Labour and Trade Unionism* (Macmillan: 1987), p. 133.

38. National Union of Sheet Metal Workers, Coppersmiths, Heating and Domestic Engineers, Minutes of the No. 6 District Committee, 30 August 1975.
39. *Financial Times*, 27 April 1978.
40. P. Higgs, Union Convenor, 'Why You Should Reject the Company's Offer', Bulletin sent to union members at Rolls- Royce, Parkside, Coventry, on behalf of the Parkside Negotiating Committee, 30 March 1978.
41. *Coventry Evening Telegraph*, 29 April 1978.
42. Bristol Survival Plan, Rolls Royce Ltd., 1982.
43. B. Franks, *The Measured Day Work and Productivity Deal Swindle: How it works and how to fight it* (All Trades Unions Alliance pamphlet, Workers Press: November 1970), p. 21.
44. *Royal Commission on Trade Unions and Employers' Associations 1965–1968*, p. 106.
45. *Ibid.*, p. 262.
46. S. Bowden, J. Foreman-Peck, and T. Richardson, 'The Post-War Productivity Failure: Insights from Oxford (Cowley)', *Business History* 43:3 (2001), p. 59.
47. *Ibid.*, p. 67.
48. A. Thornett, *From Militancy to Marxism: a Personal and Political Account of Organising Car Workers* (Left View Books: 1987), p. 107.
49. R. Hyman and T. Elger, 'Job Controls, the Employers' Offensive and Alternative Strategies', *Capital & Class*, 15 (Autumn 1981), p. 116.
50. Bowden, Foreman-Peck, and Richardson, 'The Post-War Productivity Failure', p. 64.
51. *Ibid.*, p. 59.
52. *Ibid.*, pp. 60–63.
53. Hyman and Elger, 'Job Controls, the Employers Offensive and Alternative Strategies', p. 134.
54. P. Willman, and G. Winch, *Innovation and Management Control: Labour Relations at BL Cars* (Cambridge University Press: 1985), pp. 65–84.
55. Thornett, *From Militancy to Marxism*, p. 108.
56. *Ibid.*, p. 210.
57. S. Johns, *Victimization at Cowley* (Workers Revolutionary Party pamphlet: 1975), p. 24.
58. According to Willman and Winch, *Innovation and Management Control*, Measured Day Work received a mixed response with some 'commentators' feeling that 'the scheme created considerable problems, and contributed to the reduction of productivity observed throughout the industry in the early 1970s', p. 66.
59. Johns, *Victimization at Cowley*, p. 39; Thornett, *From Militancy to Marxism*, pp. 209–10.
60. Johns, *Victimization at Cowley*, pp. 41–42; Thornett, *Inside Cowley: Trade Union Struggle in the 1970s:Who Really Opened the Door to the Tory Onslaught?* (Porcupine Press: 1998), p. 27.
61. Thornett, *Inside Cowley*, p. 28.
62. M. Barratt Brown and K. Coates, *The Blair Revelation: Deliverance for whom?* (Spokesman: 1996), p. 61.
63. Willman and Winch, *Innovation and Management Control*, p. 5.

64. J. McIlroy, 'Notes on the Communist Party and Industrial Politics' in J. McIlroy, N. Fishman and A. Campbell (eds). *British Trade Unions and Industrial Politics: Vol. 2: The High Tide of Trade Unionism, 1964–79* (Ashgate: 1999), p. 240.

65. Hyman and Elger, 'Job Controls, the Employers' Offensive and Alternative Strategies', p. 139.

66. M. Edwardes, *Back from the Brink* (Collins: 1983), p. 74.

67. *Ibid.*, p. 37.

68. B. Rudder, 'The Inside Story at Toyota and BL' Book Review, *Labour Review* 1:7 (August 1983), p. 45.

69. J. Lovering, 'The Restructuring of the Defence Industries and the Role of the State', Working Paper 59 (University of Bristol, School for Advanced Urban Studies: 1986), p. 20.

Index

absenteeism, in railway industry, 18
aerospace industry, 3, 198
    capital-labour relations in, 182–3
    informality and localism in, 183–7
    payment systems, 187–92
agricultural workers, 24
Agricultural Workers' Union, 66
Amalgamated Society of Engineers
    (ASE), 7
Amalgamated Society of Paper Makers
    (ASPM), 85
Annan Report, 146, 148
Apsley, 84–90
Arch, Joseph, 75
aristocracy, 5
Arrowsmith, J. W., 108–9
Arrowsmith-Brown, J. A., 109, 111,
    113–15, 120, 125
Askwith, George, 61
Association of Broadcasting Staff
    (ABS), 145
Association of Cinemagraphic
    Television and Allied Technicians
    (ACTT), 145
authority, 2, 3, 7, 16, 18, see also
    management authority;
    management control
automobile industry, 3, 182–7
    capital-labour relations in, 182–3
    informality and localism in, 183–7
    payment systems, 192–7

banking industry
    assets held by, 35
    branch network, 34, 49–52
    consolidation in, 32, 50
    cost savings in, 51–2, 55
    deregulation, 35
    female labour in, 32–3, 36, 38–49,
        52–6
    gender discrimination in, 41–2, 44,
        48–9
    interwar years, 48–52

    male employees in, 47–9
    management, 50–1
    office mechanization in, 33–4,
        36–8, 43, 51–2, 55
    railways and, 11, 13
    transformation of, 32–6, 52–3
    twentieth century, 32–59
Basset Vincent, Christopher,
    24–5, 27
BBC, see British Broadcasting
    Company (BBC)
BBC Staff Association, 143
Beard, John, 68
Bedaux, Charles, 156
Bedaux system, 97
Beveridge, William, 144
Bliss, William, 63, 65–7
Bliss Tweed Mill, 2
    historical development of, 63–5
    management changes, 65–7
    union organization at, 67–8
    wages at, 64–5
Bliss Tweed Mill strike, 60–82
    causes of, 62–7
    events of, 67–75
    impact of, 70–4
    results of, 75–7
Bradbury, Lizzie, 73
Braverman, Harry, 4
Bristol, 92–7
Bristol Chamber of Commerce, 93
Bristol Master Printers' Association,
    94
Bristol Typographical Association
    (BTA), 93, 108, 117
British Aircraft Corporation (BAC)
    Guided Weapons, 185, 189
British Broadcasting Company (BBC),
    2–3, 130–53
    conflict at, 147–9
    consensus at, 142, 143, 146
    growth of, 142, 144, 146
    history of, 130–3